T0214396

Lecture Notes in Computer Science 10789

Commenced Publication in 1973
Founding and Former Series Editors:
Gerhard Goos, Juris Hartmanis, and Jan van Leeuwen

Editorial Board

More information about this series at http://www.springer.com/series/7408

Alessandro Ricci · Philipp Haller (Eds.)

Programming with Actors

State-of-the-Art
and Research Perspectives

 Springer

Editors
Alessandro Ricci
University of Bologna
Cesena
Italy

Philipp Haller
KTH Royal Institute of Technology
Stockholm
Sweden

ISSN 0302-9743   ISSN 1611-3349   (electronic)
Lecture Notes in Computer Science
ISBN 978-3-030-00301-2   ISBN 978-3-030-00302-9   (eBook)
https://doi.org/10.1007/978-3-030-00302-9

Library of Congress Control Number: 2018954065

LNCS Sublibrary: SL2 – Programming and Software Engineering

This Springer imprint is published by the registered company Springer Nature Switzerland AG
The registered company address is: Gewerbestrasse 11, 6330 Cham, Switzerland

Preface

More than 40 years after their invention, *actors* have become a common reference model for designing and developing concurrent and distributed systems.

The actor model was introduced by Carl Hewitt and colleagues in 1973 [7], as a mathematical model of concurrent computation in which *actors* play the role of universal primitives of concurrent computation. In response to a message that it receives, an actor can: make local decisions, create more actors, send more messages, and determine how to respond to the next message received. Actors may modify their own private state, but can only affect each other through messages (avoiding the need for locks or other synchronization mechanisms). Since its conception, the model served both as a framework for a theoretical understanding of computation and as the theoretical basis for several practical implementations of concurrent systems [6].

In the 1980s and 1990s the model helped researchers understand and define the extension of object-oriented programming towards concurrency, e.g., in the form of concurrent object-oriented programming [1, 2, 4, 11].

In the mainstream, meanwhile, the panorama was dominated by sequential programming until the middle of the 2000s, when the "concurrency revolution" began [5, 9]. Since then, concurrent, asynchronous, and distributed programming have gradually become part of everyday design and programming.

If the 1980s and 1990s were dominated by a vision in which mainstream programming and programming paradigms could abstract from concurrency and distribution, in recent years there has been an increasing awareness that this is not feasible (e.g., when building reactive applications[1]), and – moreover – first-class concurrency abstractions, such actors and message passing, provide effective modeling and designing power to deal with the complexity of modern applications and application domains [3, 10].

The AGERE! workshop started in 2011 at the SPLASH conference to investigate the definition of suitable levels of abstraction, programming languages, and platforms to support and promote a decentralized mindset in solving problems, designing systems, as well as programming applications, including the teaching of computer programming [8]. That is, the question is how to think about problems and programs embracing decentralization of control and interaction as the most essential features. To this end, actors and agents were taken as key references, recognized as two main broad families of concepts, abstractions, and programming tools described in the literature, which explicitly promote such decentralized thinking.

The set of papers collected in this issue originated from the AGERE! workshop series – the last edition was held in 2017 – and concern the application of actor-based approaches to mainstream application domains and the discussion of related issues.

---

[1] For example, see https://www.reactivemanifesto.org.

The issue is divided into two parts. The first part concerns selected application domains:

- *Web Programming* – Parallel and Distributed Web Programming with Actors by Florian Myter, Christophe Scholliers, and Wolfgang De Meuter
- *Data-Intensive Parallel Programming* — OpenCL Actors: Adding Data Parallelism to Actor-Based Programming with CAF by Raphael Hiesgen, Dominik Charousset, and Thomas Schmidt
- *Mobile Computing* — AmbientJS: A Mobile Cross-Platform Actor Library for Multi-networked Mobile Applications by Elisa Gonzalez Boix, Kevin De Porre, Wolfgang De Meuter, and Christophe Scholliers
- *Self-Organizing Systems* — Programming Actor-Based Collective Adaptive Systems by Roberto Casadei and Mirko Viroli

The second part concerns selected issues:

- *Scheduling* — Pluggable Scheduling for the Reactor Programming Model by Aleksandar Prokopec
- *Debugging* — A Study of Concurrency Bugs and Advanced Development Support for Actor-Based Programs by Carmen Torres Lopez, Stefan Marr, Hanspeter Mössenböck, and Elisa Gonzalez Boix
- *Communication and Coordination* — A Model for Separating Communication Concerns of Concurrent Systems by Hongxing Geng and Nadeem Jamali
- *Monitoring* — A Homogeneous Actor-Based Monitor Language for Adaptive Behavior by Tony Clark, Vinay Kulkarni, Souvik Barat, and Balbir Barn

References

1. G. Agha. Concurrent object-oriented programming. Commun. ACM, 33:125–141, September 1990.
2. G. Agha, P. Wegner, and A. Yonezawa, editors. Research directions in concurrent object-oriented programming. MIT Press, Cambridge, MA, USA, 1993.
3. J. Armstrong. Erlang. Commun. ACM, 53(9):68–75, Sept. 2010.
4. J.-P. Briot, R. Guerraoui, and K.-P. Lohr. Concurrency and distribution in object-oriented programming. ACM Comput. Surv., 30(3):291–329, Sept. 1998.
5. K. B. Bruce, A. Danyluk, and T. Murtagh. Introducing concurrency in CS 1. In Proceedings of the 41st ACM Technical Symposium on Computer Science Education, SIGCSE '10, pages 224–228, New York, NY, USA, 2010. ACM.
6. C. Hewitt. Viewing control structures as patterns of passing messages. Artif. Intell., 8(3):323–364, 1977.
7. C. Hewitt, P. Bishop, and R. Steiger. A universal modular actor formalism for artificial intelligence. In Proceedings of the 3rd International Joint Conference on Artificial Intelligence, IJCAI'73, pages 235–245, San Francisco, CA, USA, 1973. Morgan Kaufmann Publishers Inc.

8. A. Ricci, R. H. Bordini, and G. Agha. AGERE! (Actors and aGEnts REloaded): SPLASH 2011 workshop on programming systems, languages and applications based on actors, agents and decentralized control. In Proceedings of the ACM International Conference Companion on Object Oriented Programming Systems Languages and Applications Companion, OOPSLA '11, pages 325–326, New York, NY, USA, 2011. ACM.

9. H. Sutter and J. Larus. Software and the concurrency revolution. ACM Queue: Tomorrow's Computing Today, 3(7):54–62, Sept. 2005.

10. V. Vernon. Reactive Messaging Patterns with the Actor Model: Applications and Integration in Scala and Akka. Addison-Wesley Professional, 1st edition, 2015.

11. A. Yonezawa and M. Tokoro, editors. Object-oriented concurrent programming, Cambridge, MA, USA, 1987. MIT Press.

June 2018   Alessandro Ricci
                                                                         Philipp Haller

Contents

Actors and Programming – Selected Domains

Parallel and Distributed Web Programming with Actors

Florian Myter[1]([⊠]), Christophe Scholliers[2], and Wolfgang De Meuter[1]

[1] Vrije Universiteit Brussel, Pleinlaan 2, Elsene, Belgium
{fmyter,wdmeuter}@vub.ac.be
[2] Universiteit Gent, 281 S9, Krijgslaan, Gent, Belgium
christophe.scholliers@ugent.be

Abstract. JavaScript is the predominant language when it comes to developing applications for the web. Many of today's web-based systems are implemented solely in JavaScript due to its applicability to both client and server-side development. Programmers have an ever-growing need to express parallelism due to the computationally intensive nature of modern web applications. Currently, JavaScript tries to satisfy this need through actor-based parallelism constructs. However, we argue that these constructs suffer from design flaws which hamper programmers to elegantly express parallelism in web applications. In this paper we present Spiders.ts, a unified actor framework to express both parallelism and distribution. In Spiders.ts, programmers can easily specify the coarse-grained parallelism needs of modern web applications. Moreover, Spiders.ts' built-in distribution features allow programmers to express client-to-server, server-to-server and client-to-client communication simply by using actors. Through benchmarks we show that our framework is able to substantially improve the performance of web applications. Moreover, we demonstrate its expressive power by comparing implementations of a distributed case study application.

Keywords: Actor framework · Web · Distributed programming
Parallel programming · Communicating event loops

1 Introduction

Roughly 94% of all websites use JavaScript [1]. Although it was originally designed as a scripting language to be used in web browsers, JavaScript has since evolved into a general purpose language adopted in a range of contexts far beyond client-side web applications (e.g. server-side applications [16], mobile applications [18], etc.).

Similarly, the kind of applications written in JavaScript evolved since its inception. Where the web used to consist of static HTML pages, it has now

F. Myter—Funded by Innoviris (the Brussels Institute for Research and Innovation) through the Doctiris program (grant number 15-doct-07).

A. Ricci and P. Haller (Eds.): Programming with Actors, LNCS 10789, pp. 3–31, 2018.
https://doi.org/10.1007/978-3-030-00302-9_1

evolved into a platform for full-fledged distributed applications. Google's Gmail and WebOS (an operating system built entirely in JavaScript) are prototypical examples of such applications. To enable this transition from web 1.0 to web 2.0, browsers have evolved from simple graphic displayers to interpreters which execute complete JavaScript programs.

In order to maintain the responsiveness of these in-browser applications, a lot of work has focused on optimising the execution of JavaScript code. Examples of these optimisations include just-in-time JavaScript compilers [6] and thread-level speculation [10]. Besides language or runtime-level optimisations, Java-Script shows great promise to optimise application-level code through the use of parallelisation [5].

JavaScript programmers are only able to fulfil this promise through the use of two actor-based parallel constructs: *web workers* for client-side JavaScript and *child processes* for server-side technology (i.e. Node.js, which is the most prominent server-side implementation of JavaScript). However, these constructs severely limit the programmer in three ways. First, programmers are forced to employ a different API depending on the tier for which the parallel application is written (i.e. client or server). Moreover, neither of these APIs can be used by JavaScript actors to communicate across tiers. Second, programmers do not have fine-grained control over how values in messages are passed. JavaScript enforces pass-by-copy semantics for values sent between actors. However, this only applies for primitive data types (e.g. numerals, strings). All other data types (e.g. functions) must be serialised manually by the programmer. Third, an actor only has the built-in capability of sending messages to the actor that spawned it, or to any actors it spawns. Communication between arbitrary actors is not supported.

In this paper we present Spiders.ts[1], an actor framework in TypeScript[2] which solves the aforementioned three problems as follows:

- Spiders.ts exposes the same API and semantics regardless of the tier (i.e. client or server) in which it is used. Moreover, Spiders.ts' underlying message passing system can handle both *vertical* as well as *horizontal* distribution. The former allows for traditional client-to-server communication while the latter allows for server-to-server and client-to-client communication.
- Programmers are freed from the burden of manually serialising objects. Objects are either passed between two actors by reference (e.g. a function object) or by copy (e.g. a numeral value). In both cases the programmer is unaware of the underlying serialisation.
- Actor references are first class. This entails that all actors are able to exchange references between and send messages to each other.

---

[1] https://github.com/myter/Spiders.js.
[2] A typed superset of JavaScript which compiles to standard JavaScript.

2   Problem Statement

Spiders.ts addresses the following software engineering problems related to programming parallel applications in JavaScript:

Non-uniform distribution and parallelism. One of the strengths of the actor model is that it unifies distribution and parallelism. Two actors employ the same message passing scheme regardless of their locations (i.e. whether they reside on the same machine or not). Actors in JavaScript break this uniformity on two levels. First, depending on the tier (i.e. server or client-side) the API used by actors differs. Client-side actors (i.e. web workers) employ HTML5 message channels, while communication between server-side actors (i.e. child processes) is traditionally implemented using web sockets. Second, JavaScript actors lack the native constructs to communicate across single machine boundaries. This burdens the programmer with the task of providing communication between server and client-side actors.

Coarse-grained message passing semantics. Programmers are unable to specify how values should be sent across actors. A value is first copied before it is passed between actors. However, this is only guaranteed for primitive data types (e.g. numerals, strings). All other data types (i.e. functions, object methods) must be serialised manually by the programmer which quickly leads to a number of error-prone situations. For example, manual serialisation of objects forces the programmer to take care of possible scoping issues (e.g. an object having a method which refers to variables defined in its lexical scope). Client-side actors support additional message passing semantics which *transfers* objects between actors. Transferring an object between actors can be compared to pass-by-reference semantics where the sender loses its reference to the transferred object. However, this feature is primarily used for performance reasons, as it only applies to a limited number of objects (i.e. ArrayBuffers, MessagePorts or ImageBitmap).

Second class actor references. Message sends between actors are natively supported only between parent and child. Upon spawning an actor the spawning actor obtains a reference to the newly spawned actor through which messages can be sent. Similarly the spawned actor is able to reference the spawning actor. However, JavaScript disallows such references to be copied between actors (e.g. as part of a message send).

This burdens the programmer with the task of implementing arbitrary actor-to-actor communication. For client-side actors this typically entails the use of HTML5 message channels (i.e. a tuple of ports), which creates a communication channel between two web workers. In a nutshell, both actors must obtain a port of the same message channel to be able to send messages. For server-side actors one traditionally achieves communication between arbitrary actors through the use of web sockets.

3   Communicating Event Loops

Spiders.ts solves the aforementioned issues with JavaScript's parallel constructs by implementing actors as communicating event loops (CEL) [12]. We first provide a more in-depth explanation of the CEL model before detailing its reification in Spiders.ts.

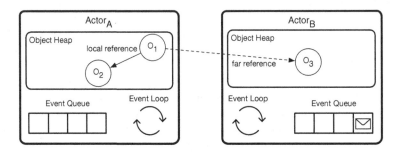

Fig. 1. Actors as communicating event loops [4]

Figure 1 gives an overview of the CEL model. Each actor is an independent entity supported by its own thread of control and contains a heap of objects, an event queue and an event loop. Each event in the queue is the result of a method invocation or field access on an object owned by another actor. The event loop continuously picks the first event from the queue and performs the invocation or field access contained in the dequeued event.

The CEL model specifies two kinds of references: *local* references and *far references*. As Fig. 1 shows, the reference that O_1 holds to O_2 is a local one since both objects are owned by $Actor_A$. This entails that all method invocations or fields accesses by O_1 on O_2 happen in a standard sequential fashion. The reference which O_1 holds to O_3 is a far reference since O_3 is owned by $Actor_B$. When O_1 invokes a method or accesses a field of O_3 this invocation is translated in an event sent asynchronously to $Actor_B$ (i.e. the event is queued in $Actor_B$'s event queue). Eventually $Actor_B$'s event loop will dequeue the event and the invocation will be executed.

CEL's dual referencing model extends to the return values and arguments of method invocations and field accesses. Concretely, the model discriminates between two kinds of objects: those that cross actor borders by copy and those that cross actor borders by reference. For example, O_1 invokes a method on O_3 and provides O_2 as argument to this invocation. Eventually O_3's method will be invoked with a far reference to O_2. Conversely, if O_3's method would be invoked with copyable arguments (e.g. numerals, strings, etc.) then O_3's method would obtain local references to the copies of these arguments.

4   Spiders.ts by Example

In order to showcase the applicability of our approach we outline an example application. This application, called *CoCode*[3], allows programmers to collaboratively code in their favourite language. To do so, each programmer logs in to the application after which she/he can start coding in a dedicated part of the webpage. Each coder has a consistent view of the piece of code which is collaboratively edited by all coders. Moreover, the code is syntax highlighted on the fly.

To keep our application efficient each client performs the syntax highlighting on its own view of the code. This allows the underlying synchronisation of code to work with pure text rather than highlighted code, which is substantially larger in size and would slow down communication. Each client spawns an actor dedicated to the syntax highlighting. This is to avoid blocking the UI thread, which would render the application unresponsive. Besides this core functionality CoCode also allows coders to discuss their code in a chat room or through private messages.

4.1   Basic Spiders

Listing 1.1 shows how the standalone functionality of each CoCode client (i.e. highlighting code in the webpage as a user types) is implemented. Each client can be divided into two actors: an actor responsible for updating the user interface and an actor dedicated to highlighting code. Actors in Spiders.ts are implemented as TypeScript classes which represent the actor's behaviour. We discriminate between the *application* actor which extends the *Application* class and runs under the main thread of control and *regular* actors which run under their own thread of control. This distinction serves three purposes: first, to avoid data races and glitches in the user interface only the application actor is allowed access to the global window object. Per webpage there can only be one instance of an application actor. Second, all actors except the application actor are devoid of their lexical environment. This ensures that data races between actors are impossible, given that objects are either passed by copy or by far reference between actors. Third, the application actor acts as an actor factory through its *spawnActor* method. This method accepts an extension of the generic *Actor* class as argument, spawns a new actor which behaves according to the class definition and returns a far reference to this actor. In our case we spawn a single highlighting actor by providing the *HighlightActor* class (see line 22). The *init* method, which is executed by Spiders.ts as soon as an actor is spawned, imports an external JavaScript library implementing the syntax highlighting.

The webpage which imports the script given by Listing 1.1 invokes the application actor's *newCode* method at each key stroke (the HTML code responsible for this is omitted for the sake of brevity). Subsequently, the application actor invokes the *highlight* method on the far reference to the highlighting actor with the new code as argument. Given that the code is represented by a string, which

---

[3] https://github.com/myter/Spiders.js/tree/master/CoCode.

```
 1  var spiders = require ('spiders')
 2  class CoCodeApp extends spiders.Application{
 3
 4    newCode(code : string){
 5      highlighter.highlight(code).then((highlightedCode : string) => {
 6        window.updateCode(highlightedCode)
 7      })
 8    }
 9
10  }
11  var CoCode = new CoCodeApp()
12  class HighlightActor extends spiders.Actor{
13
14    init(){
15      importScripts('./highlightLib.js')
16    }
17
18    highlight(code : string) : string{
19      return highlightLib.highlight(code).value
20    }
21  }
22  var highlighter : FarRef = CoCode.spawnActor(HighlightActor)
```

Listing 1.1. Spawning client-side actors in Spiders.ts

is a primitive data type, it is sent to the highlighting actor by copy. All method invocations on far references are translated by Spiders.ts to asynchronous message sends and return a promise. The resulting promise either resolves with the method's return value or is rejected with an error. As is the case for promises in standard JavaScript, one can install listeners on such promises through the built-in *then* and *catch* functions. In contrast to regular promises, Spiders.ts promises can span across actors. In our case the application actor registers a callback (see line 5) on a promise which is resolved with the return value of the highlighting actor's *highlight* method. Once the promise is resolved the user interface is updated by invoking *updateCode* on the *window* object representing the webpage.

4.2 Distributed Spiders

So far our CoCode application is standalone, it only responds to new code being produced by the local user. The first part in making CoCode a true web application is implementing a server. The code to do so is given in Listing 1.2. The server acts as a discovery service, allowing clients to obtain references to each other. This functionality can safely run on a single thread, therefore the server is implemented solely by an application actor. Concretely, the *register* method is invoked by a new client upon starting the application with its name and a reference to itself. The method then forwards this name and reference to all connected clients (see line 10).

```
 1  var spiders = require('spiders')
 2  class Server extends spiders.Application{
 3    coders : Map<string,FarRef>
 4
 5    constructor(){
 6      this.coders = new Map()
 7    }
 8
 9    register(newName : string,newClient : FarRef){
10      coders.foreach((client : FarRef,name : string) => {
11        client.newCoder(newName,newClient)
12        newClient.newCoder(name,client)
13      })
14      coders.set(newName,newClient)
15    }
16  }
17  new Server()
```

Listing 1.2. Implementing the CoCode server in Spiders.ts

The addition of the server requires us to update the implementation of our client-side CoCode actors. Listing 1.3 shows the additions to the original client-side code of Listing 1.1 that are needed in order to make CoCode a full-fledged web application. The code for the highlighting actor remains unchanged and is therefore omitted.

```
 1  var spiders = require('spiders')
 2  class Message extends spiders.Isolate{
 3    from : string
 4    text    : string
 5    date : Date
 6
 7    constructor(text : string){
 8      this.from   = window.name
 9      this.text   = text
10      this.date   = new Date()
11    }
12  }
13
14  class CoCodeApp extends spiders.Application{
15    coCoders : Map<string,FarRef>
16
17    constructor(){
18      this.coCoders   = Map.new()
19      remote(serverAddress,serverPort).then((serverRef : FarRef) => {
20        serverRef.register(window.coderName,this)
21      })
22    }
23
24    newCoder(name : string,coder : FarRef){
25      this.coCoders.set(name,coder)
26    }
27
28    newCode(code : string){
29      this.coCoders.forEach((coder : FarRef)=>{
30        coder.codeSync(code)
31      }
32      this.codeSync(code)
33    }
34
35    codeSync(code : string){
36      highlighter.highlight(code).then((highlightedCode : string) => {
37        window.updateCode(highlightedCode)
38      }
```

```
39    }
40
41    newMessage(msg  :  Message){
42      window.showMessage(msg.from ,msg.text ,msg.date)
43    }
44
45    sendPublicMessage(text  :  string){
46      this.coCoders.forEach((coder  :  FarRef)=>{
47        coder.newMessage(new Message(text))
48      })
49    }
50
51    sendPrivateMessage(to  :  string ,text  :  string){
52      this.coCoders.get(to).newMessage(new Message(text))
53    }
54
55  }
56  var CoCode  = new CoCodeApp()
```

Listing 1.3. Making CoCode clients distributed

Three additions are needed to complete our application:

Registering. Each client first acquires a reference to the server actor through
the *remote* function provided by Spiders.ts (see line 19). This function takes
the IP address and port number of a given server actor and returns a promise.
Eventually, this promise resolves with a far reference to the specified actor or
gets rejected with an error. In our case this reference is used by each client to
register themselves as a coder. This is done by invoking the *register* method
on the server reference (see line 20). The arguments to this invocation are the
client's name and a reference to itself, which is an instance of *CoCodeApp*.
Since the client's name is a string it is passed to the server by copy, while the
latter is an object and is therefore passed by far reference.

Code Updates. Shared code editing is handled by two methods. The *newCode*
method, which is called by the UI whenever a user types in code, invokes the
codeSync method on all of the client's peers (see line 29). This last method
ensures that each client's highlighting actor highlights the updated code.

Messaging. Through a dedicated section of the interface a user can either publicly broadcast a message (i.e. the UI invokes the *sendPublicMessage* method)
or send a private message to a particular coder (i.e. through the *sendPri-
vateMessage* method). In both cases an *isolated* object is created which contains the name of the sender, the date and the actual text of the message. In
contrast to other objects, isolated objects are sent by copy rather than by far
reference. As such, when a client receives a message through the *newMessage*
method, the message's data can directly be read from the copied object. If
messages were implemented as regular objects they would be sent by far reference. Each access to a message (e.g. getting the message's date) would then
return a promise, which would be impractical for this use case.

The code snippets given in Listings 1.1, 1.2 and 1.3 completely implement the
application logic behind CoCode. Using Spiders.ts one can implement a web
application which highlights code shared amongst clients in parallel, and supports public and private messaging between these clients, in 83 lines of code.

5   Spider.js Runtime

This section exhaustively describes the functionality provided by Spiders.ts. For each functionality we describe its use and how it is implemented using native JavaScript constructs. We divide this functionality into three categories: actors, referencing and message passing. Tables 1 and 2 summarise the API, the former contains the classes provided by Spiders.ts while the latter details the available functions.

5.1   Actors

Actors are implemented by extending one of two classes: *Application* or *Actor*. The application actor is spawned by instantiating an object from its class definition (i.e. using JavaScript's *new* operator), which can only be done once. All other actors are spawned through the application actor's *spawnActor* method which takes an extension of the Actor class as argument and spawns a new actor

Table 1. Classes provided by the Spiders.ts API

Class	Description	Functionality
Application	Generic application actor behaviour	Runs on the main thread
		Has access to the window object
		Serves as an actor factory through the *spawnWorker* method
Actor	Generic actor behaviour	Runs under its own thread of control
Isolate	Generic isolate definition	Adheres to pass by copy semantics

Table 2. Functions provided by the Spiders.ts API

Function	Description	Signature
.	asynchronous field access	far reference $\to$ symbol $\to$ promise\<any\>
	asynchronous method invocation	far reference $\to$ symbol $\to$ arguments $\to$ promise\<any\>
then	installs a *resolve* callback on a promise	promise\<any\> $\to$ (any $\to$ any) $\to$ promise\<any\>
catch	installs a *reject* callback on a promise	promise\<any\> $\to$ (exception $\to$ any) $\to$ promise\<any\>
remote	acquires a far reference to the specified server actor	string $\to$ number $\to$ promise\<far reference\>

with an instance of this class. *spawnActor* returns a far reference to the newly spawned actor. For server-side actors one can provide two optional arguments: the IP address and port number on which the actor will listen for incoming messages. By default the arguments are *localhost* and any unused port.

Part of the strength of the actor model is that programmers do not need to concern themselves with data races. In Spiders.ts this is achieved by disallowing any non-application actor access to its lexical scope. Concretely, a non-application actor can only access its own fields and methods. Moreover, Spiders.ts ensures that the DOM remains free of data races as well. Only the application actor is able to access the DOM and only one of such actors can be spawned per page.

Spawning an actor happens in two distinct steps. First, an object is instantiated from the given actor class. As is the case for regular TypeScript classes, this results in the invocation of the object's *constructor* method. At this point the actor is not yet spawned, which entails that the *constructor* method has access to its lexical scope. This allows the programmer to initialise an actor's fields with data available in the lexical scope. During the second step the actor is spawned using the instantiated object. Henceforth the actor is devoid of its lexical scope and its *init* method is invoked before any message is processed. The elements contained in the actor object's fields are then either accessible as far references (if the element is an object) or as values (if the element is a primitive data type or an isolate).

The technique employed by Spiders.ts to copy data from an actor's lexical scope closely resembles Scala's *spores* [11]. In a nutshell, spores allow programmers to create closures which can be safely distributed (e.g. by enforcing that spores and the variables they capture are serialisable). Both approaches rely on the programmer to specify which variables in the actor's or spore's lexical scope are to be captured. However, the spores approach is more substantial as it includes a type system which can enforce safety properties at compile time.

Implementation. The implementation of a Spiders.ts actor depends on whether it was spawned client or server-side. Client-side actors are built atop web workers. We differentiate between the application actor which runs on the client's main thread (and is therefore not an actual web worker) and regular actors, each of which are supported by a single web worker. Server-side actors are implemented as child processes, which entails that each server-side actor is a full-fledged Node.js instance.

In both cases the spawning of an actor happens as follows. First, a blank web worker or child process is created which will host the actor. Second, an object is instantiated from the actor's class after which it is serialised and sent to the blank web worker or child process. Lastly the object is deserialised by its host and its *init* method is called.

5.2   Referencing

Actors in Spiders.ts are implemented as communicating event loops and therefore discriminate between local and far references. Two objects within the same actor can reference each other locally as they would in any standard JavaScript application. Any method invocation or field access on a local reference is handled synchronously. An actor can obtain a far reference to an object owned by another actor implicitly or explicitly. Obtaining a far reference to a server actor can be done explicitly using the *remote* function. This function takes the server actor's IP address and port number and returns a promise which resolves with a far reference to the server actor. This functionality can either be employed by a client-side actor to obtain a reference to a server-side actor or between two server-side actors.

Since references in Spiders.ts are first-class entities one can also obtain far references implicitly. For example, in CoCode (see Sect. 4) the server actor allows all clients to obtain far references to each other. When a new coder connects to the server actor it provides a reference to itself. The server actor then forwards this reference to all other clients. In general an actor can implicitly obtain a far reference in two ways. First, if the promise resulting from a method invocation or field access on a far reference is resolved by an object. Second, if a method of one of its objects is invoked remotely (i.e. by an object residing in a different actor) with an object as argument.

In Spiders.ts all objects are passed between actors as far references while primitive data types are passed by copy. An exception to this rule is made for isolate objects, which are also passed by copy. A programmer can explicitly create such an isolate by instantiating an object from a class which extends the built-in generic *Isolate* class. Given that isolates are passed by copy it is the programmer's responsibility to make sure that the isolated object does not rely on its lexical scope (e.g. a method accessing a variable defined outside the isolate).

Implementation. A far reference is essentially a proxy to a remote object (i.e. an object owned by an actor different than the actor holding the reference). Accessing the property of a far reference (i.e. invoking a method or accessing a field) is translated into an asynchronous message send to the actor owning the proxied object.

In Spiders.ts far references are implemented using EcmaScript 6 proxies. This reflective construct allows us to define *traps* which intercept method invocations and field accesses. Accessing a far reference's property is translated to an asynchronous message which is sent to the actor owning the proxied object and results in a promise. This promise will either be resolved with the value of the property or it will be rejected with an exception.

5.3   Message Passing

Programmers never need to manually send messages between actors in Spiders.ts. It suffices for an actor to have a far reference to an object and access one if its fields or methods. Spiders.ts will ensure that this access is transformed into an asynchronous message send. Such an access or invocation is done using JavaScript's dot operator, after which a promise is returned. These promises behave as standard JavaScript promises: a programmer can listen for the resolving or rejecting of a promise using *then* and *catch*. Unlike regular promises, Spiders.ts promises can be passed between actors and can be resolved and rejected remotely.

Implementation. All actors residing in the same webpage communicate through the messaging systems provided by web workers and message channels. Communication between server actors or from a client actor to a server actor happens through web sockets. Remote client-side actors (i.e. actors residing in a different webpage or on a different machine) communicate through one or multiple server actors. Concretely, two remote client-side actors can only obtain references to each other through a server-side actor (e.g. the CoCode server which acts as a discovery service). All communication between these client-side actors is therefore routed by the server-side actor which initially introduced them.

Spiders.ts promises are implemented as wrappers on top of standard JavaScript promises. Concretely, in Spiders.ts each promise keeps track of the actor which created it and which actors are listening for its resolving or rejecting. This information is used to notify all listeners whenever a Spiders.ts promise is resolved or rejected.

6   Related Work

This work is strongly motivated by the limitations of the built-in parallelism features of JavaScript. Although we are not the first to propose an actor framework for web applications we are the first to fully implement a unified actor framework for both parallel and distributed computations. What follows is a discussion of the more prominent actor-based solutions for JavaScript.

Since HTML5, client-side JavaScript developers can employ *web workers* to execute code in parallel. At its core web workers are limited versions of actors: Given a URL to a piece of JavaScript code, the main thread is able to spawn web workers which will execute the code in their own thread of control. Web workers run in a completely isolated environment which entails that they do not have access to the lexical scope in which they are created. Moreover, scope isolation also includes graphical elements such as the DOM. This ensures that race conditions between workers are avoided. However, web workers limit programmers in a number of ways which we discuss in detail in Sect. 2.

Server-side JavaScript (i.e. Node.js) offers *child processes* which can be used to execute any system-level command. They also provide a built-in wrapper (i.e. *fork*) which spawns a new Node.js instance and returns an object used to send messages to the spawned instance. However, child processes exhibit the same limitations as web workers.

In previous work we introduced Spiders.js [14], the predecessor to Spiders.ts, which suffers from three major flaws. First, it under performs significantly compared to native web workers or child processes. Second, Spiders.js provides its own implementation of promises (called *futures*) to handle return values of asynchronous method invocations and field accesses. However, these futures are second-class and therefore limit the programmer's ability to compose them. Moreover, Spiders.js' future API differs from JavaScript's built-in promises. This complicates the integration of Spiders.js with native JavaScript code. Third, Spiders.js' API is based on EcmaScript 5 which is bombastic compared to some of the novel language features provided by EcmaScript 6. We addressed these flaws during the implementation and design of Spiders.ts as follows:

Performance. Spiders.ts is a complete reimplementation of Spiders.js which focuses heavily on efficiency. The most notable optimisation in Spiders.ts involves the use of meta-programming constructs. Spiders.js heavily relied on JavaScript meta-constructs (e.g. the *with* statement), which typically cannot be optimised by JavaScript runtimes. Throughout the design and implementation of Spiders.ts we avoided the use of such JavaScript constructs which harm performance.

Asynchronous method invocation. Spiders.js' custom implementation of futures has been forsaken in favour of first-class JavaScript promises. However, the promises offered by Spiders.ts are a superset of those offered by JavaScript. In contrast to JavaScript promises, Spiders.ts promises can be distributed across actors and tiers. For example, an actor residing on the server can resolve a promise which subsequently triggers callbacks on client actors.

API. Spiders.js uses regular JavaScript objects to implement actors. In Spiders.ts actors are implemented by means of TypeScript classes. This allows programmers to use traditional object-oriented concepts (e.g. field visibility, inheritance, etc.) to implement their actors. Additionally, Spiders.ts benefits from TypeScript tooling support (e.g. type checkers).

The integration of the CEL model in web applications has already been discussed by related work [13]. So far, the most notable step towards this integration comes in the form of the Q-connection[4] library. As is the case for Spiders.ts, q-connection differentiates between local and far references for objects. Moreover, far references can be exchanged between web workers. However, in q-connection web workers must explicitly export an object before another worker can acquire a far reference to it. Furthermore, in q-connection actor references are second class. We discuss this problem in detail in Sect. 2

Akka.js [15] is an actor framework that allows one to deploy Akka actors in any JavaScript environment. To do so it employs Scala.js to compile the Scala/Akka code to JavaScript. Akka.js' main goals closely resemble ours. First, it strives for in-browser parallelism by mapping actors onto web workers. Second, it allows for different actor runtimes (i.e. server and client runtimes) to seamlessly communicate. With Spiders.ts we provide JavaScript developers the means to easily write parallel applications. However, Akka.js aims to provide Akka/Scala programmers the means to easily deploy their application to JavaScript

---

[4] https://github.com/kriskowal/q-connection.

runtimes. Another difference between Spiders.ts and Akka.js is the communication between remote client-side actors. As explained in Sect. 5.3, two remote client-side Spiders.ts actors communicate via one or multiple server-side actors. Akka.js employs a routing tree mechanism which allows two remote client-side actors to directly communicate with each other.

Generic workers [17] strive to unify the way in which communication happens between parallel entities (i.e. web workers) and distributed entities (i.e. client/server) in JavaScript. To do so, it introduces the notion of a *generic* worker which can run both in the browser and on a server. Furthermore, generic workers provide the same communication API regardless of the tier in which the communication partner resides. Although we share the vision that a unified parallelism framework is needed for web applications, Spiders.ts explicitly steps away from the traditional web worker interface in favour of a more expressive API through CEL actors.

Syndicate [7] is a novel actor language tailored towards reactive programs. It extends upon functional actors with a number of reactive and event-driven features. Furthermore, it provides a JavaScript implementation of its model. However, Syndicate applications run their actors on the main thread and therefore only provide concurrency. Syndicate lacks the parallel capabilities sought after in Spiders.ts.

Connect.js [2] is a JavaScript/Titanium[5] library which allows the development of cross-platform mobile applications. Spiders.ts resembles Connect.js in two ways: both are heavily influenced by the AmbientTalk [3] actor language and both implement CEL actors. However, both the aim as well as the implementation of Connect.js differs widely from Spiders.ts. First, Connect.js operates in the context of mobile applications where peers are homogeneous (i.e. there is no client/server distinction). Second and most importantly, actors in Connect.js do not operate under their own thread of control and are therefore unsuitable for parallel applications.

Reo@JS [9] is a coordination language for web workers. As is the case for Spiders.ts, it aims to provide high-level abstractions to implement parallelism for web applications. Reo@JS focuses on communication patterns between web workers and offers abstractions to easily implement these patterns. However, it does not allow to coordinate workers across different clients or to coordinate client and server workers.

7   Evaluation

Spiders.ts provides a uniform solution for both parallelism and distribution in JavaScript. Programmers are able to parallelise their application by distributing workload over multiple actors. Moreover, Spiders.ts actors can be used to implement full-stack (i.e. server and client) distributed web applications.

To evaluate the former we measure the speedup obtained by parallelising an example application. Moreover, we compare the runtime results for three

---

[5] http://www.appcelerator.com.

implementations of the Savina benchmark suite [8]: one using web workers, one using child processes and one using Spiders.js. To evaluate the latter we compare the implementation of a multiplayer version of the arcade game *Pong*.

Using Spiders.ts we were able to speed up the example application fourfold. This clearly showcases Spiders.ts' potential as a parallel programming framework. Moreover, as our *Pong* case study shows, Spiders.ts allows one to write complete web applications more effectively than is the case for regular JavaScript. The Savina benchmark suite results show that there is still room for improving Spiders.ts' actor creation and messaging overhead compared to native JavaScript actors.

7.1   Performance

All client-side benchmarks were performed in Google Chrome (version 56.0.2924.87) on a Macbook Pro with a 2,8 GHz intel core i7 processor, 16 GB of RAM memory running Mac OSX Sierra (version 10.12.3). All server-side benchmarks were performed on an Ubuntu 14.04 server with two dual core Intel Xeon 2637 processors at 3.5 GHz with 265 GB of RAM memory.

Parallelism. To measure the parallel performance of Spiders.ts we used an application which approximates pi using the *monte carlo* method. We compare the time needed by a sequential application to approximate pi a given number of times with a parallel version which spreads the same workload across a variable amount of actors.

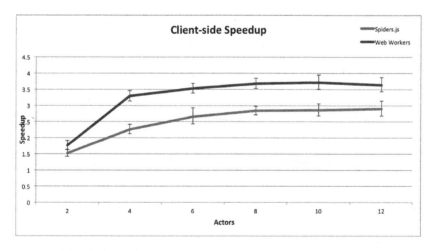

Fig. 2. Speedup obtained by comparing the sequential monte carlo application with parallel versions using Spiders.ts and web workers. Error bars indicate the 95% confidence interval.

Figure 2 shows the measured results while running this comparison in-browser. Comparing the speedup obtained by the Spiders.ts and web workers implementation, one clearly denotes an overhead induced by Spiders.ts. This overhead is also present with regards to child processes, as shown by Fig. 3. Overall the results clearly showcase Spiders.ts' applicability to parallelise both client and server-side web application.

Runtime Overhead. To measure the overhead induced by Spiders.ts we compared the runtime performance of a Spiders.ts implementation and a web workers implementation of the Savina benchmark suite. Figure 4 shows the mean run time to completion for each implementation of each application in the suite. The run times were normalised to the results obtained by web workers to better highlight the overhead introduced by Spiders.ts. The results immediately show Spiders.ts' biggest overhead: actor creation (as shown by the *Fork Join (actor creation)* application). Web workers are simply spawned by providing the path to a JavaScript source file containing their behaviour. As explained in Sect. 5.1, in Spiders.ts the object representing the actor must first be serialised and sent to a newly spawned web worker which will deserialise the object before accepting any messages. Moreover, Spiders.ts also introduces an overhead with regards to messaging overhead and throughput (respectively shown by the *counting actor* and *Fork Join (throughput)* applications). This is due to Spiders.ts' underlying runtime, which requires a considerable amount of meta-data to be attached to every message sent between actors (e.g. to handle the return values of asynchronous method invocations). These weaknesses of Spiders.ts are further showcased by our server-side comparison using a child process implementation of the Savina

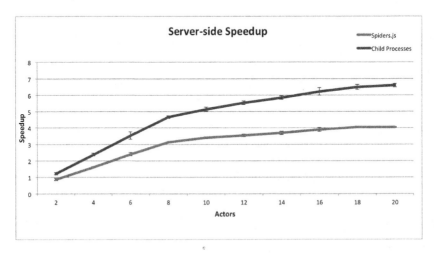

Fig. 3. Speedup obtained by comparing the sequential monte carlo application with parallel versions using Spiders.ts and child processes. Error bars indicate the 95% confidence interval.

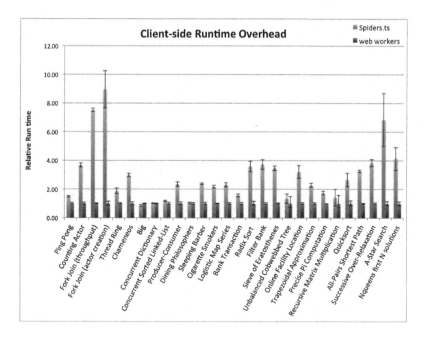

Fig. 4. Comparing Spiders.ts and web workers in the Savina Benchmark Suite. Run times are normalised to web workers results. Error bars indicate the 95% confidence interval.

suite. As Fig. 5 shows, the overhead is less pronounced but still substantial when comparing Spiders.ts and child processes

Spiders.js Comparison. Figure 6 provides the comparison between Spiders.js (i.e. Spider.ts' predecessor) and web workers. Through the improvements discussed in Sect. 6 we were able to significantly reduce the overhead induced by our framework. On average, Spiders.ts performs roughly twice as well compared to Spiders.js. However, these improvements hardly affect messaging throughput and actor creation.

7.2 Coding Complexity

To measure the expressive power of Spiders.ts over native JavaScript we implemented and compared a multiplayer version of the arcade game *Pong*[6]. We divided each implementation into three different categories of code:

Message Handling. Code that implements how a part of the application is to respond to a given message. This includes implementing and registering callbacks, dispatching on message types and implementing actor methods.

---

[6] https://github.com/myter/Spiders.js/tree/master/SpiderPong.

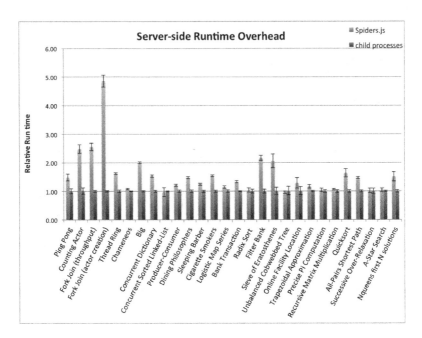

Fig. 5. Comparing Spiders.ts and child processes in the Savina Benchmark Suite. Run times are normalised to child processes results. Error bars indicate the 95% confidence interval.

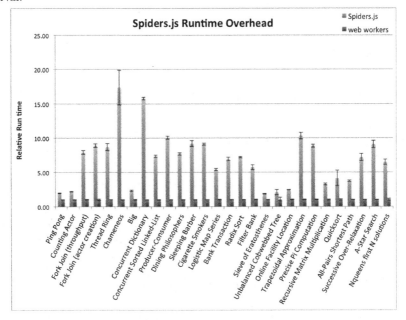

Fig. 6. Comparing Spiders.js and web workers in the Savina Benchmark Suite. Run times are normalised to web worker results. Error bars indicate the 95% confidence interval.

Message Sending. Code which implements the communication between clients and between the clients and the server. This includes creating and sending messages, opening sockets and invoking methods on far references or defining *isolate* objects.

Application Logic. Code which implements the game's core functionality (e.g. updating the user interface when a player's score has changed).

To compare both implementations we measure the proportion of each category of code to the application's total lines of code. Ideally an application should mostly be comprised of *application logic* code. Appendices A and B contain both implementations highlighted according to the three categories.

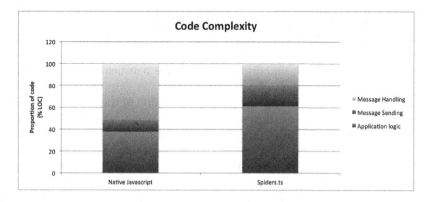

Fig. 7. Proportion, in percentage of the total lines of code, dedicated to each category of code for a native JavaScript and Spider.ts implementation of multiplayer *Pong*

Figure 7 shows how each implementation is divided into the three categories. For each category of code, the figure shows the percentage it represents with regards to the application's total lines of code. The biggest difference between both version is the portion of the application dedicated to message handling. In contrast to regular JavaScript, message handling in Spiders.ts is done implicitly (i.e. an actor's methods act as message handlers). Moreover, in Spiders.ts two clients are able to send messages to each other simply by using far references. For our pong example this entails that a client can directly send updates to his opponent, Spiders.ts will ensure that the server routes messages correctly. In the version implemented using plain JavaScript this routing must be implemented manually, adding additional code for message handling on both server and client. In conclusion, Spiders.ts allows programmers to focus on the inherent complexity and logic of their application while delegating message handling and routing to the Spiders.ts runtime.

8   Conclusion

As the web continues its evolution from a thin to a thick client model, the need for efficient and parallel web applications increases. The majority of web applications are currently implemented using JavaScript. It provides two constructs allowing programmers to write parallel web applications: *web workers* and *child processes*. However, these two constructs suffer from three major deficiencies. First, in contrast with most actor systems, distribution and parallelism are not handled uniformly in JavaScript. Depending on the tier (i.e. client or server), the API used to program JavaScript actors differs. Moreover, JavaScript actors cannot reuse the communication constructs used for local actor-to-actor communication to communicate with remote or distributed actors. Second, actors employ very coarse-grained message passing semantics. Concretely only primitive data types contained within a message are passed by copy, all other data types must be serialised manually by the programmer. Third, actor references are second class and cannot be copied as part of a message send. This entails that JavaScript lacks the built-in ability to support communication between any two arbitrary actors.

In this paper we introduce Spiders.ts, a continuation of the work done in [14]. Spiders.ts differentiates itself from other JavaScript actor frameworks in three ways. First, Spiders.ts provides a unified actor API for both client and server-side web development. Moreover, Spiders.ts exposes a single messaging API regardless of an actor's physical location. This allows programmers to express client-to-server, server-to-server and client-to-client communication. Second, using Spiders.ts programmers never need to manually serialise values passed between actors. Isolated objects and primitive data types are passed by copy. All other objects are passed by far reference, for which Spiders.ts ensures asynchronous access through promises. Third, references to actors are first class which allows communication between all actors in an application.

The results for the Savina benchmark suite indicate that there is room for improving Spiders.ts' overhead compared to native JavaScript actors. However, through speedup experiments we showcase that Spiders.ts is more than apt as a framework for parallel web applications. Using Spiders.ts we were able to considerably speed up a client and server-side example application. Moreover, by comparing implementations of a distributed case study application we show that Spiders.ts enables programmers to significantly reduce the boilerplate code associated with developing web applications.

A Highlighted Native Implementation of Pong

A.1 Server Implementation

```javascript
var io = require('socket.io');
var socket = io(8000);
var clients = new Map();
var games = new Map();
var occupation = new Map();
class Player {
    constructor(ref, name) {
        this.ref = ref;
        this.name = name;
    }
}
function newClient(nickName, ref) {
    clients.set(nickName, new Player(ref, nickName));
    games.forEach((creator, roomName) =>
        ref.emit('message', ["newGameCreated", roomName, creator.name]);
        if (occupation.get(roomName) > 1) {
            ref.emit('message', ["updateRoomInfo", roomName]);
        }
    });
}
function createNewGame(roomName, creatorRef, creatorName) {
    games.set(roomName, new Player(creatorRef, creatorName));
    occupation.set(roomName, 1);
    clients.forEach((client) => {
        if (client.name != creatorName) {
            client.ref.emit('message', ["newGameCreated", roomName, creatorName]);
        }
    });
}
function playerJoined(roomName, playerName) {
    var otherPlayer = games.get(roomName);
    occupation.set(roomName, occupation.get(roomName) + 1);
    clients.forEach((client) => {
        if (client.name != playerName && client.name != otherPlayer.name) {
            client.ref.emit('message', ["updateRoomInfo", roomName]);
        }
    });
}
function forwardPlayerJoins(to, playerNick) {
    var player = clients.get(to);
    player.ref.emit('message', ["playerJoins", playerNick]);
}
function forwardGetPortal(to, playerNick) {
    var player = clients.get(to);
    player.ref.emit('message', ["getPortal", playerNick]);
}
function forwardReceivePortal(to, x, y, r, c) {
    var player = clients.get(to);
    player.ref.emit('message', ["receivePortal", x, y, r, c]);
}
function forwardReceiveBall(to, x, y, vx, vy) {
    var player = clients.get(to);
    player.ref.emit('message', ["receiveBall", x, y, vx, vy]);
}
function forwardScoreChange(to, score) {
    var player = clients.get(to);
    player.ref.emit('message', ["scoreChange", score]);
}
function forwardReceivePowerup(to, type) {
    var player = clients.get(to);
```

A.2   Server Implementation

```
    player.ref.emit('message', ["receivePowerup", type]);
}
socket.on('connect', (client) => {
    client.on('message', (data) => {
        switch (data[0]) {
            case "newClient":
                newClient(data[1], client);
                break;
            case "createNewGame":
                createNewGame(data[1], client, data[2]);
                break;
            case "playerJoined":
                playerJoined(data[1], data[2]);
                break;
            case "forwardPlayerJoins":
                forwardPlayerJoins(data[1], data[2]);
                break;
            case "forwardGetPortal":
                forwardGetPortal(data[1], data[2]);
                break;
            case "forwardReceivePortal":
                forwardReceivePortal(data[1], data[2], data[3], data[4], data[5]);
                break;
            case "forwardReceiveBall":
                forwardReceiveBall(data[1], data[2], data[3], data[4], data[5]);
                break;
            case "forwardScoreChange":
                forwardScoreChange(data[1], data[2]);
                break;
            case "forwardReceivePowerup":
                forwardReceivePowerup(data[1], data[2]);
                break;
            default:
                console.log("Server did not understand message : " + data[0]);
        }
    });
});
```

A.3   Client Implementation

```
import {Socket} from "net";
var graph = require('./graphics')

class NativePongClient{
    serverRef    : Socket
    nickName     : string
    currentGame

    constructor(nickName : string){
        this.serverRef = require('socket.io-client')('http://127.0.0.1:8000')
        this.nickName  = nickName
        var that       = this
        this.serverRef.on('message',(data)=>{
            switch(data[0]){
                case "updateRoomInfo":
                    that.updateRoomInfo(data[1])
                    break
                case "newGameCreated":
                    that.newGameCreated(data[1],data[2])
                    break
                case "playerJoins":
                    that.playerJoins(data[1])
                    break
                case "getPortal":
                    that.getPortal(data[1])
                    break
                case "receivePortal":
                    that.receivePortal(data[1],data[2],data[3],data[4])
                    break
                case "receiveBall":
                    that.receiveBall(data[1],data[2],data[3],data[4])
                    break
                case "scoreChange":
                    that.scoreChange(data[1])
                    break
                case "receivePowerup":
                    that.receivePowerup(data[1])
                    break
                default:
                    console.log("Client did not understand message : " + data[0])
            }
        })
        this.serverRef.emit('message',["newClient",this.nickName])
        document.getElementById("newRoomButton").onclick = {} => {
            var roomName = (document.getElementById('roomName') as
HTMLTextAreaElement).value
            this.currentGame = new graph.game(that,roomName)
            this.serverRef.emit('message',["createNewGame",roomName,this.nickName])
            this.currentGame.start(true)
        }
    }

    private joinGame(roomName : string,gameCreator : string){
        this.currentGame             = new graph.game(this,roomName)
        this.currentGame.setOpponentReference(gameCreator)
        this.serverRef.emit('message',["playerJoined",roomName,this.nickName])
        this.serverRef.emit('message',["forwardPlayerJoins",gameCreator,this.nickName])
        this.serverRef.emit('message',["forwardGetPortal",gameCreator,this.nickName])
        this.currentGame.start(false)
    }
}
```

A.4   Client Implementation

```
newGameCreated(roomName : string,gameCreator : string){
    var row                   = (document.getElementById('roomList') as
HTMLTableElement).insertRow()
    var nameCell              = row.insertCell()
    var noPlayersCell         = row.insertCell()
    row.id                    = roomName
    nameCell.innerHTML        = roomName
    noPlayersCell.innerHTML   = "1/2"
    var that                  = this
    row.onclick               = function() {
        if(noPlayersCell.innerHTML === "1/2") {
            that.joinGame(roomName,gameCreator)
        }
    };
}

playerJoins(nickName : string){
    this.currentGame.setOpponentReference(nickName)
    this.currentGame.playerJoined(nickName)
}

updateRoomInfo(roomName){
    (document.getElementById(roomName) as any).cells[1].innerHTML = "2/2"
}

getPortal(requester : string){
    var gamePortal = this.currentGame.getPortal()
    this.serverRef.emit('message',
["forwardReceivePortal",requester,gamePortal.x,gamePortal.y,gamePortal.r,gamePortal.c])
}

receivePortal(x,y,r,c){
    this.currentGame.receivePortal({x:x,y:y,r:r,c:c})
}

receiveBall(x,y,vx,vy){
    this.currentGame.receiveBall({ x: x, y: y, vx: vx, vy: vy })
}

//Invoked by the UI
sendBallTo(opponent : string,x,y,vx,vy){
    this.serverRef.emit('message',["forwardReceiveBall",opponent,x,y,vx,vy])
}

//Invoked by the UI
sendScoreChangeTo(opponent : string,score){
    this.serverRef.emit('message',["forwardScoreChange",opponent,score])
}

//Invoked by the UI
sendPowerupTo(opponent : string,type){
    this.serverRef.emit('message',["forwardReceivePowerup",opponent,type])
}

scoreChange(score : number){
    this.currentGame.receiveOpponentScore(score)
}

receivePowerup(type : string){
```

A.5   Client Implementation

```
        this.currentGame.receivePowerup(type)
    }
}
(window as any).start = ()=>{
    var nickName             = (document.getElementById('nickname') as
HTMLTextAreaElement).value
    new NativePongClient(nickName)
}
```

B   Highlighted Spiders.ts Implementation of Pong

B.1   Server Implementation

```
import {SpiderLib, FarRef} from "../src/spiders";
var spiders : SpiderLib = require("../src/spiders")

class Player{
    ref     : FarRef
    name    : string
    constructor(ref,name){
        this.ref    = ref
        this.name   = name
    }
}
class SpiderPongServer extends spiders.Application{
    games       : Map<string,Player>
    occupation  : Map<string,number>
    clients     : Map<string,Player>

    constructor(){
        super()
        this.games       = new Map()
        this.clients     = new Map()
        this.occupation = new Map()
    }

    newClient(nickName : string,ref : FarRef){
        this.clients.set(nickName,new Player(ref,nickName))
        this.games.forEach((creator : Player,roomName : string)=>{
            ref.newGameCreated(roomName,creator.ref)
            if(this.occupation.get(roomName) > 1){
                ref.updateRoomInfo(roomName)
            }
        })
    }

    createNewGame(roomName : string,creatorRef : FarRef,creatorName){
        this.games.set(roomName,new Player(creatorRef,creatorName))
        this.occupation.set(roomName,1)
        this.clients.forEach((client : Player)=>{
            if(client.name != creatorName){
                client.ref.newGameCreated(roomName,creatorRef)
            }
        })
    }

    playerJoined(roomName : string,playerRef : FarRef,playerName : string){
        var otherPlayer : Player = this.games.get(roomName)
        this.occupation.set(roomName,this.occupation.get(roomName)+1)
        this.clients.forEach((client : Player)=>{
            if(client.name != playerName && client.name != otherPlayer.name){
                client.ref.updateRoomInfo(roomName)
            }
        })
    }
}
new SpiderPongServer()
```

B.2   Client Implementation

```
import {SpiderLib, FarRef} from "../../../src/spiders";
var spiders : SpiderLib = require("../../../src/spiders")
var graph              = require("./graphics")


class PortalIsolate extends spiders.Isolate{
    x
    y
    r
    c
    constructor(x,y,r,c){
        super()
        this.x = x
        this.y = y
        this.r = r
        this.c = c
    }
}

class SpiderPongClient extends spiders.Application{
    serverRef    : FarRef
    nickName     : string
    currentGame

    constructor(nickName : string){
        super()
        this.nickName = nickName
        this.remote("127.0.0.1",8000).then((serverRef : FarRef)=>{
            this.serverRef = serverRef
            serverRef.newClient(this.nickName,this)
        })
        document.getElementById("newRoomButton").onclick = () => {
            var roomName = (document.getElementById('roomName') as
HTMLTextAreaElement).value
            this.currentGame = new graph.game(roomName,this)
            this.serverRef.createNewGame(roomName,this,this.nickName)
            this.currentGame.start(true)
        }
    }

    private joinGame(roomName : string,gameCreator : FarRef){
        this.currentGame = new graph.game(roomName,this)
        this.currentGame.setOpponentReference(gameCreator)
        this.serverRef.playerJoined(roomName,this,this.nickName)
        gameCreator.playerJoins(this,this.nickName)
        gameCreator.getPortal().then((portal)=>{
            this.currentGame.receivePortal(portal)
        })
        this.currentGame.start(false);
    }

    newGameCreated(roomName : string,gameCreator : FarRef){
        var row                = (document.getElementById('roomList') as
HTMLTableElement).insertRow()
        var nameCell           = row.insertCell()
        var noPlayersCell      = row.insertCell()
        row.id                 = roomName
        nameCell.innerHTML     = roomName
        noPlayersCell.innerHTML = "1/2"
        var that               = this
```

B.3   Client Implementation

```
        row.onclick              = function() {
            if(noPlayersCell.innerHTML === "1/2") {
                that.joinGame(roomName,gameCreator)
            }
        };
    }

    playerJoins(player : FarRef,nickName : string){
        this.currentGame.setOpponentReference(player)
        this.currentGame.playerJoined(nickName)
    }

    updateRoomInfo(roomName){
        (document.getElementById(roomName) as any).cells[1].innerHTML = "2/2"
    }

    getPortal(){
        var gamePortal = this.currentGame.getPortal()
        return new PortalIsolate(gamePortal.x,gamePortal.y,gamePortal.r,gamePortal.c)
    }

    receiveBall(x,y,vx,vy){
        this.currentGame.receiveBall({ x: x, y: y, vx: vx, vy: vy })
    }

    scoreChange(score : number){
        this.currentGame.receiveOpponentScore(score)
    }

    receivePowerup(type : string){
        this.currentGame.receivePowerup(type)
    }

    //Invoked by UI
    sendBall(x,y,vx,vy,ref){
        ref.receiveBall(x,y,vx,vy)
    }

    //Invoked by UI
    sendScoreChange(score,ref){
        ref.scoreChange(score)
    }

    //Invoked by UI
    sendPowerup(type,ref){
        ref.receivePowerup(type)
    }
}

(window as any).start = ()=>{
    var nickName              = (document.getElementById('nickname') as
HTMLTextAreaElement).value
    new SpiderPongClient(nickName)
}
```

References

1. Usage of JavaScript for websites. https://w3techs.com/technologies/details/cp-javascript/all/all. Accessed 3 June 2016
2. Boix, E.G., Scholliers, C., Larrea, N., De Meuter, W.: Connect. js. Technical report, Vrije Universiteit Brussel (2015). http://soft.vub.ac.be/AGERE15/papers/AGERE_2015_paper_20.pdf
3. Cutsem, T.V., et al.: AmbientTalk: programming responsive mobile peer-to-peer applications with actors. Comput. Lang. Syst. Struct. **40**(3–4), 112–136 (2014)
4. De Koster, J., Van Cutsem, T., De Meuter, W.: 43 years of actors: a taxonomy of actor models and their key properties. In: Proceedings of the 6th International Workshop on Programming Based on Actors, Agents, and Decentralized Control, AGERE 2016, pp. 31–40. ACM, New York (2016)
5. Fortuna, E., Anderson, O., Ceze, L., Eggers, S.: A limit study of JavaScript parallelism. In: Proceedings of the IEEE International Symposium on Workload Characterization, IISWC 2010, pp. 1–10. IEEE Computer Society, Washington, DC (2010)
6. Gal, A., et al.: Trace-based just-in-time type specialization for dynamic languages. In: Proceedings of the 30th ACM SIGPLAN Conference on Programming Language Design and Implementation, PLDI 2009, pp. 465–478. ACM, New York (2009)
7. Garnock-Jones, T., Felleisen, M.: Coordinated concurrent programming in SYNDICATE. In: Thiemann, P. (ed.) ESOP 2016. LNCS, vol. 9632, pp. 310–336. Springer, Heidelberg (2016). https://doi.org/10.1007/978-3-662-49498-1_13
8. Imam, S., Sarkar, V.: Savina-an actor benchmark suite. In: 4th International Workshop on Programming based on Actors, Agents, and Decentralized Control, AGERE! (2014)
9. Krauweel, M., Jongmans, S.-S.T.Q.: Simpler coordination of JavaScript web workers. In: Jacquet, J.-M., Massink, M. (eds.) COORDINATION 2017. LNCS, vol. 10319, pp. 40–58. Springer, Cham (2017). https://doi.org/10.1007/978-3-319-59746-1_3
10. Martinsen, J.K., Grahn, H., Isberg, A.: An argument for thread-level speculation and just-in-time compilation in the Google's V8 JavaScript engine. In: Proceedings of the 11th ACM Conference on Computing Frontiers, CF 2014, pp. 25:1–25:2. ACM, New York (2014)
11. Miller, H., Haller, P., Odersky, M.: Spores: a type-based foundation for closures in the age of concurrency and distribution. In: Jones, R. (ed.) ECOOP 2014. LNCS, vol. 8586, pp. 308–333. Springer, Heidelberg (2014). https://doi.org/10.1007/978-3-662-44202-9_13
12. Miller, M.S., Tribble, E.D., Shapiro, J.: Concurrency among strangers: programming in E as plan coordination. In: De Nicola, R., Sangiorgi, D. (eds.) TGC 2005. LNCS, vol. 3705, pp. 195–229. Springer, Heidelberg (2005). https://doi.org/10.1007/11580850_12
13. Miller, M.S., Van Cutsem, T.: Communicating event loops, an exploration in JavaScript (2011). http://soft.vub.ac.be/tvcutsem/talks/presentations/WGLD_CommEventLoops.pdf
14. Myter, F., Scholliers, C., De Meuter, W.: Many spiders make a better web: a unified web-based actor framework. In: Proceedings of the 6th International Workshop on Programming Based on Actors, Agents, and Decentralized Control, AGERE 2016, pp. 51–60. ACM, New York (2016)

15. Stivan, G., Peruffo, A., Haller, P.: Akka.js: towards a portable actor runtime environment. In: Proceedings of the 5th International Workshop on Programming Based on Actors, Agents, and Decentralized Control, AGERE! 2015, pp. 57–64. ACM, New York (2015)
16. Tilkov, S., Vinoski, S.: Node.js: using JavaScript to build high-performance network programs. IEEE Internet Comput. **14**(6), 80 (2010)
17. Welc, A., Hudson, R.L., Shpeisman, T., Adl-Tabatabai, A.R.: Generic workers: towards unified distributed and parallel JavaScript programming model. In: Programming Support Innovations for Emerging Distributed Applications, PSI EtA 2010, pp. 1:1–1:5. ACM, New York (2010)
18. Xanthopoulos, S., Xinogalos, S.: A comparative analysis of cross-platform development approaches for mobile applications. In: Proceedings of the 6th Balkan Conference in Informatics, BCI 2013, pp. 213–220. ACM, New York (2013)

AmbientJS
A Mobile Cross-Platform Actor Library
for Multi-Networked Mobile Applications

Elisa Gonzalez Boix[1]([⊠]), Kevin De Porre[1], Wolfgang De Meuter[1],
and Christophe Scholliers[2]

[1] Vrije Universiteit Brussel, Pleinlaan 2, 1050 Brussel, Belgium
{egonzale,kevin.de.porre,wolfgang.de.meuter}@vub.be
[2] Ghent University, St. Pietersnieuwstraat 33, 9000 Gent, Belgium
christophe.scholliers@ugent.be

Abstract. In this paper, we argue that due to technological advances programmers today are faced with a ninth fallacy of distributed computing: *"there is only one fixed application architecture throughout the lifetime of the application"*. Mobile devices are nowadays equipped with wireless technology which allows them to interact with one another in both a peer-to-peer way (e.g. Wi-Fi-direct, bluetooth, etc.), and via a server in the cloud. Distributed software engineering abstractions, however, do not aid the programmer in developing mobile applications which communicate over multiple networking technologies. This paper introduces AmbientJS, a mobile cross-platform actor library which incorporates a novel type of remote reference, called network transparent references (NTRs), which allows to seamlessly combine multiple application architectures. We give an overview of the NTR model, detail their implementation in a novel actor library called AmbientJS and assess the performance of AmbientJS with benchmarks.

1 Introduction

Today we are witnessing a convergence in mobile technology and cloud computing trends. One the one hand, mobile devices have become ubiquitous. Many of them have more computing power than high end (fixed) computers developed a decade ago. Moreover, they are equipped with multiple wireless network capabilities such as cellular network (3G/4G), Wi-Fi, bluetooth, Wi-Fi-direct, and NFC. As to be expected with any new technology, multiple implementation platforms are currently available (being the most relevant ones Android, and iOS). Important for the programmer is that each of these platforms have a radically different programming environment (e.g., Java in Android, Objective C in iOS). In order to minimize the software development costs, mobile cross-platform tools have emerged which allow the programmer to develop applications which can run on multiple mobile platforms. Many of these mobile cross-platform tools make use of web-based technologies such as Javascript and HTML5 [30]. While these

A. Ricci and P. Haller (Eds.): Programming with Actors, LNCS 10789, pp. 32–58, 2018.
https://doi.org/10.1007/978-3-030-00302-9_2

tools ease the development of certain application aspects like GUI construction, they still fall short with respect to support for distributed programming.

In this paper, we focus on a new breed of mobile applications which make use of both peer-to-peer communication and centralised wireless network access to coordinate and share data. Such *multi-networked* mobile application enable communication over both infrastructure-less networks of mobile devices, and the cloud. Note that many distributed programming abstractions already abstract away the details of the underlying network technology. For example, a socket abstracts the details of communication over a Wi-Fi connection or a bluetooth connection. However, sockets do not aid the developer in simultaneously using a Wi-Fi and bluetooth connection and seamlessly switch between them based on the connectivity. Developing rich mobile applications thus burdens developers with the following tasks:

- Programmers need to implement a different version of the network layer for each network technology (Bluetooth, Wi-Fi, 3G, etc.).
- Programmers need to adapt the application to support multiple architectures (peer-2-peer, client-server) depending on the network layer employed.
- Programmers need to write complex failure handling code to be able to reliably combine multiple network interfaces and application architectures.

To overcome these issues we propose AmbientJS, a mobile cross-platform development library for multi-networked mobile applications based on the actor model. In order to be able to seamlessly communicate over multiple networking technologies, AmbientJS introduces a novel kind of *extensible remote object reference* which abstracts over the kind of network interface being used. We call such object references network transparent references (NTR). As a result, applications can seamlessly communicate over the cloud or use an infrastructureless mobile network depending on the underlying available networking technology. NTRs offer reliable communication and as such, programmers do not need to manually verify the delivery of each message sent over multiple network interfaces. In this paper we argue that the use of NTRs implemented in the AmbientJS middleware greatly simplifies the creation of multi-networked rich mobile applications.

2   Motivation

Mobile cloud computing was initially employed for applications such as Google's Gmail which run on a rich server and the mobile device acts as a thin client connecting to it via 3G. However, due to the recent availability of networking capabilities on mobile devices, mobile cloud computing is converging to what we call *rich mobile applications*, in which the mobile devices themselves can also act as service providers and communicate with one another. In this section, we highlight the need for programming abstractions for rich mobile applications. Based on the analysis of an illustrative application, we derive a number of software engineering issues that programmers face when implementing such applications.

2.1 Case Study: Coupon Go

We now introduce an industrial case study, called *Coupon Go*, devised together with a Brussels Region company specialized in digital vouchers. This application allows the distribution and redemption of digital, electronic coupons. Figure 1, provides an architectural overview of the system.

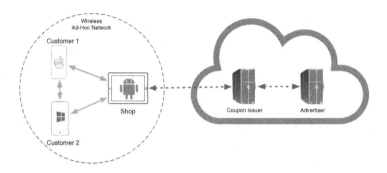

Fig. 1. Coupon Go architectural overview

As shown in the figure, the architecture of Coupon Go consists of four different actors:

- *Coupon Issuer.* The coupon issuer is in charge of the distribution of coupons to the different users upon request of an advertiser. The issuer maintains the digital wallets of the customers, and has access to the shopping history of the customer which can be used for constructing user profiles.
- *Customers.* The users of the electronic coupon system hold a digital wallet on their mobile device, which is populated in two ways: (1) users receive a coupon from the coupon issuer or from a merchant while they are in a shop, and (2) they can get coupons from other digital wallets, e.g. members of the same family transferring a coupon from one wallet to another one.
- *Shops.* Shops notify the coupon issuer when customers redeem a valid coupon. This can happen instantly if there is an internet connection available at the store, or asynchronously, e.g. at the end of the day with all the sales. Once a redeemed coupon is accepted by the issuer, the coupon is said to be *granted*, and process of repaying the store can be initiated.
- *Advertisers.* Advertisers request the generation of digital coupons to the coupon issuer for a specific product or group of products. An advertiser can also make use of the user profiles constructed by the coupon issuer to allow for more targeted advertising.

Note that the envisioned electronic coupon system, the digital coupons are first created by the coupon issuer but customers receive a copy of the coupon which is stored in their wallet. This provides offline functionality so that coupons can be validated at stores or transfer between wallets in the absence of an internet connection.

2.2   Analysis

The programmer of a rich mobile application is faced with all the traditional software engineering problems of distributed applications. However, rich mobile applications like the Coupon Go application exhibit several properties that distinguishes them from other types of distributed applications.

– First, the entities of the distributed system employ various network technologies to communicate (i.e. WPAN, WLAN etc.).
– Second, they combine multiple distributed application architectures within the same system, i.e. client-server and peer-to-peer.
– Finally, those applications need to be deployed on multiple software platforms e.g. iOS, Android, Windows mobile devices, back-end servers.

This puts extra burden on software developers. As a matter of fact, these properties act as different dimensions impacting software development.

Figure 2 shows the design space of rich mobile applications. From the point of view of the software platform, the tools and environments provided by the different platforms are often not compatible with each other. In many cases the implementation language itself is different, e.g., Java for Android devices and Swift for iOS devices. Moving from one platform to another requires programmers to rewrite the application from scratch.

From the distributed application architecture perspective, programming a traditional client-server application is very different from programming a peer-to-peer application over e.g. Wi-Fi-direct. A peer-to-peer application includes a discovery process which is not required when contacting a centralised server in a client-server architecture. When the application is not designed from scratch with multiple network technologies large portions of the application need to be rewritten.

Finally, from the network technology perspective, the networking libraries available for communicating over a bluetooth connection are very different from

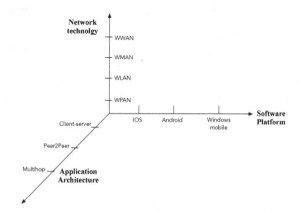

Fig. 2. Design space of rich mobile applications

the libraries for creating HTTP request. Again when the application is not written with these different application requirements from the start there is a big impact on the overall architecture of the application when using a different network technology.

2.3 Problem Statement

There is a long history in distributed computing in order to pinpoint appropriate methodologies and software practices for writing distributed applications. One particular important seminal article called "the fallacies of distributed computing" gives an overview of a number of misconceptions that traditional programmers have when first implementing a distributed application. These fallacies are: the network is reliable, latency is zero, bandwidth is infinite, the network is secure, topology doesn't change, there is one administrator, transport cost is zero and the network is homogeneous [5].

Traditional distributed applications typically only exhibit one single application architecture which does not change during the lifetime of the application. In a rich mobile application, on the other hand, the kind of architecture evolves during the applications lifetime depending on the networking technology available for communication. Moreover, these network architectures can be active a the same time. For example, a device could communicate with a nearby device with ad hoc networking technology while communicating with a centralized server. In our case study, a customer can get coupons directly from a shop or a nearby digital wallet. However, when that user moves out of direct communication range, the application can seamlessly switch communication through a centralized server available on the Internet by 3G or Wi-Fi connection. These kind of scenarios were not within the reach of everyday mobile applications when the eight fallacies of distributed computing were conceived. Today, however, every mobile device has a multitude of network facilities which can only be put to good use when developers are given the right software engineering principles. We argue that due to the technological advances programmer today are faced with a ninth fallacy when writing rich mobile applications. **The Ninth Fallacy of Distributed Computing:**

> There is only one fixed application architecture throughout the lifetime of the application.

In the rest of this paper we formulate our answer to tackle this ninth fallacy of distributed computing under the form of a new distributed library called AmbientJS. AmbientJS introduces a novel extensible remote object reference which abstracts over the kind of network interface being used.

3 AmbientJS

AmbientJS is a mobile cross-platform library for JavaScript specially designed to ease the development of rich mobile applications. The library embodies the principles of ambient-oriented programming model from the AmbientTalk language [4] and extends them to support multiple distributed application architectures employing different network technologies. The idea of AmbientJS is that programmers can write their rich mobile applications in JavaScript as *one single application* which consists of different *actors* that can be distributed over mobile devices (iOS and Android devices). At server side, AmbientJS can be used in combination with `node.js`. Communication between different distributed actors employs a uniform distributed object model which abstracts over the different networking technologies employed by the application architecture. This includes *direct* peer2peer communication and *indirect* communication through a server. We will first introduce the general architecture of AmbientJS and then focus on its programming support.

3.1 AmbientJS General Architecture

In order to deal with the diversity of software platforms, AmbientJS has been integrated as a JavaScript library to be used on top of mobile cross-platform technology. However, mobile cross-platforms frameworks are not homogenous. There exists two big families of approaches: interpreted and hybrid technologies [30]. Nevertheless, AmbientJS has been designed as a mobile cross-platform agnostic library. This means it can be used on top of the most relevant incarnations of interpreted and hybrid mobile cross-platform technologies, namely Cordova and Titanium.

Figure 3 shows the general architecture of AmbientJS which consists of three main components:

1. AmbientJS's core which provides distributed programming abstractions on top of ambient-oriented programming model,
2. the platform bridge which is in charge of loading the right mobile cross-platform framework, either Titanium or Cordova and dispatches distributed communication from the core to the corresponding networking layer,
3. the AmbientJS networking layer built in JavaScript which provides service discovery and communication services to the core. This layer is implemented on top of the underlying networking libraries for each mobile cross-platform frameworks (namely, Bonjour and NSD for Titanium, and zeroconf and Chrome sockets for Cordova).

AmbientJS's core in turn consists of three cornerstones components:

1. An actor model translating the principles of ambient-oriented programming to rich mobile applications (explained in Sect. 3.2).
2. A novel object referencing abstraction called *Network Transparent References* (NTRs) which abstracts away the complexities of the basic networking facilities. NTRs are the main abstraction to help developers deal with the different distributed application architectures as we explain Sect. 3.3.
3. A metalevel interface on which NTRs have been built. The meta-level interface is the key feature in order to allow for extensibility of NTRs as we explain in Sect. 3.5.

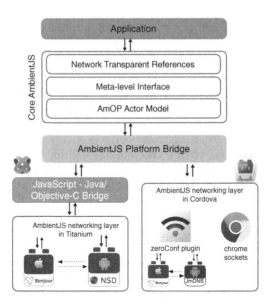

Fig. 3. Architectural overview of AmbientJS

Before delving into each of the main components of AmbientJS' core, let us briefly explain the development process of AmbientJS application for each platform. Titanium applications consists of a number of JavaScript modules in which GUI and device specific APIs are offered by the platform as JavaScript modules. AmbientJS applications are just regular Titanium applications which import the AmbientJS library in their project as shown below.

```
1  var AmbientJS = require('js/AmbientJS/AmbientJS');
2  AmbientJS.online();
3  // ... use AmbientJS ...
```

AmbientJS is packaged as a third party Titanium plugin which, once loaded, it can be accessed as any default APIs supported by Titanium (e.g. for GUI construction and accessing phone APIs). In the code snippet, the `online` function is called to connect the library to the network and start exporting and discovering service objects by means of the underlying networking facilities. AmbientJS then relies on the JavaScript - Java/ObjectiveC bridge from Titanium (marked in grey in Fig. 3) to transform such JavaScript library code into native applications in the targeted mobile platform. Note that the same kind of code is required to load AmbientJS on top of `node.js`.

In contrast, when using AmbientJS in Cordova, programmers are required to use an asynchronous programming style since the platform only execute code upon all required libraries are ready (i.e. when the `deviceready` is emitted).

As such, when employing AmbientJS in Cordova, programmers need to first register to the `AmbientJSready` event as follows:

```
1  var AmbientJS = require('./AmbientJS/AmbientJS');
2  AmbientJS.events.addListener('AmbientJSready', function() {
3  // ... use AmbientJS ...
4  });
```

The `AmbientJSready` event is emitted once Cordova notifies that AmbientJS is available in the platform. Cordova's development environment is also different than Titanium since it expects a HTML5 file for the UI code and a JavaScript file for the application logic. In AmbientJS, application logic is divided in a number of JavaScript files. It then relies on the Browserify library[1] to create a packaged file used as input to Cordova.

3.2   Ambient-Oriented Actor Model

As previously mentioned, AmbientJS incorporates the Ambient-Oriented Programming (AmOP) paradigm at the heart of its programming model. The model advocates a non-blocking communication model to ensure autonomy of devices in face of partial failures so frequent in a mobile environment. Similar to the AmbientTalk language, the unit of concurrency and distribution is an actor represented by an event loop which encapsulates one or more objects. As such, two objects are said to be *remote* when they are owned by different actors. All distributed communication is enqueued in the message queue of the owner of the object and processed by the owner itself. To this end, AmbientJS reuses the already existing event loop concurrency from JavaScript. As such, AmbientJS assumes one event loop per device and does not provide dedicated support to spawn new event loops in the library.

Communication between remote objects happens by means of the so-called *far references*. Far references are a special kind of remote object references which can be only used by sending asynchronous messages. Figure 4 shows the conceptual representation of a far reference with a dashed line. A far reference is reified into two meta-objects encapsulating all aspects of interactions between senders and receivers, called a *transmitter-receptor* pair. Any message sent via a far reference to an object is first enqueued by the far reference itself (by its transmitter) which then delivers it to the receiver actor using the underlying communication channel (depicted with a double line). When the message is received at the recipient actor, the receptor will first receive the message on its mailbox, and further invoke a method on the remote object when appropriate.

By manipulating these two metaobjects, developers can handle remote interactions between two objects in a *modular way* as they encapsulate the whole distributed behaviour of a remote object and the references that are handed to client objects. We use them to implement the programming abstractions to support multiple application architectures in an object-oriented programming style. We will further explain their API in Sect. 3.5.

---

[1] http://browserify.org.

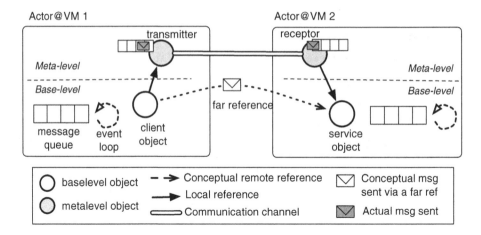

Fig. 4. Event loop concurrency in AmbientJS

In AmbientJS, objects are by default passed by far reference to objects owned by other actors. Objects can also be sent to a different AmbientJS VM by (deep) copy, which allows the recipient actor to operate on the copy by means of regular synchronous communication. Like in AmbientTalk, we refer to those objects as *isolates*.

3.3   Network Transparent References (NTRs)

As previously mentioned, the only type of communication allowed on far references is asynchronous message passing. AmbientJS extends the concept of a far reference with support for implementing different application architectures which in turn can use multiple networking technologies. This allows AmbientJS actors to communicate with one another over wireless links or mobile broadband access. As such, remote references in AmbientJS abstract the underlying networking technology being used for communication. Such *network transparent references* (NTRs) are resilient to network fluctuations by default.

Basic Network Transparent References. In order to illustrate the workings of the NTR model consider Fig. 5. Figure 5(i) shows the far reference model, in which a conceptual remote reference (dashed arrow) between objects is actually implemented by two meta-level objects. Those meta-level objects acts as proxies at each side of the reference, and enqueue messages sent from client to a service object over a communication channel. Those communication channels are built on top of one networking facilities, e.g. Wi-Fi. In such a model, if the application can communicate over different communication channels, programmers needs to do manual bookkeeping for every far references being created over each network technology.

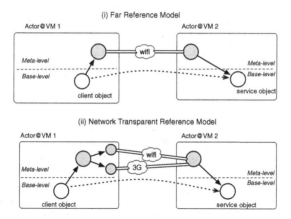

Fig. 5. Far references vs. network transparent references

Figure 5(ii) illustrates the network transparent references model. Instead of having a network reference per network technology there is conceptually only one reference. The conceptual far reference abstracts away the network technology for the programmer. Note that the network transparent reference is a distributed referencing abstraction which is active at both the sender and receiver. Part of the difficulty of having multiple references to the same object is to make sure that messages are not duplicated or lost. Therefore there is a part of the network transparent reference which is active at the receiver side in order to filter possible duplicate messages.

A NTR appears as a far reference which enqueues and transmits asynchronous messages sent to the remote object. Unlike normal far references when a network technology (e.g. bluetooth) is not available, the NTR attempts to transmit messages sent to it using another networking technology, e.g. 3G. If all network interfaces are down, the remote reference starts buffering all messages sent to it. When the network partition is restored at a later point in time, the NTR flushes all accumulated messages to the remote object in the same order as they were originally sent. As such, temporary network failures or fluctuations on the availability of the different network interfaces does not have an immediate impact on the applications' control flow. In order to distinguish partial failures from permanent failures the programmer can make use of leasing. The inner workings of this leasing mechanism are however, outside of the scope of this paper.

Network Transparent References over Multiple Network Architectures. When direct communication between two entities is not possible the traditional way of establishing a communication link with each other is by making use of known centralised server. The *network architecture* of such a distributed application is quite different from the network architecture used for a peer-to-peer application. As shown in the Coupon Go scenario both network architectures are useful during the life time of the application. The situation where communication is possible both over a centralised server and through Wi-Fi direct is sketched in Fig. 6.

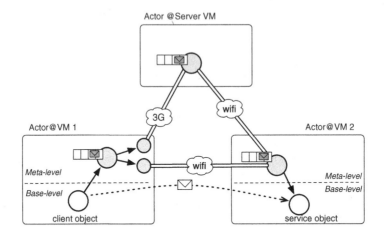

Fig. 6. Indirect network transparent references

As shown in this figure when adding a centralised sever there is a step increase in the possible ways packages can travel over the different communication channels. Important to note is that even in this complex architecture conceptually there is still only one reference between the distributed objects.

Unfortunately with existing distribution libraries the programmer needs to completely rewrite his application in order to account for the different ways that communication can be established. Because the server acts as a broker between the different communication partners it becomes even more difficult for the programmer to know exactly from which sender each message comes. For each exported object there might be multiple incoming links from the server to the object. Moreover, for each sender there might be multiple ways from the sender to the sever. The programmer thus manually needs to keep track of which messages are received in order to avoid executing the same message multiple times for each communication path. With NTR the programmer does not need to be concerned about the details of routing the messages through the centralised server and can think in terms of the conceptual reference.

3.4   NTRs in Action

To illustrate NTRs and the different distributed programming constructs in AmbientJS consider the following code snippet from a rich mobile chat application.

```
1  var buddyList = {};
2  var Ambient = require("js/AmbientJS/AmbientJS");
3  function initializeMessenger(name) {
4   //....
5   Ambient.wheneverDiscovered("MESSENGER",
6    function(ntr){
7      var msg = Ambient.createMessage(getName,[]);
8      var future = ntr.asyncSend(msg,"twoway");
9      future.whenBecomes(function(reply) {
10     buddyList[reply] = ntr;
11     // send a salute message
12     });
13    });
14 }
```

Listing 1.1. Example use of asynchronous message passing over NTRs language

In this application the programmer keeps a list of buddies (`buddylist`) of all the available communication partners (line 1). After initialising the library the programmer registers a callback function to be notified about the discovery of nearby communication partners (line 5). The `wheneverDiscovered` function takes as arguments a string representing the service type and a function serving as callback. Whenever an actor is encountered in the ad hoc network that exports a matching object, the callback function is executed. The `ntr` parameter of the function is bound to a network transparent reference to the exported messenger object of another device. This means that while the programmer conceptually receives one reference there might be multiple underlying network technologies to the same remote object.

Once the programmer has obtained the network transparent reference he proceeds by sending a message `getName` over the NTR (line 7–8). The result of sending this asynchronous message is a future on which the programmer registers a callback to receive the reply (line 8–9). When the remote object returns the result of processing the `getName` message the callback function is applied and the return value is bound to the variable `reply`. The programmer then simply stores the network transparent reference into the buddy list and uses the name of the remote buddy as a key (line 10). Note that in a real application care needs to be taken to make these names unique. This concludes the discovery part of the chat application.

We now show how programmers can export a local object so that other mobile phones can discover it. In order to export objects to the network, the `exportAs` function is employed. The code snippet below shows how to create an object which implements a service corresponding to the chat application. Then we export this object with MESSENGER string as service type so that other devices in the neighbourhood can discover it (line 5).

```
1  var remoteObj = Ambient.createObject({
2    "getName": function () { return myName; },
3    "talkTo": function (msg) { displayMessage(msg);}
4  });
5  Ambient.exportAs(remoteObj, "MESSENGER");
```

Extending the Peer-to-Peer Chat Application to Use a Centralised Server. So far our chat application exhibits a peer to peer architecture. With the code provided two phones can already communicate with each other when they are within direct communication range. However, when the phones are not in direct communication range, AmbientJS allows the phones to communicate with each other through a centralised node server. To this end, the programmer needs to configure a node server so that service objects can also be exported via an intermediary server in the cloud. The entire code to configure the server is shown below.

```
1  var Ambient=require("js/AmbientJS/AmbientJS"),
2  express = require("express"),
3  nodeServer = require("http").Server(express());
4  nodeServer.listen(3000);
5  Ambient.initServer(nodeServer);
```

The only change needed at the client side of the application is to add one line in the configuration object of AmbientJS. For example the following configuration file is sufficient for the clients to be able to connect to the software languages lab server to discover each other. Because the application was written with network transparent references there are no further changes necessary to the application.

```
1  var configuration = {
2    serverurl : 'http://soft.vub.ac.be:3000'
3  };
```

3.5   Meta-level Interface

AmbientJS features a meta-level interface inspired by the transmitter-receptor meta model [10] which reifies the most important aspects of distributed communication amongst remote objects. As illustrated in Fig. 4, a remote reference is represented at the meta level as a pair of metaobjects, named *transmitter* and *receptor*, representing the source and the target of a far reference, respectively. Transmitter and receptors provide a meta-object protocol (MOP) [15] that allows developers to modify message sending semantics via far references as well as how references are shared in the network. It has been used to implement NTRs and provide them as the default kind of communication mechanism in AmbientJS.

Each service object is bound to at least one receptor. The receptor intercepts each asynchronous message received by its associated service object in a transparent way. It can then perform actions before or after the service object sends or receives a message to handle aspects such as persistence, replication, security, etc. A transmitter, on the other hand, is transparently created on the client device when a receptor is unmarshalled, and is used to transmit asynchronous messages to the service object (via the receptor). A transmitter can perform some actions before or after a message send to handle communication aspects such as providing one-to-many communication, applying delivery guarantees, logging successful message sends, etc. In addition, a transmitter exposes the network connectivity of the physical communication with the device hosting the service object.

We now explain the core API exposed by transmitters and receptors and explain their relevance to implement NTRs.

onReceive(message) This hook allows changing the default behaviour of the reference when a message is sent to the reference. The default behaviour at transmitter side is to remove a letter from the far reference's mailbox containing the message and receiver, and transmits it. At receptor side, it makes the service object accept the delivery of an asynchronous message. We employ this hook to ensure message order and eliminate duplicates at the receptor side of NTRs.

onPassReference(reference) This hook reifies the act of marshalling objects when they are passed as argument of a message sent to another actor, or passed via the service discovery mechanism. It returns either the receptor or the transmitter to be marshalled instead of this receptor or transmitter. This hook is employed in NTRs to be able to implement indirect access via a server.

Programmers can employ such MOP to extend NTRs to support other application architectures, or to build other families of referencing abstractions. In the context of the Coupon Go, we employed such a meta-level interface to implement different consistency policies for objects distributed between virtual wallets. For example, we built a *single use* object to model transferable coupons which can only be redeemed once, even if they are transferred amongst the wallets of the members of a family. Listing 1.2 shows a simplification of the implementation of the reference abstraction allowing for single use objects.

```
1   function singleUseConsistencyRef(){
2       var receptor = AmbientJS.createReferenceProxy(function(delegate){
3           var blocked = false;
4           this.onReceive = function(msg){
5               if (!this.blocked) {
6                   delegate.onReceive(msg);
7                   if (msg == "redeem") {
8                       this.blocked = true
9                   }
10                  return true;
11              } else { return false;}
12          }
```

```
13      /// rest code
14      }
15  }
```

Listing 1.2. Creating a custom far reference abstraction for a single use consistency object.

createReferenceProxy function creates a receptor for a delegate object (which is passed by parameter). The receptor then mediates all distributed message passing and serialization of the delegate object. In this case, the receptor keeps a boolean to limit the access to the delegate object after receiving the message redeem. To this end, it overrides the onReceive function to block the object upon reception of the first redeem message. Listing below shows how to use the newly created receptor for creating a twix coupon object. The code employs extended version of the createObject function in which we can pass a custom receptor which will control the reception of messages sent to the twixCoupon (which acts as the delegate object from the point of view of the receptor).

```
1  var twixCoupon = AmbientJS.createObject({
2      "getDescription" : function() {...},
3      "getStockCount" : function() {...},
4      "redeem" : function(amount) {...}
5  }, receptor);
```

4   Developing Applications with AmbientJS

In this section, we describe the implementation of a rich mobile application developed with AmbientJS. This application is a mobile variant of the well known arcade game called pong. In our explanation we stress the distributed aspects of the application and omit the details of the application logic.

4.1   wePong Application

Similar to pong, wePong allows two players to defeat each other by playing table tennis. The player controls a paddle to hit a ball back and forth in a game field. The game differentiates from the original game in two fundamental aspects: (1) players control the paddle by moving the mobile device, and (2) the table field is distributed amongst players. Each player's mobile device represents the game field for one player, which can interact with the game field of another player nearby (by means of ad-hoc networking technology) or a remote player (over the Internet).

Figure 7 shows the game field of a player which initially contains a paddle, a portal and one ball. A portal is a special object located somewhere on the game field (depicted by a green circle in the figure). When a ball traverses the portal, the ball is sent to the opponent. To make the game more competitive, each player has a power-up bar which contains the following types of items:

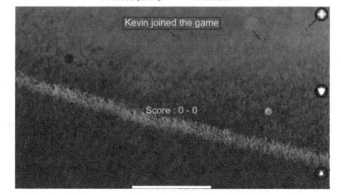

Fig. 7. Screenshot of the wePong game

- extra ball power-up, which adds an extra ball to the game field of the player.
- multi-ball power-up, which adds three to five new balls to the game.
- long pallet power-up, which enlarges pallet for a duration of 20 s.
- score power-up, which appears for few seconds on the field game and allows the player to earn extra 100 points when it is hitted.

Power-ups appear randomly in the bar of each player. The figure shows the power-up bar on the left hand side of the field with unused 3 power-ups, and an active score power-up on the game field. In order to use power-ups in the game, a player can either tap it or drag it to a portal. When a power-up is tapped, the effect is applied to the player's own game field. A power-up can also be dragged to the portal which will apply it to the opponent.

4.2   Implementation

The first step in the implementation of wePong, is to create and export a game object to representing a playing session in the network. When the user clicks on the `newRoomButton` button, the application creates a game session and waits for an opponent to join it. Listing 1.3 shows the code exporting the game object to other wePong applications instances. The game object is stored in the `remoteInterface` variable at line 3 and contains four methods that can be called by remote wePong applications: (1) `getGameName` returns the name of the game session being exported so that a list of available games is shown to the user, (2) `joiningGame` is called by an opponent who wants to join the game session, (3) `scoreChange` is used to receive the score updates from an opponent, and (4) `receiveGameElement` is used to receive power-ups or balls sent by the opponent. As shown in line 11 power-ups are model by `gameElement` objects which need to implement the `doAction` function.

```
1   function startGame(roomName) {
2       currentGame = new game(AmbientJS, roomName, instrumenting);
3       var remoteInterface = AmbientJS.createObject(
4           "getGameName":
5               function () { return roomName; },
6           "joiningGame" :
7               function (nickname) { currentGame.playerJoined(nickname);
                    }
8           "scoreChange" :
9               function (score) { currentGame.receiveOpponentScore(score)
                    ; },
10          "receiveGameElement" :
11              function(gameElement) { gameElement.doAction(currentGame)
                    },
12      });
13      AmbientJS.exportAs(remoteInterface, "WePong_Game");
14      currentGame.start(true);
15  }
```

Listing 1.3. Exporting a wePong game session on the network

Listing 1.4 shows the discovery of a wePong game instance. Upon discovery, the application requests the name of the game session being exported by a player by sending the **getGameName** message (line 2). Once the future for that asynchronous message is resolved, the **addRoomToTable** method adds a new name to the list of available game sessions (line 5), and the **joinGame** is called if the user selects that game session by clicking on the name, and will notify the opponent of the wish to join the game session.

```
1   AmbientJS.wheneverDiscovered("WePong_Game", function(reference) {
2       var getNameMsg = AmbientJS.createMessage("getGameName", []);{}
3       var future     = reference.asyncSend(getNameMsg, "twoway");
4       future.whenBecomes(function(name) {
5           var row = addRoomToTable(name);
6           row.addEventListener('click', function(e) {
7               joinGame(name, reference);
8           });
9       });
10  });
```

Listing 1.4. Discovering a wePong game session on the network

The application contains a gameloop which periodically updates the position of the balls and the pallet. The gameloop also detects collisions between a ball and some game object. When a collision happens between a ball and the portal, the ball is sent to the opponent by calling the sendBall function.

Listing 1.5 shows the sendBall function. Each applications keeps an array of balls being displayed on the game field. Before sending the ball to the opponent, it is first remove from the player's game field (in lines 2–3). Line 4 creates an AmbientJSobject which is a copy of the ball to be passed to the opponent. In this case the createObjectTaggedAs function is used to send the ball by copy. The teleportedBall implements the required doAction method which will basically add the ball to the opponent's game field upon arrival. Lines 10 and 12 create the receiveGameElement message which carries the teleportedBall and sends it as one way message (i.e. we do not request a future for the result of the function). The similar implementation strategy is followed to send power-ups to the opponents when they are dragged into a portal.

```
1  function sendBall(ball) {
2      var i = balls.indexOf(ball);
3      balls.splice(i, 1);
4      var teleportedBall = AmbientJS.createObjectTaggedAs({
5          var copyBall = [ball.x, ball.y, ball.vx, ball.vy];
6          "doAction" : function (opponentsGame) {
7              opponentsGame.receiveBall(copyBall);
8          }
9      }, [Isolate]);
10     var ballMsg = AmbientJS.createMessage(
11         "receiveGameElement", [teleportedBall]);
12     opponent.reference.asyncSend(ballMsg, "oneway");
13     delete ball;
14 }
```

Listing 1.5. Sending a ball to an opponent through a portal

This concludes the relevant parts of the distribution aspects of wePong. We have actually built two variants of wePong application, one to be deployed on mobile devices natively with Titanium and one as a web application with Cordova. Both variants employ the same AmbientJS code for implementing the game functionality and distribution aspects. Only native functionality like acceleration data, screen touches and user interface elements are different.

5   Performance Evaluation

Recall that AmbientJS is implemented on top of two existing cross-platform technology: Cordova and Titanium. Cordova is a hybrid technology where the application is written in a mixture between HTML5 and Javascript while Titanium is an so called interpreted approach where all the UI elements are native components and the application logic is written in Javascript. In order to showcase the usability of AmbientJS we performed benchmarks with respect to CPU-load, memory consecution and network throughput for both implementations.

Each benchmark is conducted by monitoring the execution performance of the wePong game running on an iPhone 4S and an iPhone 6S. Note that the implementation of the game does not rely on the GPU. Therefore, all calculations of the trajectory of the balls, the collision detection and the network connections with other players need to be handled by the CPU.

In order to ensure that the game is executing exactly the same code on both platforms, the user interaction is completely automated. The automated script goes through a typical scenario where two users connect with each other and play the wePong game. The script fully automates all the interactions including the device orientation and user touches such as tapping and dragging. Every source of randomness was also removed from the game i.e. we ran it with the same seed.

All performance experiments were measured with the Xcode performance tools[2]. For each run of the benchmark, the **CPU**, **memory usage** and **network throughput** is measured. A first observation is that *both versions of AmbientJS are able to run the wePong game smoothly at 80 frames per second.* There are, however, small differences between the interpreted version and the hybrid approach. We give an overview of these difference in the following sections.

5.1   CPU Usage

The CPU usage is determined by measuring the CPU load at discrete time intervals during the execution of the application. Each execution of the wePong game lasts a bit more than a minute. During that time the Xcode Activity Monitor is able to make 38 measurements of the CPU-load. We take the average CPU

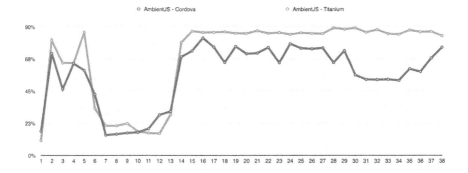

Fig. 8. Average CPU-usage over time

---

[2] https://tinyurl.com/instrumentsUserGuide.

load at each time interval for multiple runs of the application. Figure 8 shows the average CPU-loads for both the Cordova and Titanium implementation.

From this graph it is clear that the CPU-load for both Cordova and Titanium has a similar shape. At the start of the application there is a heavy startup-cost after which the CPU-load becomes less intensive. When the connection between the phones is established and the wePong game is running, the CPU load peeks again. The graph clearly shows that the CPU load for wePong is less for Cordova than for the Titanium implementation. The reason for this difference probably lies in the fact that the Cordova version runs inside an HTML5 canvas, while in Titanium it uses native UI elements. Hence, Titanium needs glue code to communicate between the JavaScript interpreter and native components which requires more CPU-load than its browser-based counterpart.

5.2   Memory Usage

To monitor memory usage throughout a wePong game, we used the Allocations instrument included in Xcode Instruments. This instrument reports every memory allocation together with its size and timestamp. We processed the output of this tool and imported them into SPSS. We then further processed these files in order to measure the overall memory usage. Figure 9 shows the memory consumption of the wePong application in three different runs of the benchmarked scenario.

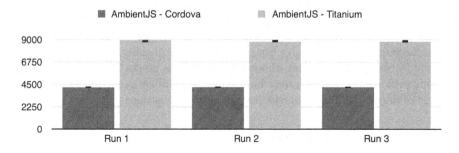

Fig. 9. Memory consumption of the wePong application

Based on Fig. 9, we conclude that the Titanium implementation of wePong is using significantly more memory than the Cordova one. This is because Titanium uses native UI elements to provide a better looking UI and bundles a self contained JavaScript interpreter, while Cordova does not use any extra styling to make the user interface look better and relies on the built in JavaScript interpreter. Hence, as Titanium provides a full SDK the memory usage is significantly higher than with plain HTML5 and CSS.

5.3 Network Throughput

The last performance benchmark we conducted measures the network through-put during the lifetime of the wePong application. Again the network throughput is measured by taking discrete slices of the application and measure the through-put at that time slice. Note that the data that is being sent is exactly the same for each of the implementations. The result of measuring the throughput is shown in Fig. 10.

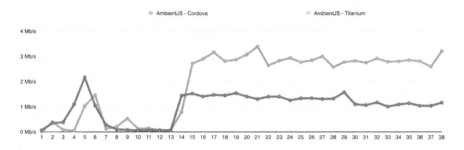

Fig. 10. Network throughput

From this benchmarks we can conclude that our network layer implemented on top of Titanium performs significantly better with respect to throughput. The most probable reason for this difference in throughput is that for the imple-mentation in Titanium we directly access the native libraries of the phone. In the case of Cordova we make use of the web sockets library which seems to per-form a bit worse than the native libraries. Note that in practice both versions of AmbientJS run the application smoothly and there is no noticeable network lag. But this performance impact may be noticed by applications transferring large amount of data like sharing or video streaming applications.

5.4 Benchmark Conclusions

Our benchmarks unveiled that making use of the native UI components is not necessarily more performant. In the wePong application there are many calls from the Javascript to the UI component to draw on the screen. In the Titanium implementation all these calls need to be translated to calls to the UI component which is less efficient than directly using a HTML5 webview. We also noticed that making use of Titanium implies a significant memory overhead compared to the Cordova approach. Finally, we observed that employing native components as done by Titanium does pay off in terms of network throughput which is significantly higher than in the Cordova implementation.

When one has to choose a suited mobile cross-platform approach for his appli-cation, various factors need to be considered. Important factors are performance as well as user experience. Because in Titanium the GUI components are native the user experience is much better.

6 Related Work

In what follows we describe the different advances in the field of mobile and cloud computing with respect to the design space of rich mobile applications. We give an overview of the related work in three dimensions: the network technology, distributed application architectures and the software platforms.

Network Technology. Mobile rich applications employ a wide variety of connection protocols, being the most relevant ones Wi-Fi, Bluetooth, and 3G [8]. Wi-Fi was intended as replacement for cabling amongst computers for wireless local area networks (WLANs). Wi-Fi's communication range is within 100 m and supports up to 11 Mbps data rates. Bluetooth, on the other hand, was intended for wireless personal area networks (WPAN) uses and it is characterized by low-power shorter communication range (up to 10 m) requirements. Bluetooth Low Energy (BLE) has reduced power consumption while keeping a similar range. Finally, 3G provide broadband access to mobile devices of several Mbps, which is slower than Wi-Fi but can be deployed over wider areas.

Since energy consumption varies amongst those technologies (e.g. 3G has been shown to be higher than Wi-Fi), many research in mobile cloud computing has focused on offloading workload from mobile devices depending on the connection protocols used [8]. Satyanarayanan et al. proposed the concept of a *cloudlet* [24] in which part of the computation of the cloud is offloaded to several multi-core computers which has access to the cloud (forming a cloudlet). This solution advocates VM technology which automatically offloads application workload from the mobile device (which acts as a thin client) to a nearby cloudlets situated on designated places like coffee shops or airports. Such VM migration technique is employed by many mobile computing frameworks since it requires no or very little application rewriting [8]. Common to our approach their VM migration techniques can be deployed over several network interfaces. Their approach is to hide the complexity in the VM while we offer it at the middleware layer. Moreover, they do not provide any cross-platform facilities.

Distributed Application Architectures. An application architecture basically materializes the abstraction of a communication link used to represent the interactions between entities of a distributed system [3]. In traditional distributed applications, interactions are often established between two entities or process. The most representative case of this type of interactions are client-server applications, supported by point-to-point communication abstractions. One of the most recurrent communication abstractions for building distributed client-server applications has been Remote Procedure Call(RPC). RPC-based solutions include distributed middleware like RMI [25], or RBI [13], but it has been also employed in the context of web programming in service-oriented architectures like SOAP [29] and Apache Thrift developed by Facebook[3]. Nevertheless, RPC

---

[3] http://thrift.apache.org/.

has been repeatedly highlighted to be unappropriated for distributed programming [27,28]. Several extensions were proposed to overcome the so-criticized synchronous request-response messaging promoted by RPC like queueing RPCs [14]. In the context of rich mobile applications, one of the main critique on RPC is the lack of support for disconnected operations [8].

Peer-to-peer architectures, one the other hand, considers that processes can both provide and request services. Those architectures are often supported by group communication abstractions. One of the representative approach of this kind of interactions is the publish/subscribe communication paradigm [6] which allows processes to interact by publishing event notification (often called *events*) and subscribing to the type of events they are interested in. The first publish/subscribe systems assumed that components comprising an application are stationary and interact by means of a fixed, reliable network of event brokers. Adaptations for mobile computing does not rely on intermediate infrastructure, but rely on broadcasting of subscriptions to reachable hosts (e.g. EMMA [20]), or to a certain geographical area closeby the producer, e.g. STEAM [17]. Such group communication abstractions have recently penetrated mainstream SDKs like allJoyn2, Qeo library3, Intel CCF SDK4.

Another group of models and languages in mobile computing are based on the concept of *coordination* in which interactions are established between two or more process by means of a shared tuple space [9] by reading and writing tuples. Mobile middleware such as LIME [19] and TOTA [16] are the most representative examples based on distributed peer-to-peer variants of the original, shared memory tuple space model. Mobile tuple space systems that have adopted a replication model [11,16,18] allow for multi-hop architectures in which devices in the network can be used as routers of messages.

Although variations of RPC, publish/subscribe and tuple spaces are plentiful, the integration of those interactions has received very attention. Eugster et al. [7] proposed support for publish/subscribe programming into an object-oriented language. However, that work does not integrate the paradigms, rather allows programmers to use both event notifications and message passing and objects. To the best of our knowledge, reconciling the communication properties of point-to-point and group communication models has only been studied in the context of distributed programming language AmbientTalk [4]. Van Cutsem et al. [26] explored a novel remote object reference abstraction called *ambient reference* which unifies point-to-point with group communication for mobile ad hoc networking applications. The main novelty of *ambient references* lies in the declarative designation of a group of communication partners. Ambient references, however, do not provide any means to combine multiple network technologies and present it as a single reference abstraciton to the programmer. In the context of mobile RFID-enabled applications, *multiway references* [21,22] were introduced as a reference abstraction that allows to address RFID-enabled objects through different networking technologies. This paper builds on this work and applies it in the context of rich mobile applications.

Software Platforms. From the platform perspective, developing rich mobile applications entails developing one mobile application for each platforms. However, this is costly and requires deep knowledge of several operating systems and programming languages, and imposes redudancy at the whole software development cycle from design to testing [1]. In oder to reduce that cost, mobile cross-platform frameworks have emerged as a solution to alleviate the issue [30]. They advocate the use of a single code base which can be deployed on multiple mobile plaftorms.

There are two different kinds of mobile cross-platform solutions: hybrid approaches and interpreted approaches (also called "self-contained runtime environments" [12]). The most prominent exponent of the hybrid approach is Phone-Gap (currently developed in Apache Cordova) which combines web technology and native functionality. More precisely, hybrid mobile applications combine HTML5 web applications inside a native container (UIWebView in iOS and WebView in Android). On the other hand, the most relevant interpreted technology is Appcelerator Titanium mobile which generates native code for the UI and application logic implemented using JavaScript. Interpreted applications are said to be more efficient and provide better user experience than hybrid approaches because of the native user interfaces. However, they are mainly criticized by the complete dependence on the software development environment as the UI is implemented completely programmatically using the provided APIs.

What both families of mobile cross-platform frameworks have in common is that they provide a number of built-in APIs for GUI construction and accessing the underlying hardware without requiring detailed knowledge of the targeted platform. However, developers still need to deal with many of the difficulties for distributed programming, as they only provide low-level libraries directly on top of networking protocols for communication (e.g. HTTP request and TCP/IP sockets in Titanium, WebRTC or Chrome sockets in the case of Cordova).

While most popular mobile cross-platform solutions are built for JavaScript, alternatives exists employing other languages like C# in Xamarin[4], or C/C++ in Marmalade SDK[5]. Employing JavaScript has the potential to allow developers to write both mobile client and back-ends on the same programming language (e.g. by Cordova and `node.js` at client and server side respectively). Note, however, there is no distributed object model that can be used on both mobile clients and back-end JavaScript code running on `node.js`. Recent trends include the use of reactive programming libraries [2] for JavaScript for communication between client and server. However, distributed reactive programming is its infancy [23], and developers need to manually program the interactions, ensuring consistency and offline functionality.

---

[4] https://www.xamarin.com/.

[5] https://marmaladegamestudio.com/tech/.

7   Conclusion

In this paper, we argued that due to mobile computing advances, programmers today are faced with a ninth fallacy of distributed computing: *"there is only one fixed application architecture throughout the lifetime of the application"*. When programmers do not take into account that their mobile applications can operate both in a peer-to-peer fashion as well as in a client-server architecture adding support for both kinds of application architecture usually requires a rewrite of the networking layer. We have shown that such problems do not arise when making use our mobile cross-platform actor library called AmbientJS. The main innovation of AmbientJSis the embodiment of a special kind of extensible remote reference, called network transparent references (NTRs), which abstracts away from the underlying network technology used. We have given an overview of the NTR model, detailed their implementation in AmbientJS and assessed the performance of AmbientJS with benchmarks.

References

1. Abolfazli, S., Sanaei, Z., Gani, A., Xia, F., Yang, L.T.: Review: rich mobile applications: genesis, taxonomy, and open issues. J. Netw. Comput. Appl. **40**, 345–362 (2014)
2. Bainomugisha, E., Carreton, A.L., Van Cutsem, T., Mostinckx, S., De Meuter, W.: A survey on reactive programming. ACM Comput. Surv. **45**(4), 52:1–52:34 (2013). https://doi.org/10.1145/2501654.2501666. Article no: 52
3. Cachin, C., Guerraoui, R., Rodrigues, L.: Introduction to Reliable and Secure Distributed Programming, 2nd edn. Springer, Heidelberg (2011). https://doi.org/10.1007/978-3-642-15260-3
4. Van Cutsem, T., Gonzalez Boix, E., Scholliers, C., Carreton, A.L., Harnie, D., Pinte, K., De Meuter, W.: AmbientTalk: programming responsive mobile peer-to-peer applications with actors. Comput. Lang. Syst. Struct. **40**(34), 112–136 (2014). https://doi.org/10.1016/j.cl.2014.05.002
5. Deutch, P.: The eight fallacies of distributed computing (1994). https://blogs.oracle.com/jag/resource/Fallacies.html. Captured Feb 2017
6. Eugster, P.T., Felber, P.A., Guerraoui, R., Kermarrec, A.: The many faces of publish/subscribe. ACM Comput. Surv. **35**(2), 114–131 (2003)
7. Eugster, P.T., Guerraoui, R., Damm, C.H.: On objects and events. SIGPLAN Not. **36**(11), 254–269 (2001)
8. Fernando, N., Loke, S.W., Rahayu, W.: Mobile cloud computing: a survey. Futur. Gener. Comput. Syst. **29**(1), 84–106 (2013). Including Special section: AIRCC-NetCoM 2009 and Special section: Clouds and Service-Oriented Architectures
9. Gelernter, D.: Generative communication in Linda. ACM Trans. Program. Lang. Syst. **7**(1), 80–112 (1985)
10. Gonzalez Boix, E.: Handling partial failures in mobile ad hoc network applications: from programming language design to tool support. Ph.D. thesis, Vrije Universiteit Brussel, Faculty of Sciences, Software Languages Lab, October 2012
11. Gonzalez Boix, E., Scholliers, C., De Meuter, W., D'Hondt, T.: Programming mobile context-aware applications with TOTAM. J. Syst. Softw. SCI Impact factor in 2013:1.135 (5-year impact factor 1.322) **92**, 3–19 (2014)

12. Heitkötter, H., Hanschke, S., Majchrzak, T.A.: Evaluating cross-platform development approaches for mobile applications. In: Cordeiro, J., Krempels, K.-H. (eds.) WEBIST 2012. LNBIP, vol. 140, pp. 120–138. Springer, Heidelberg (2013). https://doi.org/10.1007/978-3-642-36608-6_8

13. Ibrahim, A., Jiao, Y., Tilevich, E., Cook, W.R.: Remote batch invocation for compositional object services. In: Drossopoulou, S. (ed.) ECOOP 2009. LNCS, vol. 5653, pp. 595–617. Springer, Heidelberg (2009). https://doi.org/10.1007/978-3-642-03013-0_27

14. Joseph, A.D., Tauber, J.A., Kaashoek, M.F.: Mobile computing with the Rover toolkit. IEEE Trans. Comput. **46**(3), 337–352 (1997)

15. Kiczales, G., Paepcke, A.: Open implementations and metaobject protocols. Tutorial slides and notes, Software Design Area, Xerox Corporation (1996). http://www.parc.xerox.com/csl/groups/sda/publications

16. Mamei, M., Zambonelli, F.: Programming pervasive and mobile computing applications: the TOTA approach. ACM Trans. Softw. Eng. Methodol. **18**(4), 15:1–15:56 (2009)

17. Meier, R., Cahill, V.: Steam: event-based middleware for wireless ad hoc networks. In: 22nd International Conference on Distributed Computing Systems, pp. 639–644. IEEE Computer Society, Washington, DC (2002)

18. Murphy, A.L., Picco, G.P.: Using LIME to support replication for availability in mobile ad hoc networks. In: Ciancarini, P., Wiklicky, H. (eds.) COORDINATION 2006. LNCS, vol. 4038, pp. 194–211. Springer, Heidelberg (2006). https://doi.org/10.1007/11767954_13

19. Murphy, A., Picco, G., Roman, G.-C.: LIME: a middleware for physical and logical mobility. In: Proceedings of the 21st International Conference on Distributed Computing Systems, pp. 524–536. IEEE Computer Society (2001)

20. Musolesi, M., Mascolo, C., Hailes, S.: EMMA: epidemic messaging middleware for ad hoc networks. Pers. Ubiquitous Comput. **10**(1), 28–36 (2005)

21. Pinte, K., Harnie, D., D'Hondt, T.: Enabling cross-technology mobile applications with network-aware references. In: De Meuter, W., Roman, G.-C. (eds.) COORDINATION 2011. LNCS, vol. 6721, pp. 142–156. Springer, Heidelberg (2011). https://doi.org/10.1007/978-3-642-21464-6_10

22. Pinte, K., Harnie, D., Gonzalez Boix, E., De Meuter, W.: Network-aware references for pervasive social applications. In: Second IEEE Workshop on Pervasive Collaboration and Social Networking (PERCOM Workshops), pp. 537–542, March 2011

23. Salvaneschi, G., Drechsler, J., Mezini, M.: Towards distributed reactive programming. In: De Nicola, R., Julien, C. (eds.) COORDINATION 2013. LNCS, vol. 7890, pp. 226–235. Springer, Heidelberg (2013). https://doi.org/10.1007/978-3-642-38493-6_16

24. Satyanarayanan, M., Bahl, P., Caceres, R., Davies, N.: The case for VM-based cloudlets in mobile computing. IEEE Pervasive Comput. **8**(4), 14–23 (2009)

25. Sun Microsystems: Java RMI specification (1998). http://java.sun.com/j2se/1.4.2/docs/guide/rmi/spec/rmiTOC.html

26. Van Cutsem, T., Dedecker, J., De Meuter, W.: Object-oriented coordination in mobile ad hoc networks. In: Murphy, A.L., Vitek, J. (eds.) COORDINATION 2007. LNCS, vol. 4467, pp. 231–248. Springer, Heidelberg (2007). https://doi.org/10.1007/978-3-540-72794-1_13

27. Vinoski, S.: RPC under fire. IEEE Internet Comput. **9**(5), 93–95 (2005)

28. Waldo, J., Wyant, G., Wollrath, A., Kendall, S.: A note on distributed computing. In: Vitek, J., Tschudin, C. (eds.) MOS 1996. LNCS, vol. 1222, pp. 49–64. Springer, Heidelberg (1997). https://doi.org/10.1007/3-540-62852-5_6
29. World Wide Web Consortium: Simple Object Access Protocol (SOAP) 1.2 W3C Recommendation (2007). https://www.w3.org/TR/soap12//
30. Xanthopoulos, S., Xinogalos, S.: A comparative analysis of cross-platform development approaches for mobile applications. In: Proceedings of the 6th Balkan Conference in Informatics, BCI 2013, pp. 213–220. ACM, New York (2013)

OpenCL Actors – Adding Data Parallelism to Actor-Based Programming with CAF

Raphael Hiesgen, Dominik Charousset, and Thomas C. Schmidt[✉]

Department Computer Science,
Hamburg University of Applied Sciences, Hamburg, Germany
{raphael.hiesgen,dominik.charousset,t.schmidt}@haw-hamburg.de

Abstract. The actor model of computation has been designed for a seamless support of concurrency and distribution. However, it remains unspecific about data parallel program flows, while available processing power of modern many core hardware such as graphics processing units (GPUs) or coprocessors increases the relevance of data parallelism for general-purpose computation.

In this work, we introduce OpenCL-enabled actors to the C++ Actor Framework (CAF). This offers a high level interface for accessing any OpenCL device without leaving the actor paradigm. The new type of actor is integrated into the runtime environment of CAF and gives rise to transparent message passing in distributed systems on heterogeneous hardware. Following the actor logic in CAF, OpenCL kernels can be composed while encapsulated in C++ actors, hence operate in a multi-stage fashion on data resident at the GPU. Developers are thus enabled to build complex data parallel programs from primitives without leaving the actor paradigm, nor sacrificing performance. Our evaluations on commodity GPUs, an Nvidia TESLA, and an Intel PHI reveal the expected linear scaling behavior when offloading larger workloads. For sub-second duties, the efficiency of offloading was found to largely differ between devices. Moreover, our findings indicate a negligible overhead over programming with the native OpenCL API.

Keywords: Actor model · C++ · GPGPU Computing · OpenCL Coprocessor

1 Introduction

The stagnating clock speed forced CPU manufacturers into steadily increasing the number of cores on commodity hardware to meet the ever-increasing demand for computational power. Still, the number of parallel processing units on a single GPU is higher by orders of magnitudes. This rich source of computing power became available to general purpose applications as GPUs moved away from

© Springer Nature Switzerland AG 2018
A. Ricci and P. Haller (Eds.): Programming with Actors, LNCS 10789, pp. 59–93, 2018.
https://doi.org/10.1007/978-3-030-00302-9_3

single purpose pipelines for graphics processing towards compact clusters of data parallel programmable units [36].

Many basic algorithms like sorting and searching, matrix multiplication, or fast Fourier transform have efficient, massively parallel variants. Also, a large variety of complex algorithms can be fully mapped to the data parallel architecture of GPUs with a massive boost in performance. Combined with the widespread availability of general-purpose GPU (GPGPU) devices on desktops, laptops and even mobiles, GPGPU computing has been widely recognized as an important optimization strategy. In addition, accelerating coprocessors that better support code branching established on the market.

Since not all tasks can benefit from such specialized devices, developers need to distribute work on the various architectural elements. Managing such a heterogeneous runtime environment inherently increases the complexity. While some loop-based computations can be offloaded to GPUs using OpenACC [10] or recent versions of OpenMP [15] with relatively little programming effort, it has been shown that a consistent task-oriented design exploits the available parallelism more efficiently. Corresponding results achieve better performance [27] while they are also applicable to more complex work loads. However, manually orchestrating tasks between multiple devices is an error-prone and complex task.

The actor model of computation describes applications in terms of isolated software entities—actors—that communicate by asynchronous message passing. Actors can be distributed across any number of processors or machines by the runtime system as they are not allowed to share state and thus can always be executed in parallel. The message-based decoupling of software entities further enables actors to run on different devices in a heterogeneous environment. Hence, the actor model can simplify software development by hiding the complexity of heterogeneous and distributed deployments.

In this work, we take up our previous contribution [22] about actors programmed with OpenCL—the Open Computing Language standardized by the Khronos Group [41]. We enhance the integration of heterogeneous programming with the C++ Actor Framework [11] by a fully effective encapsulation of OpenCL kernels within C++ actors—the OpenCL actor. OpenCL actors can be transparently used at regular actor programming (e.g., like a library or toolset). They can be composed like standard CAF actors, which leads to a multi-staging of OpenCL kernels. We present indexing as a realistic use case for this elegant programming approach. Furthermore, we thoroughly examine the runtime overhead introduced by our abstraction layer, and justify our integration of heterogeneous hardware to the existing benefits of CAF such as network-transparency, memory-efficiency and high performance.

The remainder of this paper is organized as follows. Section 2 introduces the actor model as well as heterogeneous computing in general and OpenCL in particular. Our design goals and their realization are laid out in Sect. 3. Along these lines, benefits and limitations of our approach are thoroughly discussed. An application use case that is composed of many data parallel primitives is described in Sect. 4. In Sect. 5, we evaluate the performances of our work with a focus on overhead and scalability. Finally, Sect. 6 concludes and gives an outlook to future work.

2   Background and Related Work

Before showing design details, we first discuss the actor model of computation, heterogeneous computing in general, and OpenCL.

2.1   The Actor Model

Actors are concurrent, isolated entities that interact via message passing. They use unique identifiers to address each other transparently in a distributed system. In reaction to a received message, an actor can, (1) send messages to other actors, (2) spawn new actors and (3) change its own behavior to process future messages differently.

These characteristics lead to several advantages. Since actors can only interact via message passing, they never corrupt each others state and thus avoid race conditions by design. Work can be distributed by spawning more actors in a divide and conquer approach. Further, the actor model addresses fault-tolerance in distributed systems by allowing actors to monitor each other. If an actors dies unexpectedly, the runtime system sends a message to each actor monitoring it. This relation can be strengthened through bidirectional monitors called links. By providing network-transparent messaging and fault propagation, the actor model offers a high level of abstraction for application design and development targeted at concurrent and distributed systems.

Hewitt et al. [21] proposed the actor model in 1973 as part of their work on artificial intelligence. Later, Agha formalized the model in his dissertation [2] and introduced mailboxing for processing actor messages. He created the foundation of an open, external communication [3]. At the same time, Armstrong took a more practical approach by developing Erlang [6].

Erlang is a concurrent, dynamically typed programming language developed for programming large-scale, fault-tolerant systems [5]. Although Erlang was not build with the actor model in mind, it satisfies its characteristics. New actors, called processes in Erlang, are created by a function called spawn. Their communication is based on asynchronous message passing. Processes use pattern matching to identify incoming messages.

To combine the benefits of a high level of abstraction and native program execution, we have developed the C++ Actor Framework (CAF) [11]. Actors are implemented as sub-thread entities and run in a cooperative scheduler using work-stealing. As a result, the creation and destruction of actors is a lightweight operation. Uncooperative actors that require access to blocking function calls can be bound to separate threads by the programmer to avoid starvation. Furthermore, CAF includes a runtime inspection tool to help debugging distributed actor systems.

In CAF, actors are created using the function spawn. It creates actors from either functions or classes and returns a network-transparent actor handle. Communication is based on message passing, using send or request. The latter function expects a response and allows setting a one-shot handler specifically for the response message. This can be done in two ways: either the actor maintains its normal behavior while awaiting the response or it suspends its behavior until the response is received.

CAF offers dynamically as well as statically typed actors. While the dynamic approach is closer to the original actor model, the static approach allows programmers to define a message passing interface which is checked by the compiler for both incoming and outgoing messages.

Messages are buffered at the receiver in order of arrival before they are processed. The behavior of an actor specifies its response to messages it receives. CAF uses partial functions as message handlers, which are implemented using an internal domain-specific language (DSL) for pattern matching. Messages that cannot be matched stay in the buffer until they are discarded manually or handled by another behavior. The behavior can be changed dynamically during message processing.

In previous work [12], we compared CAF to other actor implementations. Namely Erlang, the Java frameworks SALSA Lite [17] and ActorFoundry (based on Kilim [40]), the Scala toolkit and runtime Akka [42] and Charm++ [24]. We measured (1) actor creation overhead, (2) sending and processing time of message passing implementations, (3) memory consumption for several use cases and (4) picked up a benchmark from the Computer Language Benchmarks Game. The results showed that CAF displays consistent scaling behavior, minimal memory overhead and very high performance.

2.2 Heterogeneous Computing

Graphic processing units (GPUs) were originally developed to calculate high resolution graphic effects in real-time [33]. High frame rates are achieved by executing a single routine concurrently on many pixels at once. While this is still the dominant use-case, frameworks like OpenCL [37] or CUDA (Compute Unified Device Architecture) [25] offer an API to use the available hardware for non-graphical applications. This approach is called general purpose GPU (GPGPU) computing.

The first graphics cards were build around a pipeline, where each stage offered a different fixed operation with configurable parameters [29]. Soon, the capabilities supported by the pipeline were neither complex nor general enough to keep up with the developing capabilities of shading and lighting effects. To adapt to the challenges, each pipeline stage evolved to allow individual programmability and include an enhanced instruction set [8]. Although this was a major step towards the architecture in use today, the design still lacked mechanisms for load balancing. If one stage required more time than others, the other stages were left idle. Further, the capacities of a stage were fixed and could not be shifted depending on the algorithm. Eventually, the pipelines were replaced by data parallel programmable units to achieve an overall better workload and more flexibility [36]. All units share a memory area for synchronization, while in addition each unit has a local memory area only accessible by its own processing elements. A single unit only supports data parallelism, but a cluster of them can process task parallel algorithms as well.

By now, this architecture can be found in non-GPU hardware as well. Accelerators with the sole purpose of data parallel computing are available on the market. While some have a more similar architecture to GPUs, for example the Nvidia Tesla devices [34], others are build closer to x86 machines, most prominently the Intel Xeon Phi coprocessors [23]. Both have many more cores than available CPUs and require special programming models to make optimal use of their processing power.

Naturally, algorithms that perform similar work on independent data benefit greatly from the parallelism offered by these architectures. Since most problems cannot be mapped solely to this category, calculations on accelerators are often combined with calculations on the CPU. This combination of several hardware architectures in a single application is called heterogeneous computing.

2.3 OpenCL

The two major frameworks for GPGPU computing are CUDA (Compute Unified Device Architecture) [25]—a proprietary API by Nvidia—and OpenCL [37]—a standardized API. In our work, we focus on OpenCL, as it is vendor-independent and allows us to integrate a broad range of hardware. The OpenCL standard is developed by the OpenCL Working Group, a subgroup of the non-profit organization Khronos Group [41]. Universality is the key feature of OpenCL, but has the downside that it is not possible to exploit all hardware-dependent features. The OpenCL framework includes an API and a cross-platform programming language called "OpenCL C" [31].

A study by Fang et al. [18] examines the performance differences between OpenCL and CUDA. Their benchmarks are divided into two categories. The first category consists of synthetic benchmarks, which measure peak performance and show similar results for OpenCL and CUDA. The second category includes real-world applications and shows a better overall performance for CUDA. However, the author explain the gap with differences in the programming model, optimizations, architecture and compiler. They continue to define a fair comparison that includes several steps such as individual optimizations and multiple kernel compilation steps.

Figure 1 depicts a computing device from the perspective of OpenCL. Each device is divided into compute units (CU), which are further divided into processing elements (PE) that perform the actual calculations. OpenCL defines four different memory regions, which may differ from the physical memory layout. The global memory is accessible by all PEs and has a constant memory region with read-only access. Each local memory region is shared by the PEs of a single CU. In addition, each PE has a private memory region which cannot be accessed by others.

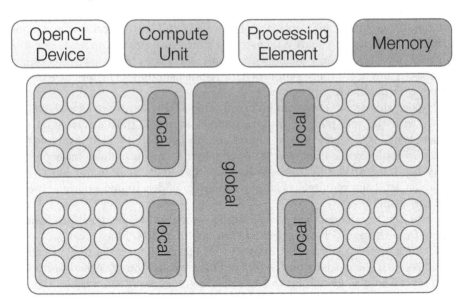

Fig. 1. The OpenCL view on a computation device, dividing the hardware into groups of Processing Elements called Compute Units that have access to shared local memory.

Each OpenCL program consists of two parts. One part runs on the host, normally a CPU, and is called host program. The other part consists of any number of kernels that run on an OpenCL device. A kernel is a function written in an OpenCL-specific C dialect. OpenCL does not require a binary interface, as kernels can be compiled at runtime by the host program for a specific GPGPU device.

A kernel is executed in an N-dimensional index space called "NDRange". Derived from three dimensional graphic calculations, N can be either one, two or three. Each tuple (n_x, n_y, n_z) in the index space identifies a single kernel execution, called work-item. These tuples are called global IDs and allow the identification of work-items during the kernel execution. Further organization is achieved through work-groups. The number of work-items per work-group cannot exceed the number of processing elements in a compute unit. Similar to the global index space, work-items can be arranged in up to three dimensions inside a work-group. All items in a work-group run in parallel on a single CU. Depending on the available hardware, work-groups may run sequentially or in parallel.

The host program initializes data on the device, compiles kernels, and manages their execution. This requires a series of steps before running a kernel on an OpenCL device. Available device drivers offer an entry point in form of different platforms. These can be queried through the OpenCL API. Once a platform is chosen, all associated device IDs can be acquired. The next step is to create a context object for managing devices of the platform in use.

Communication with a device requires a command queue. The number of command queues per context or device is not limited, though a queue is associated with a single device. Multiple commands can be organized with events. Each command can generate an event which can then be passed to another command to define a dependency between them. Alternatively, OpenCL allows associating an event with a callback. In this way, an asynchronous workflow can be implemented.

Before a kernel—usually stored as source code in the host application—can run on a device, it needs to be compiled using the API of OpenCL. The compilation is then wrapped in a program object. Each program can compile multiple kernels at once and allows their retrieval by name. Running a kernel requires the transfer of its input argument to the target device, as the memory regions of host and GPGPU device are usually disjoint. OpenCL organizes chunks of memory as memory buffer objects that can be created independently and set as read-write, read-only or write-only. Once each argument is assigned to a buffer and the programmer has specified all dimensions in the index space, the kernel can be scheduled. The last step in this process is copying any produced results from the GPGPU device back to the host.

OpenCL offers reference counted handles for its components using the prefix "cl_", e.g., a kernel is stored as a cl_kernel. The internal reference count needs to be managed manually. In a similar manner, functions are prefixed with cl, e.g., clGetPlaformIDs. Most API calls can be executed blocking as well as non-blocking.

The Khronos Group is actively working on advancing OpenCL. The next version of the specification is available as a provisional document since April 2016. In addition to OpenCL itself, the group supports projects that build upon or support OpenCL. SYCL (C++ Single-source Heterogeneous Programming for OpenCL) [28] aims to provide the same source code for the CPU and device part, compared to a separate code base for the OpenCL kernels. Since the code for all targets is written with C++ templates, it can be shared across platforms. However, the specification keeps to the familiar execution model from OpenCL and imposes the same restrictions to the SYCL device code as to OpenCL C.

2.4   Nested Parallelism

The index space (NDRange) specified to execute a kernel can be much larger than the parallelism offered by the hardware. In these cases, processing works by slicing the index space into work groups, which are then executed subsequently or partially in parallel—depending on the hardware characteristics. This concept works well for simple independent calculations. Typical examples that easily scale with the vast parallelism on GPUs are matrix multiplications or calculating fractal images such as the Mandelbrot set. The restrictions of this approach become apparent when moving to more complex applications.

Algorithms that process large amounts of data with dependencies between subsequent computation steps dependent on sequential execution of different kernels. A limiting factor is the number of work items that can be executed in parallel on a device. This number depends on the available compute units and the work items per unit—both vary greatly on different hardware. A problem is the synchronization of processing steps over the total amount of data, which might be much larger than the number of work items that can actually run in parallel. Sorensen et al. [39] discuss these limitations and propose an inter-workgroup barrier that synchronizes all threads running in parallel by estimating the *occupancy*, i.e., the number of work items that can run in parallel, and building a barrier using OpenCL atomics.

The traditional work-flow for complex computations manages this by splitting algorithms into multiple kernel execution stages. Each stage executes all work items before moving to the next stage to ensure that all data has been processes and all work items have a consistent view on the memory. Between each stages the data is kept on the device to prevent expensive copy operations.

Modern GPGPU programming models address this limitation. They allow the creation of new kernels from the device context without additional interaction from the CPU context. This can be seen in the *dynamic parallelism* offered in CUDA or the *nested parallelism* of OpenCL. The OpenCL 2.0 specification introduced the function enqueue_kernel for this purpose [32]. It can be used to enqueue new kernels to the command queue from the GPU, specifying a new index space for the execution. Moreover, the enqueued kernel can be run asynchronously, after all work items of the current kernel have finished, or after the work items of the work group have finished. Subsequent kernel executions initiated from the GPU context provide the same guarantees as for subsequent kernel executions from the CPU with regard to synchronization. From the CPU context, nested parallelism looks like a single kernel execution. Thus, waiting for the parent kernel to finish waits for all child kernels as well.

2.5 Approaches to Heterogeneous Computing

As with multi-core machines, accelerators can be programmed through many different frameworks. The above-mentioned frameworks OpenCL and CUDA are the mainstream solutions. They offer specialized functions and the opportunity for optimizations at the price of an extensive API. Many libraries have emerged that use OpenCL or CUDA as a back end to offer a higher level API and implementations of often-used algorithms. Examples are Boost.Compute[1] or VexCL[2].

The projects Aparapi [4] and PyOpenCL [26] provide interfaces for writing OpenCL kernels in their respective language, Java and Python. By avoiding the use of OpenCL C they ease the entrance to heterogeneous computing for developers not familiar with OpenCL. Having this level of abstraction further allows the execution of code on CPUs in case no suitable OpenCL devices is available. While Aparapi provides an interface similar to Java Threads, PyOpenCL relies on annotations to define which functions are offloaded. In contrast, OCCA [30] has the goal to provide portability and flexibility to developers. They contribute

---

[1] https://github.com/boostorg/compute (Feb. 2017).

[2] https://github.com/ddemidov/vexcl (Feb. 2017).

a uniform interface for programming OpenMP, CUDA and OpenCL. Writing the offloaded code in macros allows translation depending on the target platform at runtime. An extensible approach allows the addition of new languages in the future.

A pragma-based approach uses code annotations to specify which code should be parallelized by the compiler. A major advantage is the portability of existing code by adding the annotations to the offloaded code blocks. At the same time, the developer has much less control over the execution and less potential for optimization. OpenACC [35] is a such standard. It supports data parallel computations distributed on many cores as well as vector operations. A comparison between OpenCL and OpenACC can be found in the work of Wienke et al. [44]. Although OpenCL showed much better performance in their tests, the authors conclude that OpenACC opens the field to more programmers and will improve in performance over time.

Opening C++ to GPU programming has been approached from several directions. The C++ framework CuPP [9] contributes both low-level and high-level interfaces for accessing CUDA to support data parallel applications. With AMP^3, Microsoft extends Visual C++ to allow for programming parallel kernels without any knowledge of hardware-specific languages. CAPP [14] uses aspects to manage and integrate OpenCL kernels in AspectC++. Also, an interface is provided for executing OpenCL kernels from the C++ code. First steps towards executing OpenCL kernels within the C++ Actor Framework were presented in [13]. The basic concept of an OpenCL Actor in CAF [22] is now re-examined and extended to execute composable actor chains on resident memory, allowing dynamic execution of data parallel operations.

Integrating GPU computing into the actor model is also explored by other scientists. For example, Harvey et al. [20] showed actors running OpenCL code as part of the actor based programming language Ensemble. By adding an additional compiler step, they allow the device code to be written in the same language as the rest of their code. This approach simplifies the development as it allows the use of language features such as multi-dimensional arrays. Further optimizations allow the language to keep messages sent between OpenCL actors on the device instead of copying it back and forth. The code used as the actors behavior still must be written to address the parallel nature of OpenCL devices. Their benchmarks compare OpenACC, Ensemble and native OpenCL. In most cases Ensemble performs close to OpenCL while OpenACC lacks behind in performance.

3   The Design of OpenCL Actors

We are now ready to introduce our approach in detail, discuss its rationales and implementation challenges along with its benefits as well as its limitations.

---

^{3} http://msdn.microsoft.com/en-us/library/hh265136.aspx (Feb. 2017).

3.1   Design Goals and Rationales

OpenCL is a widely deployed standard containing a programming language (OpenCL C) and a management API. Unlike other approaches such as OCCA [30], CAF does neither attempt to build a new language unifying CPU and GPGPU programming nor to abstract over multiple GPGPU frameworks. Instead, our approach allows programmers to implement actors using data parallel kernels written in OpenCL C without contributing any boilerplate code. Hence, CAF is hiding the management complexity of OpenCL. We want to keep CAF easy to use in practice and confine tools to a standard-compliant C++ compiler with available OpenCL drivers. In particular, we do not require a code generator or compiler extensions.

A possible design option would be to specify a domain-specific language (DSL) for GPGPU programming in C++ based on template expressions. Such a DSL essentially allows a framework to traverse the abstract syntax tree (AST) generated by C++ in order to enable lazy evaluation or to generate output in a different language such as OpenCL C. However, programmers would need to learn this DSL in the same way they need to learn OpenCL C. Further, we assume GPGPU programmers to have some familiarity or experience with OpenCL or CUDA. Introducing a new language would thus increase the entry barrier instead of lowering it. Also, this would force users to re-write existing OpenCL kernels. For this reason, we chose to support OpenCL C directly.

Our central goals for the design of OpenCL actors are (1) hiding complexity of OpenCL management and (2) seamless integration into CAF with respect to access transparency as well as location transparency.

Hiding Complexity. The OpenCL API is a low-level interface written in C with a style that does not integrate well with modern C++. Although OpenCL does offer a C++ header that wraps the C API, it shows inconsistencies when handling errors and requires repetitive manual steps. The initialization of OpenCL devices, the compilation and management of kernels as well as the asynchronous events generated by OpenCL can and should be handled by the framework rather than by the programmer. Only relevant decisions shall be left to the user and remain on a much higher level of abstraction than is offered by OpenCL.

Seamless Integration. OpenCL actors must use the same handle type as actors running on the CPU and implement the same semantics. This is required to make both kinds of actors interchangeable and hide the physical deployment at runtime. Further, using the same handle type enables the runtime to use existing abstraction mechanism for network-transparency, monitoring, and error propagation. Additionally, the API for creating OpenCL actors should follow a conformal design, i.e., the OpenCL abstraction should provide a function that is similar to spawn.

3.2   Core Approach to the Integration of OpenCL

The asynchronous API of OpenCL maps well to the asynchronous message passing found in actor systems. For starting a computation, programmers enqueue a task to the command queue of OpenCL and register a callback function that is invoked once the result has been produced. This naturally fits actor messaging, whereas the queue management is done implicitly and a response message is generated instead of relying on user-provided callbacks.

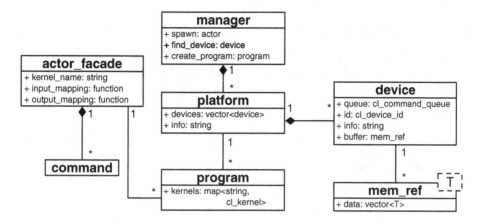

Fig. 2. Class diagram for the OpenCL integration.

OpenCL actors introduce easy access to heterogeneous computing within the context of CAF actors. Our main building block is the class `actor_facade` which is shown in Fig. 2. The facade wraps the kernel execution on OpenCL devices and provides a message passing interface in form of an actor. For this purpose, the class implements all required interfaces to communicate with other components of CAF (omitted in the diagram for brevity). Whenever a facade receives a message, it creates a `command` which preserves the original context of a message, schedules execution of the kernel and finally produces a result message. The remaining classes implement the bookkeeping required by OpenCL.

- `manager` is a module of an actor system that performs platform discovery lazily on first access and offers an interface to spawn OpenCL actors;
- `platform` wraps an OpenCL platform and manages a `cl_context` that stores OpenCL-internal management data as well as the devices related to the platform;
- `device` describes an OpenCL device and provides access to its command queue;
- `program` stores compiled OpenCL kernels and provides a mapping from kernel names to objects;
- `mem_ref` represents a buffer storing data of type `T` on an OpenCL device and allows its retrieval, both usually handled by the framework.

CAF handles all steps of the OpenCL workflow automatically, but allows for fine-tuning of key aspects. For example, developers can simply provide source code and names for kernels and have CAF create a `program` automatically by selecting a device and compiling the sources. Particularly on host systems with multiple co-processors, programmers may wish to query the `manager` object for accessible devices manually and explicitly create a `program` object by providing a device ID, source code, kernel names, and compiler options.

3.3   Illustration: Matrix Multiplication with OpenCL Actors

We illustrate our concepts and give source code examples for multiplying square matrices. This problem is a straight-forward fit and a common use case for this programming model as each index of the result matrix can be calculated independently.

Listing 1.1. OpenCL kernel to multiply two square matrices.

```
 1  constexpr const char* name = "m_mult";
 2  constexpr const char* source = R"__(
 3  __kernel void
 4  m_mult(__global float* matrix1,
 5         __global float* matrix2,
 6         __global float* output) {
 7    size_t size = get_global_size(0);
 8    size_t x = get_global_id(0);
 9    size_t y = get_global_id(1);
10    float result = 0;
11    for (size_t idx=0; idx<size; ++idx) {
12      result += matrix1[idx + y * size]
13              * matrix2[x + idx * size];
14    }
15    output[x+y*size] = result;
16  })__";
```

Listing 1.1 shows an OpenCL kernel for multiplying two square matrices stored as string in the variable `source`. Additionally, the variable `name` stores the in-source name of the function implementing the kernel. OpenCL requires all kernels to return `void` and use the prefix `__kernel`. The first two arguments to the function `m_mult` are two input matrices and the last argument is the result. All matrices are placed in the global memory region to be accessible by all work-items (GPU cores). Since OpenCL does not support multi-dimensional arrays, the matrices are represented as one-dimensional arrays and the position is calculated from the x and y coordinate. At runtime, each instruction will run in parallel on multiple GPU cores but use different memory segments (single instruction, multiple data) identified by the function `get_global_id`. In this example, we use two dimensions, which can be queried as index 0 for the x axis and 1 for the y axis. Since we multiply square matrices `get_global_size` returns the same value for both axes.

3.4   Programming Interface

While the OpenCL interface can be translated to actor-like communication in a straightforward way, generating the behavior of the actor is more complex. Since OpenCL source code is compiled at runtime from strings, the C++ compiler needs additional information regarding input and output types.

OpenCL actors are created using a variant of spawn that is available through the OpenCL manager when the module is loaded. The execution of a kernel requires configuration parameters like the number of work-items for executing it. Listing 1.2 illustrates how to create an actor for the kernel shown in Listing 1.1. It creates an actor_system with a config that loads the module in lines 3–5.

Listing 1.2. Spawning OpenCL actors.

```
1  constexpr size_t mx_dim = 1024;
2  actor_system_config cfg;
3  cfg.load<opencl::manager>();
4  actor_system system{cfg};
5  auto& mngr = system.opencl_manager();
6  auto worker = mngr.spawn(
7    source, name,
8    nd_range{dim_vec{mx_dim, mx_dim}},
9    in<float>{}, in<float>{}, out<float>{});
10  auto m = create_matrix(mx_dim * mx_dim);
11  scoped_actor self;
12  self->request(worker, m, m).receive(
13    [](const vector<float>& result) {
14      print_as_matrix(result);
15    });
```

The first two arguments to the OpenCL spawn are strings containing source code and kernel name. CAF will automatically create a program object from this source code. For more configuration options, programmers can also create a program manually and pass it as the first argument instead. The third argument—the nd_range—describes the distribution of work-items in three dimensions. A nd_range always contains the global dimensions and optionally offsets for the global IDs and local dimensions (to override defaults and fine-tune work-groups in OpenCL). The dimensions are passed as instances of dim_vec, which is a tuple consisting of either one, two, or three integers. Our example creates one work-item for each index, i.e., $matrix\_size \times matrix\_size$ items, meaning that one GPU core computes one element of the result matrix at a time.

The remaining arguments must represent the kernel signature as list of in, out, in_out, local and priv declarations. This type information allows CAF to automatically generate a pattern for extracting data from messages and to manage OpenCL buffers. While input arguments are provided by the user, storage for output buffers must be allocated by CAF. By default, CAF assumes output buffers to have a size equal to the number of work-items. This default can be overridden by passing a user-defined function to an `out` declaration which calculates the output size depending on the inputs at runtime. The types `local` and `priv` provide buffers in local or private memory for the kernel. In addition to the type of the relate kernel argument, optional template parameters modify the accepted and forwarded types of arguments on the CPU. Specifically, the programmer can choose between values and references to on-device memory. As an example, this enables actors to accept data as a `std::vector<T>` and forward it efficiently to another OpenCL actor as a `mem_ref<T>`.

In our example, the kernel expects two input arguments and one output argument, all represented by one-dimensional dynamic arrays of floating point numbers—in C++ named `std::vector<float>`. The template arguments provided here only determine the type of the arguments and thus default to value types (`std::vector<T>`) for receipt and answer. In line 13 of Listing 1.2, we send two input matrices to the OpenCL actor using `request`. The message handler for the result in line 14 awaits the resulting matrix and prints it.

Optionally, programmers can pass two conversion function following the `spawn_config` argument as shown in Listing 1.3. The first function is then responsible for extracting data from a message while the second function converts the output generated by the kernel to a response message. This mapping gives users full control over the message passing interface of the resulting actor. Per default, these functions are generated by CAF. A message is then matched against all `in` and `in_out` kernel arguments, while the output message is generated from all `in_out` and `out` arguments.

Listing 1.3. Pre- and post-processing in OpenCL actors.

```
1  template <size_t Size>
2  class square_matrix { /* ... */ };
3  using fvec = vector<float>;
4  constexpr size_t mx_dim = 1024;
5  using mx = square_matrix<mx_dim>;
6  auto preprocess = [](message& msg)
7                          -> optional<message> {
8    return msg.apply([](mx& x, mx& y) {
9      return make_message(move(x.data()),
10                         move(y.data()));
11 });};
12 auto postprocess = [] (fvec& res)
13                        -> message {
14   return make_message(mx{move(res)});
15 };
16 auto worker = mngr.spawn(
17   kernel_source, kernel_name,
18   nd_range{dim_vec{mx_dim, mx_dim}},
19   preprocess, postprocess,
20   in<float>{}, in<float>{}, out<float>{});
```

The example in Listing 1.3 introduces the class square_matrix, which is used for message passing. Since OpenCL does not allow custom data types, the OpenCL actor needs to convert the matrix to a one-dimensional float array before copying data to the GPU and do the opposite after receiving the result from OpenCL. This pattern matching step is modeled by the two functions preprocess, which converts two input matrices to arrays, and postprocess, which maps a computed array to a matrix.

An OpenCL actor usually sends the result message to the actor that requested the calculation. This behavior can be adapted in multiple ways. First, CAF offers a client side approach for such behavior using the function send_as. Second, the postprocess functions can be used to send messages to other actors using the computed result. Further, automatically sending a response message can be suppressed by returning a default-constructed message. And finally, CAF offers the composition of actor to describe the message flow between a number of actors. This concept will be discussed in more detail in the next section.

3.5   OpenCL Actors as Kernel Stages

The basic OpenCL actor offers stateless computation. It transfers the required data between the CPU and the OpenCL device before and after each kernel invocation. This section extends the basic concept by applying OpenCL actors stage-wise and introduces memory objects that can persist over multiple kernel invocations. References to persistent memory are not confined to a specific actor, but represent state available to the execution pipeline. A reference type (see type mem_ref<T> depicted in Fig. 2) represents data on the GPU device at the CPU, and allows messaging between OpenCL actors to execute subsequent kernels on the same memory. An OpenCL actor that receives such a reference type in a message matches the data type of the reference against the signature of its kernel as it would match incoming data. For this purpose, a reference type includes type information about the data it references in addition to the amount of bytes it refers to and memory access rights. This provides an efficient way to use the output of one kernel as the input for the next kernel.

While each OpenCL stage is a single actor, the composition API of CAF allows to construct a new, composed actor of multiple others. This reduces the need for an additional supervising actor that passes messages from stage to stage. The composition of CAF actors works as follows: Normally, each actor is expected to return its result from a message handler (with void explicitly meaning no result). If a result is not immediately available, though, actors may return a 'promise' instead. Such 'promise' indicates that a result will be produced later, or that the result was delegated to another actor which then becomes responsible for responding to the sender. This allows CAF to correlate input with output messages and enables a powerful composition primitive similar to function composition. We denote $C = B \odot A$ to define an actor C which takes any messages it receives as input of A and uses the result as input for B. This definition of actors in terms of other actors is intuitively similar to function composition, i.e., $h = f \circ g \equiv h(x) = f(g(x))$.

In the context of OpenCL actors, we need to include the memory transfer to and from the GPU into the actor chain. For this purpose, the first actor in the chain accepts the input data in a message and transfers it to the OpenCL device before forwarding memory references to the next stage. When the references reach the last actor in the pipeline, it reads the results back and sends them to the initial requester, fulfilling the promise. In the composition of $C \odot B \odot A$, the first actor A would transfer the data to the device, perform its computations, and send references to the results to B. In turn, B executes its kernel and passes its results to C where the data is read back when C has processed it according to its behavior.

Although the newly composed actor represents a pipeline of kernel executions, it requires messaging between the related CPU actors to pass memory references from one stage to the following. Unless a result from one stage is required to configure the next, kernel executions can be scheduled asynchronously. This allows actors to forward memory references to the next actor before the execution on the device is finished. OpenCL offers an event-based system to express relationships between commands. Here, we use these events to schedule data transfer to devices, followed by a sequence of kernel executions and the final transfer of the results. This allows OpenCL to chain tasks efficiently without downtime for interaction with the CPU.

Listing 1.4 depicts how kernels are enqueued into the OpenCL command queue for asynchronous execution. The class command is used by an actor_facade to wrap a single execution and let it run asynchronously. Only its function enqueue is shown here which enqueues the kernel, sets a callback and forwards the arguments to the next actor. It omits error handling for brevity. A reference count manages the lifetime of the command and is incremented when the function is called (line 3) which represents the reference held by the OpenCL command queue. Next, the command calls the function clEnqueueNDRangeKernel to pass the kernel to OpenCL. The kernel arguments were already set by the actor that created the command and require no additional handling here. The first two arguments are the command queue and kernel for the execution, followed configuration of the index space for the execution. This includes the number of dimensions (line 6), potential offsets for the global index space (line 7), the global dimensions (line 8) and the number of work items in a work group (line 9). The last three arguments enable asynchronous event management in OpenCL: the number of events the kernel has to await, the events themselves and an event that represents the kernel execution itself.

Listing 1.4. Enqueue commands for asynchronous execution.

```
1  class command : public ref_counted {
2  void enqueue() {
3    this->ref(); // reference held by the OpenCL command queue
4    clEnqueueNDRangeKernel(
5      queue, kernel,
6      range.dimensions().size(),
7      range.offsets(),
```

```
8      range.dimensions(),
9      range.local_dimensions(),
10     events.size(), events.data(), &event);
11   clSetEventCallback(
12     event, CL_COMPLETE,
13     [](cl_event, cl_int, void* data) {
14       auto cmd = reinterpret_cast<command*>(data);
15       cmd->deref();
16     },
17     this);
18   clFlush(queue);
19   forward_arguments();
20 }
21 };
```

After the kernel execution is enqueued, the function `clSetEventCallback` allows registration of a callback when an event is set to a specific execution status. Here, we set a callback to be performed after the event produced by the function `clEnqueueNDRangeKernel` is set to CL_COMPLETE, i.e., the kernel execution finished. The third argument is the callback itself in form of a C++ lambda. The last argument of the callback is user data that is passed as the last argument when setting the callback, a pointer to the command itself. Inside the callback, this allows decrementing the reference count of the command, thus releasing its resources. After registering the callback, the function `clFlush` ensures that the commands are passed to OpenCL without awaiting their completion. Finally, the function `forward_arguments` sends the memory references expected to be returned by the actor to the next one, bundling the kernel execution event. This enables subsequent kernel stages to schedule their kernels asynchronously to the execution on the device. The return types of kernel executions can be calculated from the arguments of the spawn function. This allows us to choose a different enqueue implementation when the results of the execution are not limited to reference types. In that case, the callback will only forward the results after the execution has finished and the required data is read back by the CPU from the OpenCL device.

The algorithms performed by stages may differ greatly in complexity, execution time and interface. While the first two characteristics are part of the user implementation without affecting the composition of stages, the last one impacts the compatibility between subsequent stages. Simply passing the output of one kernel to the next may not work. A kernel may produce new data or require local memory for its computations in addition to input arguments and configuration passed along the pipeline. In this case, an incoming message may not contain all arguments required for the execution. For this purpose, stages can create non-input arguments for internal use similar to the basic OpenCL actor. A pre-processing function that is passed to OpenCL actors can add, remove or configure the arguments for the execution while the post-processing function could drop unnecessary output or reorder arguments to fit the next stage. Dropping a reference argument simply releases its memory on the device.

A restriction of pipelining computations is the locality of its kernel execution. A memory reference type is bound to the process memory where it is created as it references a memory object managed by the local OpenCL context. A different process or remote node would have no use of it. This makes pipelines unsuitable for distribution over multiple nodes as is. There are three approaches to handle this: (a) prohibit serialization of the reference type to raise an error when a reference would be sent over the network, (b) introduce automatic memory transfer from the device to the CPU memory before sending the message—this changes the messages content and type—or, (c) include host information of the memory references to allow lazy transfer of the memory should a remote OpenCL actor attempt to use it. The first approach offers the easier solution making expensive copy operations explicit.

While not as efficient as the dynamic parallelism offered by new standards, introducing OpenCL actors as kernel stages raises the expressiveness of CAF and widens its application context to complex GPU-based applications, thereby relying on a widely available version of OpenCL.

3.6 Design Discussion

CAF achieves a much higher level of abstraction than the management API provided by OpenCL. Only key decisions such as the work-item distribution is required by the user. The OpenCL device binding for a kernel defaults to the first discovered device, but can optionally be chosen dynamically at runtime.

The OpenCL actors presented in this section introduce data parallel intra-actor concurrency to CAF. The behavior of an OpenCL actor consists of three parts: (1) a pre-processing function that pattern-matches input messages and forwards extracted data to OpenCL, (2) a data parallel kernel that runs on an OpenCL device, and (3) a post-processing function that finalizes the message processing step and per default converts data produced by the kernel to a response message. Since the data parallel kernel is running in a separate address space and can only use the limited instruction set provided by OpenCL C, sending messages or spawning new actors from OpenCL C directly cannot be achieved. However, the pre- and post-processing functions run on the CPU and allow programmers to spawn more actors and send additional messages in the common way. These two functions can be automatically generated for convenience by deriving all message types from the signature of a kernel.

Transparent message passing and error handling are achieved in our design by mapping the mailbox of an actor to a command queue of OpenCL. From the perspective of the CAF runtime system, an OpenCL actor is not distinguishable from any other actor since it implements the same interfaces as actors running on the CPU. With the spawn function of the OpenCL manager, we provide an interface for the creation process of actors that hides most complexity while still granting access to all performance-relevant configuration options via optional parameters.

Once created, the actor handle can be used and addressed independent of its location. The creation process itself has its limitations, though. OpenCL is available for GPUs and dedicated accelerators as well as CPUs. This suggests to run OpenCL actors on the CPU if no other devices are available. While this is conceptually possible, device drivers commonly deployed do not support code compilation for the CPU. Another problem to consider is the workload caused by an OpenCL actor running on the CPU. It is not scheduled with other actors, but competes for the same resources. Alternatively, a single actor could have two implementations, one in OpenCL and one in regular C++. CAF could then choose the implementation that promises the best performance.

At the abstract actor level, the composition of kernel stages offers a way to express dependencies for processing a set of data. Our approach uses actors that wrap a single kernel as building blocks. This design closely follows the idea of the actor model, describing entities of simple functionality, and is built on top of the composition API available in CAF. It enables a high-level view on kernel pipelines and encourages the reuse of actors for different parts of an algorithm. The downside of this approach is the messaging overhead pass memory references from actor to actor.

An alternative level of composition uses kernels as building blocks to compose a single OpenCL actor that handles multiple kernel stages. This would remove the need for message passing between kernel executions and could prevent idling of the OpenCL device in between kernel executions. To allow such composition a suitable API for handling kernel instances and combining them in an actor would be required. The translation from output of one kernel to the input of the next one could be defined in suitable callbacks similar to the pre- and post-processing functions available for OpenCL actors. This raises the question whether an actor should map to a single kernel—requiring message passing via the CPU—or to an algorithm by wrapping multiple kernel executions—forwarding data by use of callbacks.

In general, kernel execution and message passing can run in parallel using the event capabilities of OpenCL. Therefore, message passing should only affect execution time if the kernel execution is faster than passing the parameters to the next actor and enqueueing its kernel for execution. The payoff for calculation with heterogeneous hardware rises with the calculation time as the overhead to transfer data between the devices (or pass messages between actors) becomes smaller in comparison. To estimate the costs of message passing between stage actors, we created an actor with an empty kernel and passed it a memory reference to execute its kernel. Measuring the time from sending the message to receiving an answer should give an estimate of the baseline required to process an "empty" stage. The measurement results vary between different GPUs and vendors, but mainly remain below 1 ms. This includes the time required by the OpenCL API and leads us to believe that message passing should not be a bottleneck for most use cases. Looking only at the time between the mapping functions for the output of the first stage and the input mapping function on the second stage is called, the measurements remain around a few microseconds.

With these considerations in mind, an interface that integrates into the actor model and allows for composition based on existing functionality provides flexibility and encourages reuse of kernel stages, whereas an interface for composing kernels on the OpenCL level allows developers to choose performance over flexibility. A step further towards efficient kernel execution is the nested parallelism discussed in Sect. 2.4. It wraps multiple kernels into a single actor as the host program cannot differentiate between a simple kernel without child kernels and a kernel enqueueing child kernels from the GPU.

Overall, the introduction of multi-stage actors in addition to the basic OpenCL actor widens the realm of possibilities offered by CAF to developers. It allows to select the right approach for each application: a high level composition of OpenCL actors that fits well into the actor model, or actors that use nested parallelism to implemented kernel stages on the device itself. Implementing an OpenCL actor that wraps kernels on the CPU would provide a intermediate middle option that avoids message passing but still relies on host interaction. Note that nested parallelism depends on the availability of suitable hardware and drivers. While the standard was introduced in 2013, it is not widely available yet and especially lacks support on the hardware deployed.

An advanced aspect of OpenCL usage is scheduling kernels across multiple devices. To enqueue kernels for concurrent execution, a scheduler needs to keep track of the available resources, such as processing elements and memory, as these informations are not offered by OpenCL at runtime. The process get more complicated when using different hardware such as different GPU generations or hardware from various vendors. Depending on the target device, a kernel must be configured specifically for the target to reach optimal performance.

4   Use Case: Indexing on the GPU

We want to explore the full capabilities of OpenCL actors in CAF by closely following an implementation of a rather complex use case. The creation of bitmap indexes from large volumes of data is a challenging application of sequential kernel executions. Indexing also proved realistic for GPGPU computing, as work from Fusco et al. [19] could show. Having VAST [43] already as an application domain of CAF, we attempt to accelerate its indexing process through heterogeneous OpenCL computations.

4.1   Mapping WAH to OpenCL Actors

Fusco et al. [19] presented how WAH [45] and PLWAH [16] compressions can be created entirely on the GPU. The index consists of blocks of 32 bit values which either represent a heterogeneous sequence of zeros and ones as is—called a'literal'—or a sequence of homogeneous blocks compressed into a single'fill'. The corresponding data parallel algorithm consists of six parts applied to the index data. On a high level, it first encodes values with their input position before sorting them by value. This moves values that will be encoded in the same bitmap adjacent to each other while maintaining information about their original distance in the in form of their previous position. From this data, the literals and fills for the WHA encoding are created. The resulting index includes one bitmap for each unique value in the input data. Finally, the algorithm creates a lookup table to find the bitmap related to each value in the index. The six parts are composed from 20 stages which successively run on the GPU without control of the CPU.

For the sake of brevity, we confine our discussion to the step 'fuseFillsLiterals' for building a WAH bitmap index (see Algorithm 5 in [19]). It merges previously computed arrays to build the index. For this purpose, the algorithm interleaves two previously created arrays (chunk ids and literals) and performs a stream compaction on the resulting index. A stream compaction removes all entries from an input array that match a given value, compacting the remaining values. The resulting array should have a length less than or equal to the length of the chunk ids and literals array combined.

Listing 1.5 presents an actor composition that combines three kernels to perform this algorithm. The first actor prepares the index by merging the chunk ids and literals into the combined index array. Subsequently, the stream compaction removes all zero entries from the index. Billeter et al. [7] published a stream compaction algorithm for GPUs which is used here. The OpenCL implementation combines phases two and three in a single kernel invocation.

Lines 2 and 3 of the listing configure the index spaces for the calculation, see Sect. 3.4 for details on the configuration parameters. All kernels use a one dimensional index space. While the preparing kernel only requires k work items, each moving a value from the chunk id and literal array into the index, the subsequent stream compaction kernels use one work item per value in the index, i.e., $2 \cdot k$. The stream compaction is written to utilize work-groups of size 128, as declared in the last argument of the range_sc. Such sizing is applicable and efficient on most GPUs. Next, line 4 acquires a reference to the OpenCL manager of the local actor_system.

Three actors are created for this step, one for each kernel (Lines 6 to 21). The first actor is created from the program that contains the specific algorithms, in this case the "prepare_index" kernel, and is configured to create a one-dimensional index space with k work items. The remaining arguments describe the kernel signature, which requires three uint* as input (the first three arguments) and returns two uint*, the first and last argument. The first argument here is a configuration array passed along the pipeline that contains the number of elements to handle and is used to return newly created values such as the new length after the compaction. The other output is the prepared array for the index.

The kernel signature is not just described by the type of the argument (uint) but includes tags to specify how the kernel accepts and forwards each argument. As this stage is part of a larger algorithm, the data is forwarded in form of memory references along the pipeline. The in_out type requires one parameters for input and one for output while `in` and `out` only require one parameter for the direction they represent.

Listing 1.5. Composing an actor to perform the *fuseFillsLiterals* indexing step.

```
 1   // k is length of the arrays to merge into the index
 2   auto range = nd_range{dim_vec{k}, {}, {}};
 3   auto range_sc = nd_range{dim_vec{2 * k}, {}, dim_vec{128}};
 4   auto& mngr = sys.opencl_manager();
 5
 6   auto prepare = mngr.spawn(
 7     program_fuse, "prepare_index", range,
 8     in_out<uint, ref, ref>{},
 9     in<uint, ref>{}, in<uint, ref>{},
10     out<uint, ref>{2 * k});
11   auto count_elems = mngr.spawn(
12     program_sc, "count_elements", range_sc,
13     in_out<uint, ref, ref>{}, in_out<uint, ref, ref>{},
14     out<uint, ref>{k / 128},
15     local<uint>{128});
16   auto move_elems = mngr.spawn(
17     program_sc, "move_valid_elements", range_sc,
18     in_out<uint, ref, ref>{},
19     in<uint, ref>{}, in<uint, ref>{},
20     out<uint, ref>{2 * k},
21     local<uint>{128}, local<uint>{128}, local<uint>{128});
22
23   // create a composed actor of the three algorithmic steps
24   auto fuse = move_elems * count_elems * prepare;
```

Next, the actor to handle the first step of the stream compaction is spawned. The stream compaction is located in `program_sc` object which contains the kernels `count_elements` used here and the kernel `move_valid_elements` for the next stage. Arguments kept in local memory can neither be initialized from nor read by the CPU. Moreover, they are not persistent over multiple kernel executions. These buffers are reserved for computations by a work group. Thus, the `count_elements` kernel excepts two arguments in a message: the configuration and the data to compact. It returns an additional argument that is used in the second stage of the stream compaction and contains a value for each work group.

The third actor uses the information calculated by the `count_elem` actor to compact the index, removing all empty entries. For this purpose, it accepts the configuration parameters, the index, and the data calculated in the count stage as input. A new buffer for the compacted index is created by the actor in addition to the three local buffers for each work group. Only the configuration and the new buffer are returned by the actor, which writes the new length of the compacted index into the configuration.

Finally, the three actors are composed into a new actor `fuse`, see line 24. The overall calculation performed by the `fuse` actor can be expressed in the following equation:

$$\text{fuse}(msg) = \text{move\_elems}(\text{count\_elems}(\text{prepare}(msg))).$$

It expects the chunk ids and literals computed in an earlier step together with their length as input, and returns the index and its new length as output. The messages sent here between actors only include memory references. The actual data remains on the GPU.

4.2   Results and Insights

We implemented the complete WAH indexing algorithm using `libcaf_opencl`. The clean message passing approach provided a familiar environment for writing the algorithm and composing the stages. Standard algorithms such as the stream compaction were repeatedly needed at different stages of the algorithm, offering the opportunity to reuse the respective actors. Radix sort using a fixed cardinality of 16 bits was implemented for ordering the input. All code is publicly available on GitHub.

Going forward, actors that offer such standard algorithms could be included in the framework to provide easier access to building blocks for multi-stage OpenCL actors and GPGPU computing with CAF. The application we developed consisted mostly of OpenCL actors. When the indexing implementation is optimized and proves to be useful for VAST itself, its integration will reveal how well OpenCL actors blend into a larger code base.

While the algorithm is fully functional and produces the expected index, it would still require optimizations to reproduce the absolute performance presented in [19]. However, we are rather interested in the qualitative runtime behavior and the scaling.

Figure 3 compares the execution times of creating a WAH bitmap index on the GPU and the CPU as a function of the problem size. Inputs range from 10.000 to 20.000.000 values. Initial measurement steps include $N = 20.000$, 100.000, and 250.000 followed by increments of 250.000 for each subsequent measurement. Both axes are scaled logarithmically, depicting the means of 10 measurements as well as their standard deviations. We start the timer on the CPU with the initial invocation of indexing, and stop on the CPU after final completion including data return. A Tesla C2075 GPU running OpenCL 1.1 was used for indexing, built in a 24 core Dell server running CentOS 7. The GPU has 14 compute units that can run up to 1024 work items each, adding up to 14.336 concurrent computations.

The runtime consumption of the CPU grows linearly as expected from the algorithms in use. Asymptotically, the GPU also exhibits linear scaling with about half the slope. Correspondingly, execution times on the CPU are about twice as large as on the GPU. For small problem sizes, though, the GPU starts with a slightly higher initialization overhead and a clearly sub-linear growth due to its high inherent parallelism.

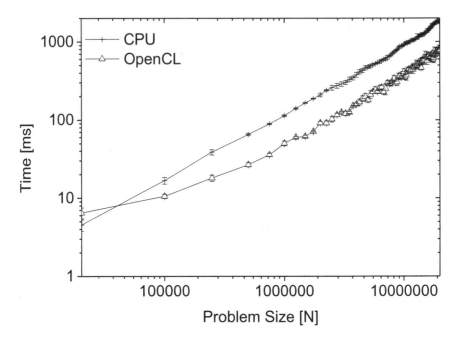

Fig. 3. Runtime for building a WAH index as a function of index size—comparing GPU with CPU performance

In summary, the results show that indexing can be successfully offloaded to a GPU, leaving the CPU idle for performing regular operations such as interactive searches and queries. GPU offloading grants a significant speedup. Keeping in mind the results of [19], the latter can be expected even higher as the algorithmically complex indexing on the GPU promises higher optimization potentials than the same on the CPU.

5   Evaluation of the OpenCL Actor

We have implemented four benchmark programs to systematically measure runtime characteristics and overhead introduced by our OpenCL wrapper.

The first benchmark compares the creation time of OpenCL actors to the event-based actors of CAF. Our next two benchmarks examine the overhead we induce compared to manually using the OpenCL API. Here, we take a look at single calculation before comparing our implementation against an optimized scenario. Our final benchmark examines the scalability in heterogeneous setups by stepwise transferring workload to a GPU and a coprocessor.

The first benchmarks were performed on a Late 2013 iMac with a 3.5 GHz Intel Core i7 running OS X and OpenCL version 1.2. The GPU is an NVIDIA GeForce GTX 780M GPU with 4096 MB memory. The last benchmarks on scalability use a machine with two twelve-core Intel Xeon CPUs clocked at 2.5 GHz equipped with a Tesla C2075 GPU, as well as a Xeon Phi 5110P coprocessor. The server runs Linux and uses the graphics drivers provided by Nvidia (version 375.20) and the Intel OpenCL Runtime 14.2.

5.1 Spawn Time

Our first benchmark focuses on the time to instantiate OpenCL actors. The creation of actors is traditionally a lightweight operation. We expect the creation of OpenCL actors to be more heavy weight than the creation of other actors in CAF. Still, we want to quantify the overhead associated with actor creation.

We compare the creation time of OpenCL actors to that of event-based actors. Both benchmarks consist of a loop that spawns one actor per iteration. Afterwards we ensure that all actors are active by sending a message to the last created actor and waiting for its response.

The time measured is the wall clock time required to spawn an increasing number of actors. This includes the time required to initialize the runtime environment. To provide an equal setup, we spawn the event-based actors with the lazy_init flag. It prevents them from being scheduled for small initialization tasks unless they receive a message, as is the case with OpenCL actors.

Figure 4 depicts the wall-clock runtime in seconds as a function of the number of spawned actors. It plots the mean of 50 runs with error bars showing the 95 % confidence intervals. In all cases, the error bars are barely visible. Both

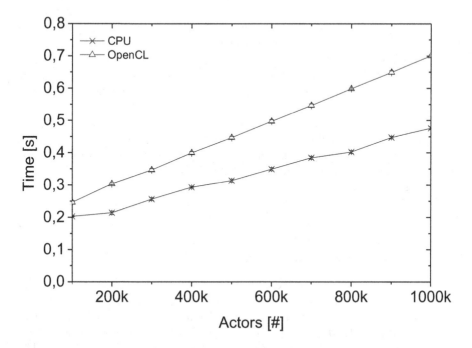

Fig. 4. Comparing the wall-clock time for spawning OpenCL versus event-based actors.

implementations show a linear dependency with minor growth. However, event-based actors take less time than OpenCL actors and exhibit a smaller slope. The difference in slope indicates a longer spawn time for each individual OpenCl actor. Similar slopes with a constant distance would have indicated a similar creation time with longer initialization time of the runtime.

Compared to the time required for a simple calculation, the creation time is reasonably small. It is worth mentioning that OpenCL actors are parallelized internally by OpenCL. They are not created as frequently as event-based actors. This limits the overhead further.

5.2   Runtime Overhead of Actors over Native OpenCL Programming

Our second benchmark measures the overhead induced by our actor approach compared to the native API of OpenCL. While the OpenCL actor uses the OpenCL API internally, it performs additional steps such as the setup of the OpenCL environment and the actor creation. This benchmark quantifies the overhead added by message passing and wrapping the OpenCL API.

It implements a program that executes a simple task on a GPU using an OpenCL actor. In this case, the benchmark kernel calculates the product of two $N \times N$ matrices with 1000, 4000, 8000 and 12000 as values for N. The increase in problem size shall test for a correlation between the message size and the overhead.

Two measurements are of interest in this case. First, the duration required for the whole calculation, from sending the message to receiving the answer. Second, the time between enqueuing the kernel until OpenCL invokes the callback, which includes data transfer as well as the kernel execution. Ideally, both times should be nearly equal.

Figure 5(a) depicts the runtime in seconds as a function of the problem size N. Each value is the mean of 50 runs, plotted with the 95 % confidence interval. The total calculation time ranges from 0.07 s up to 14.1 s. We have also plotted the time difference separately in Fig. 5(b) since the two lines in Fig. 5(a) are not distinguishable. The difference between the measured values ranges between 5.7 ms and 8.6 ms. No discernible slope can be observed in the graph and the measurements fluctuate independently of the problem size.

The results of this measurement clearly show a negligible overhead that does not depend on the problem size. Hence, our high level interface can be used at a very low cost.

5.3   Baseline Comparison

The previous benchmark examines the overhead for a single calculation by comparing the runtime distribution between CAF and OpenCL. In this benchmark we want to compare the performance when calculating a sequence of independent tasks. Two 1000×1000 matrices are multiplied with an increasing number of iterations, starting at 1000 and increasing by 1000 in each step up to 10000. The

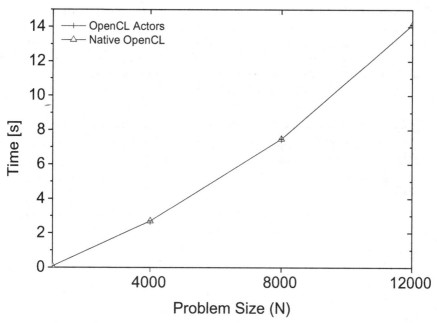

(a) Comparing CAF OpenCL Actors with pure OpenCL.

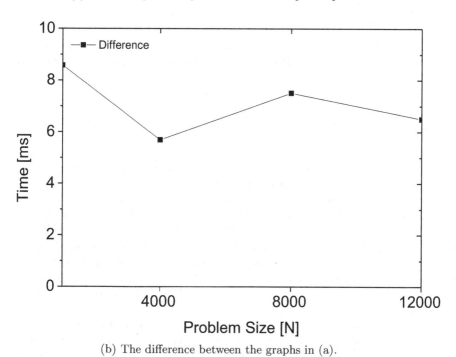

(b) The difference between the graphs in (a).

Fig. 5. Overhead of the CAF messaging when multiplying $N \times N$ matrices.

environment is only initialized once and the calculations are preformed sequentially. For CAF, an actor sends a new message when it receives the results of the last calculation. In comparison, the native OpenCL implementation initiates the next calculation as part of the callback. Both programs use the same kernel for the multiplication. We avoid simultaneous kernel executions as we want to examine the overhead in our framework.

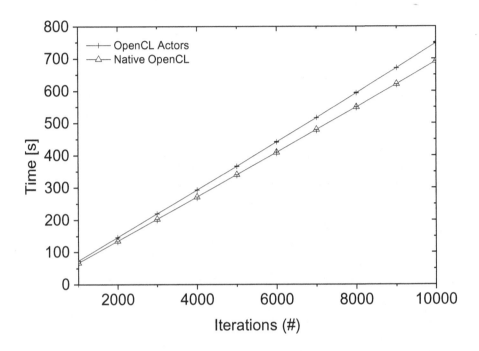

Fig. 6. Comparing the runtime of iterated tasks in CAF versus native OpenCL.

Figure 6 displays the wall-clock time as a function of the iterations performed. We plotted the average of 10 measurements as well as a 95% confidence interval. Since we use the OpenCL API within CAF, it is not possible to achieve a better performance than OpenCL itself. The OpenCL graph is the baseline we aim for with our performance. Both implementations exhibit linear growth. However, the native OpenCL implementation has a smaller slope and the runtime difference between the programs increases. This indicates a consistent overhead required for the message passing compared to the direct API usage. The relative performance difference equals 8.3 % for 1000 iterations and slightly decreases to 7.4 % at 10000 iterations.

It is worth mentioning that this micro benchmark is looking at a minimal baseline that is not a realistic application scenario. A program using OpenCL will need to include some synchronization to pass GPU-computed results to the CPU and generate the next task for the GPU. Hence, a native application will not meet the baseline simply because it uses the OpenCL API directly.

5.4   Scaling Behavior in a Heterogeneous Setup

Our last benchmark focuses on the scalability of our heterogeneous computing approach by incrementally shifting work from the CPU to an OpenCL device. OpenCL distinguishes between CPU, GPU and accelerator devices. Our system includes the two mentioned devices, an NVIDIA Tesla GPU and an Intel Xeon Phi accelerator. The difference between a GPU and an accelerator is that GPUs are traditionally used for 3D APIs such as OpenGL or DirectX, while accelerators are dedicated for offloading computations from the host. The Xeon Phi features an architecture based on x86 processors, although not a compatible one, and differs greatly from the architecture of the Tesla GPU. It consists of 60 cores with 512 bit vector registers and 4 threads each, totaling to up to 240 threads.

We use the calculation of a Mandelbrot set in the benchmark, as the workload can be easily divided into many independent tasks. The problem is a cut from the inner part of a Mandelbrot set that has a balanced processing complexity for the entire image. The workload is offloaded in 11 steps, starting with 0 % on the coprocessor and increasing by 10 % in each step up to 100 %. Each computed image of the Mandelbrot set represents the area of $[-0.5 - 0.7375i, 0.1 - 0.1375i]$. Our measurements include two different workloads, a resolution of 1920×1080 pixels in Fig. 7 and a resolution of 16000×16000 in Fig. 8, both measured with 100 iterations. In addition, we increased the number of iterations to 1000 for the larger workload to further examine the scaling behavior.

Figure 7 depicts the runtime in milliseconds as functions of the problem fraction offloaded. The problem is offloaded to the Tesla in Fig. 7(a) and to the Xeon Phi in Fig. 7(b). Each graph displays the runtime for the CPU and OpenCL device calculations separately, i.e., the time between starting all actors and their termination. Since calculations are performed in parallel, the total runtime is not a sum of the separate runtimes, but measured independently.

The problem plotted in Fig. 7(a) exhibits excellent scalability. The runtime declines until the workload is completely offloaded to the GPU. While the CPU runtime is lower than the total runtime on average, it takes longer to calculate 10 % of the problem on the CPU than is needed to calculate 100 % on the GPU. As a result, the lower bound is the time required to process the complete workload on the GPU.

In contrast, Fig. 7(b) reveals a measurable overhead. While the CPU runtime declines steadily, the runtime measured for OpenCL fluctuates heavily and the total execution time doubles when offloading 10 % of work to the Phi. Even when running 100 % of the problem size on the Phi, the computation is still slower than the initially measured 60 ms for the CPU-only setup. The initial cost of offloading computations to the Phi are not amortized by faster, parallel computations on the accelerator device. It is worth mentioning that we did not optimize the OpenCL kernel for the Phi, which might result in suboptimal performance on this device.

In summary, these experiments reveal excellent scalability of programming GPUs with CAF actors. However, offloading work to the Xeon Phi is not advisable for this problem size. Since the performance of OpenCL applications largely

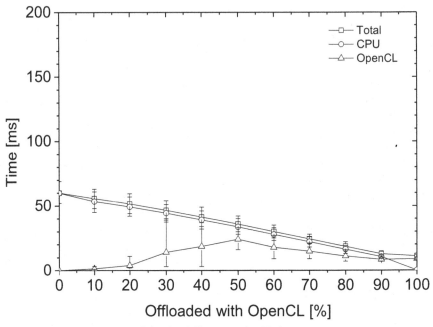

(a) Mandelbrot on the Tesla.

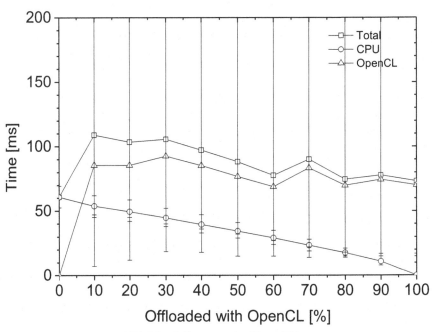

(b) Mandelbrot on the Xeon Phi.

Fig. 7. Moving a small workload to OpenCL devices.

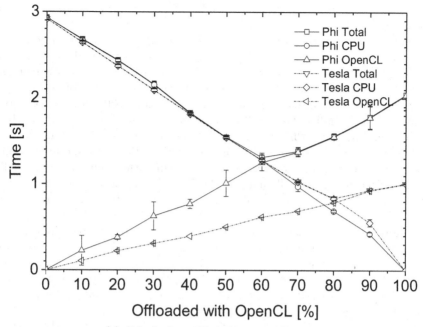

(a) Calculation with a 100 iterations.

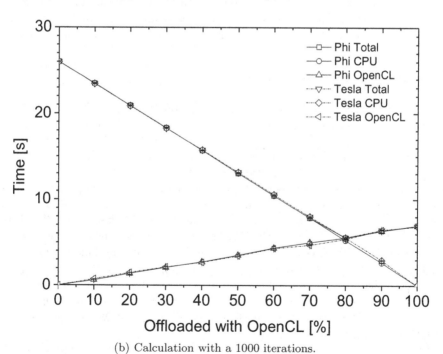

(b) Calculation with a 1000 iterations.

Fig. 8. Moving large workloads to OpenCL devices.

depends on the driver implementation and configuration, it is left to future work to examine the Phi results in more detail.

Figure 8 shows the runtime in milliseconds as a function of the offloaded problem in % for a larger Mandelbrot image. We have increased the number of pixels from 1920×1080 to 16000×16000. The larger image drastically increases the computation time on the device to offset the initial cost of offloading computations. We have run the benchmark using 100 and 1000 iterations per pixel.

Figure 8(a) visualizes the smaller measurements with 100 iterations for both the Tesla and the Xeon Phi. In difference to the previous benchmark in Fig. 7(a), the best performance is achieved at around 80 % on the GPU and around 60 % on the accelerator. Since the initial cost of offloading the computation is smaller in comparison to the overall runtime, the Xeon Phi achieves drastically better performance as shown in Fig. 7(b), but does not reach the performance of the Tesla.

Finally, the measurements with 1000 iterations are depicted in Fig. 8(b). Here, the Phi and Tesla perform equally well. Since this setup has the same data rate as before but an increased runtime on the device, it becomes evident that the data transport to the Phi did hinder better results in the previous benchmarks. Hence, this accelerator (with current drivers) is best suited for problems of small data size but large computation demands.

In a naive approach, we simply transferred a problem from the Tesla to the Phi. This proved to be inefficient for small problems, but improved with an increase in problem size. As should be noted again, optimizing kernels and configurations for the Phi may improve its performance for smaller problems.

6   Conclusions and Outlook

Integrating GPGPU computing into an application can increase its performance by orders of magnitudes while releasing the CPU. This holds on all scales from mobiles to server systems. The challenge of integrating GPGPU devices into applications, though, is left to a programmer, who is faced with an ever-growing complexity of hardware architectures and APIs.

The actor model is an important concept for taming the complexity of parallel and concurrent systems and the task-oriented work flow of actors fits the work flow of GPGPU computing very well. The present work on OpenCL actors within the C++ Actor Framework (CAF) shows that an intelligent actor runtime can manage GPGPU devices autonomously while inducing minimal performance overhead. We optimized performance by designing OpenCL actors as composable stages that pipeline data flows and avoid costly memory transfer between kernel invocations. Supporting OpenCL as first-class implementation option in CAF further broadens the scope of our native actor system by introducing data parallel intra-actor concurrency.

Our presented implementation of OpenCL actors is based on OpenCL 1.1. This version is available across Intel, NVIDIA, and AMD drivers. Our directions for future development fall into three categories: (1) improve scheduling by load balancing across multiple OpenCL devices both locally and in a network, (2) extend the use case of indexing on GPUs to common indexing algorithms such as PLWAH, and (3) provide efficient algorithmic primitives as building blocks for OpenCL actor pipelines.

A Note on Reproducibility

We explicitly support reproducible research [1,38]. Our experiments have been conducted in a transparent standard environment. The source code of our implementations (including scripts to setup the experiments, CAF measurement apps etc.) are available on GitHub at https://github.com/inetrg/Agere-LNCS-2017.

Acknowledgments. The authors would like to thank Marian Triebe and Sebastian Bartels for implementing benchmarks, testing, and bugfixing. We further want to thank Matthias Vallentin for raising the indexing use case, and the iNET working group for vivid discussions and inspiring suggestions. Funding by the German Federal Ministry of Education and Research within the projects ScaleCast and X–CHECK is gratefully acknowledged.

References

1. ACM: Result and Artifact Review and Badging, January 2017. http://acm.org/publications/policies/artifact-review-badging
2. Agha, G.: Actors: A Model of Concurrent Computation In Distributed Systems. MIT Press, Cambridge (1986)
3. Agha, G., Mason, I.A., Smith, S., Talcott, C.: Towards a theory of actor computation. In: Cleaveland, W.R. (ed.) CONCUR 1992. LNCS, vol. 630, pp. 565–579. Springer, Heidelberg (1992). https://doi.org/10.1007/BFb0084816
4. AMD: Aparapi, February 2017. http://aparapi.github.io
5. Armstrong, J.: Making Reliable Distributed Systems in the Presence of Software Errors. Ph.D. thesis, Department of Microelectronics and Information Technology, KTH, Sweden (2003)
6. Armstrong, J.: A history of erlang. In: Proceedings of the Third ACM SIGPLAN Conference on History of Programming Languages (HOPL III), pp. 6-1–6-26. ACM, New York (2007)
7. Billeter, M., Olsson, O., Assarsson, U.: Efficient stream compaction on wide SIMD many-core architectures. In: Proceedings of the Conference on High Performance Graphics 2009, HPG 2009, pp. 159–166. ACM, New York, August 2009
8. Blythe, D.: The Direct3D 10 system. In: ACM SIGGRAPH 2006 Papers, SIGGRAPH 2006, pp. 724–734. ACM, New York (2006)
9. Breitbart, J.: CuPP - a framework for easy CUDA integration. In: Proceedings of the 2009 IEEE International Symposium on Parallel & Distributed Processing (IPDPS 2009), pp. 1–8. IEEE Computer Society, Washington (2009)
10. CAPS: Cray Inc., NVIDIA and the Portland Group. The OpenACC Application Programming Interface, v1.0, November 2011
11. Charousset, D., Hiesgen, R., Schmidt, T.C.: CAF - the C++ actor framework for scalable and resource-efficient applications. In: Proceedings of the 5th ACM SIGPLAN Conference on Systems, Programming, and Applications (SPLASH 2014), Workshop AGERE! pp. 15–28. ACM, New York, October 2014

12. Charousset, D., Hiesgen, R., Schmidt, T.C.: Revisiting actor programming in C++. Comput. Lang. Syst. Struct. **45**, 105–131 (2016). https://doi.org/10.1016/j.cl.2016.01.002

13. Charousset, D., Schmidt, T.C., Hiesgen, R., Wählisch, M.: Native actors - a scalable software platform for distributed, heterogeneous environments. In: Proceedings of the 4th ACM SIGPLAN Conference on Systems, Programming, and Applications (SPLASH 2013), Workshop AGERE! pp. 87–96. ACM, New York, October 2013

14. Clucas, R., Levitt, S.: CAPP: a C++ aspect-oriented based framework for parallel programming with OpenCL. In: Proceedings of the 2015 Annual Conference on South African Institute of Computer Scientists and Information Technologists (SAICSIT 2015), pp. 10:1–10:10. ACM, New York (2015)

15. Dagum, L., Menon, R.: OpenMP: an industry standard API for shared-memory programming. Comput. Sci. Eng. IEEE **5**(1), 46–55 (1998)

16. Deliège, F., Pedersen, T.B.: Position list word aligned hybrid: optimizing space and performance for compressed bitmaps. In: Proceedings of the 13th International Conference on Extending Database Technology, pp. 228–239. EDBT 2010. ACM, New York, March 2010

17. Desell, T., Varela, C.A.: SALSA lite: a hash-based actor runtime for efficient local concurrency. In: Agha, G., et al. (eds.) Concurrent Objects and Beyond. LNCS, vol. 8665, pp. 144–166. Springer, Heidelberg (2014). https://doi.org/10.1007/978-3-662-44471-9_7

18. Fang, J., Varbanescu, A.L., Sips, H.: A comprehensive performance comparison of CUDA and OpenCL. In: Parallel Processing (ICPP), pp. 216–225 (2011)

19. Fusco, F., Vlachos, M., Dimitropoulos, X., Deri, L.: Indexing million of packets per second using GPUs. In: Proceedings of the 2013 Conference on Internet Measurement Conference (IMC 2013), pp. 327–332. ACM, New York, October 2013

20. Harvey, P., Hentschel, K., Sventek, J.: Parallel programming in actor-based applications via OpenCL. In: The 16th International Conference on Middleware. ACM, New York, December 2015

21. Hewitt, C., Bishop, P., Steiger, R.: A universal modular ACTOR formalism for artificial intelligence. In: Proceedings of the 3rd IJCAI, pp. 235–245. Morgan Kaufmann Publishers Inc., San Francisco (1973)

22. Hiesgen, R., Charousset, D., Schmidt, T.C.: Manyfold actors: extending the C++ actor framework to heterogeneous many-core machines using OpenCL. In: Proceedings of the 6th ACM SIGPLAN Conference on Systems, Programming, and Applications (SPLASH 2015), Workshop AGERE! pp. 45–56. ACM, New York, October 2015

23. Intel: Intel Xeon PhiTM Coprocessor x100 Product Family Datasheet, February 2017. http://www.intel.com/content/www/us/en/processors/xeon/xeon-phi-coprocessor-datasheet.html

24. Kale, L.V., Krishnan, S.: Charm++: parallel programming with message-driven objects. In: Parallel Programming Using C++, pp. 175–213 (1996)

25. Kirk, D.B., Hwu, W.m.W.: Programming Massively Parallel Processors, A Hands-on Approach, 2nd edn. Morgan Kaufmann, San Francisco (2013)

26. Klöckner, A., Pinto, N., Lee, Y., Catanzaro, B., Ivanov, P., Fasih, A.: PyCUDA and PyOpenCL: a scripting-based approach to GPU run-time code generation. Parallel Comput. **38**(3), 157–174 (2012)

27. Krieder, S.J., et al.: Design and evaluation of the GeMTC framework for GPU-enabled many-task computing. In: Proceedings of the 23rd International Symposium on High-performance Parallel and Distributed Computing, HPDC 2014, pp. 153–164. ACM, New York (2014)

28. Howes, L., Rovatsou, M.: SYCL integrates OpenCL devices with modern C++. Khronos Group, February 2017
29. Lindholm, E., Kilgard, M.J., Moreton, H.: A user-programmable vertex engine. In: Proceedings of the 28th Annual Conference on Computer Graphics and Interactive Techniques, SIGGRAPH 2001, pp. 149–158. ACM, New York (2001)
30. Medina, D.S., St-Cyr, A., Warburton, T.: OCCA: A unified approach to multi-threading languages. ArXiv e-prints, March 2014
31. Munshi, A.: The OpenCL Specification. Khronos OpenCL Working Group, Khronos Group (2012). http://www.khronos.org/registry/cl/specs/opencl-1.2.pdf, Version 1.2, Revision 19
32. Munshi, A., Howes, L.: The OpenCL Specification. Khronos OpenCL Working Group, Khronos Group (2015). https://www.khronos.org/registry/OpenCL/specs/opencl-2.0.pdf, Version 2.0, Revision 29
33. Nickolls, J., Dally, W.J.: The GPU computing era. IEEE Micro **30**(2), 56–69 (2010)
34. NVIDIA: Tesla C2075 Computing Processor Board (Board Specification), February 2017
35. OpenACC-standard.org: The OpenACC Application Programming Interface, February 2017
36. Owens, J.D., Houston, M., Luebke, D., Green, S., Stone, J.E., Phillips, J.C.: GPU computing. Proc. IEEE **96**(5), 879–899 (2008)
37. Scarpino, M.: OpenCL in Action: How to Accelerate Graphics and Computation. Manning Publications Company, Manning Publication Co., 20 Baldwin Road, Shelter Island, NY 11964 (2011)
38. Scheitle, Q., Wählisch, M., Gasser, O., Schmidt, T.C., Carle, G.: Towards an ecosystem for reproducible research in computer networking. In: Proceedings of ACM SIGCOMM Reproducibility Workshop. ACM, New York, August 2017
39. Sorensen, T., Donaldson, A.F., Batty, M., Gopalakrishnan, G., Rakamarić, Z.: Portable inter-workgroup barrier synchronisation for GPUs. In: Proceedings of the 2016 ACM SIGPLAN International Conference on Object-Oriented Programming, Systems, Languages, and Applications, OOPSLA 2016, pp. 39–58. ACM, New York (2016)
40. Srinivasan, S., Mycroft, A.: Kilim: isolation-typed actors for java. In: Vitek, J. (ed.) ECOOP 2008. LNCS, vol. 5142, pp. 104–128. Springer, Heidelberg (2008). https://doi.org/10.1007/978-3-540-70592-5_6
41. The Khronos Group: The Khronos Group, February 2017. http://www.khronos.org/
42. Typesafe Inc.: Akka Framework, August 2017. http://akka.io
43. Vallentin, M., Paxson, V., Sommer, R.: VAST: a unified platform for interactive network forensics. In: Proceedings of the USENIX Symposium on Networked Systems Design and Implementation (NSDI), March 2016
44. Wienke, S., Springer, P., Terboven, C., an Mey, D.: OpenACC — first experiences with real-world applications. In: Kaklamanis, C., Papatheodorou, T., Spirakis, P.G. (eds.) Euro-Par 2012. LNCS, vol. 7484, pp. 859–870. Springer, Heidelberg (2012). https://doi.org/10.1007/978-3-642-32820-6_85
45. Wu, K., Otoo, E.J., Shoshani, A.: Optimizing bitmap indices with efficient compression. ACM Trans. Database Syst. **31**(1), 1–38 (2006)

Programming Actor-Based Collective Adaptive Systems

Roberto Casadei[✉] and Mirko Viroli

Alma Mater Studiorum—Università di Bologna, Cesena, Italy
{roby.casadei,mirko.viroli}@unibo.it

Abstract. In recent years, we are witnessing a growing interest in large-scale situated systems, such as those falling under the umbrella of pervasive computing, Cyber-Physical Systems, and the Internet of Things. The actor model is a natural choice for designing and implementing such systems, thanks to the ability of actors to address distribution, autonomy of control, and asynchronous communication: namely, it is convenient to view the *pervasive cyberspace* as an environment densely inhabited by mobile *situated actors*. But how can an actor-centric development approach be fruitfully used to engineer a complex coordination strategy, where a myriad of devices/actors performs adaptive distributed sensing/processing/acting?

Aggregate computing has been proposed as an emerging paradigm that faces this general problem by adopting a global, system-level stance, allowing to specify and functionally compose collective behaviours by operating on diffused data structures, known as "computational fields". In this paper, we develop on the idea of integrating the actor model and aggregate computing, presenting a software framework where declarative global-level system specifications are automatically turned into an underlying system of Scala/Akka actors carrying complex coordination tasks involving large sets of devices spread over the pervasive computing system.

Keywords: Aggregate computing · Collective adaptive systems
Actors · Scala · Internet of Things

1 Introduction

The interplay between electronic miniaturisation and device cost reduction is leading to the diffusion into the environment of more and more elements capable of sensing, computing, and acting. This can be seen as part of the enduring goal of mankind to shape and engineer the living environment so as to make life easier or better. Nowadays, we see that a lot of opportunities arise by strengthening the connection (and mutual feedback loop) between the physical and the digital world. Multiple metaphors and buzzwords have entered the lexicon of both academia and industry that represent and evoke a similar idea, i.e., a notion of

© Springer Nature Switzerland AG 2018
A. Ricci and P. Haller (Eds.): Programming with Actors, LNCS 10789, pp. 94–122, 2018.
https://doi.org/10.1007/978-3-030-00302-9_4

programming a "computing physical world" densely inhabited by interconnected processing units: cyberspace, service ecosystem, pervasive computing, ubiquitous computing, Internet of Things (IoT), Cyber-Physical Systems (CPS), complex/-collective adaptive systems (CAS), and so on. These scenarios challenge traditional software engineering approaches, since non-trivial complexity emerges from the combination of the multiple issues that arise, such as distribution, heterogeneity, environmental unpredictability, energetic and technological constraints, scalability, and so on.

When it comes to design and implement distributed systems composed of multiple autonomous entities, the *actor model* [2] is generally considered a primary choice, for it captures the key aspects there involved: distribution, encapsulation of control, and asynchronous communication. Indeed, several works proposed actor-based abstractions and frameworks in the context of particular distributed computing scenarios, such as wireless sensor networks (WSNs) and mobile ad-hoc networks (MANETs) [5,21], as well as the IoT, for both middleware [20] and application [16] development. In IoT frameworks, for instance, physical devices and services can be wrapped or exposed as actors [16,17] in order to promote application integration [17,23], behaviour compositionality [17], and runtime adaptation [23,28,33].

To more stress the notion of (physical) *environment*, it is then natural to consider actors for situated systems, which we shall call *situated actors*. However, actor-based applications that involve complex coordination among several (potentially myriads of) entities, and requiring system adaptivity and resiliency, are still very difficult to build: development and maintenance tend to become convoluted and brittle due to the scattering of multiple concerns across many actor definitions and intricate conversational patterns [6]. Plausibly, this problem can be addressed by augmenting the actor model with effective abstractions for programming complex collective adaptative behaviours, providing resiliency and support for very-large scale sets of situated components somewhat inherently.

Aggregate computing [6] is a recent computational and programming model that tackles at its core the development of complex collective adaptive systems. It enables system-level behaviours to be specified as functional manipulations of whole "distributed data structures", known as *computational fields* [7,18]—data structures consisting in a mapping from physical devices to values across time. These program specifications are then automatically translated (by a *global-to-local* mapping) into repetitive micro-level computations of individual devices. As key advantage, it becomes possible to define decentralised algorithms and coordination strategies that are independently specified from, and thus able to adapt and react to, changes in network topology, size, and density as well as to unanticipated environmental perturbations [8]. Critically, this approach is also compositional, so that coarse-grained services can be built out of simple and safe combination of smaller functional blocks, and these in turn can be combined into a service ecosystem.

In this paper, we draw a bridge between the actor model and aggregate computing, in order to establish a disciplined approach for the injection of self-adaptive and advanced coordination capabilities in complex distributed applications. On the one hand, we propose the idea of viewing aggregate computing as a layer on top of actors that enables effective specification of complex coordination patterns. Namely, we describe an actor-based programming framework in which large sets of actors responsible of complex coordination, which we call *actor aggregates*, are programmed "in one shot" according to the aggregate computing model, to automatically and transparently interact with each other to carry on a complex computational process over space and time. With respect to traditional actor programming techniques, this approach reduces accidental complexity by fostering declarativity, separation of concerns, and modularity. On the other hand, our work suggests that a careful exposure of the actor-based view of an aggregate system can provide the means for *(i)* steering collective computation by the inputs of other non-aggregate subsystems of actors, and for *(ii)* turning the aggregate process into coordination events forwarded to the many different parts of a larger application. In a nutshell, integrating aggregate computing *on top of (as well as aside to)* actors is expected to pragmatically address open challenges in the state-of-art of IoT and CASs, by proposing a principled way to the engineering of (critical portions of) such systems.

The paper is organised as follows. First, in Sect. 2, we discuss the applicability of the actor model to nowadays distributed computing scenarios. In Sect. 3, we present a case study rooted on a CAS, and outline requirements for effectively engineering an implementation of it. Then, in Sect. 4, we introduce aggregate computing as an extension to the actor model that is suitable for tackling the problem of complex distributed computation and coordination. In Sect. 5, we present SCAFI[1], an aggregate computing framework on top of the Scala programming language, focussing on its actor-based distributed platform and then describing the language and its operational semantics through examples. Finally, in Sect. 6, we evaluate the idea of actor aggregates discussing an implementation of the case study.

2   Actors in the Pervasive Cyberspace

An *actor* [2] is a (re)active entity that represents an independent *locus of control*, encapsulates a state and behaviour, has a globally unique immutable identifier that allows for location transparency, and interacts with other actors via asynchronous message passing—each actor has a *mailbox* for message buffering. In response to a message, an actor can only (i) send a finite number of messages to other actors, (ii) create a finite number of child actors, and (iii) change its own behaviour, that is, its message processing logic. Thus, an actor system consists of an (possibly huge) evolving set of (possibly changing, mobile) autonomous actors that communicate with one another and perform some task along the way.

---

[1] https://github.com/scafi/scafi.

Actor systems very well fit highly distributed systems: since communication is based on logical identifiers, the programmer can ignore the actual physical location in which a recipient actor resides (*location transparency*). Also, actors do not share state, in that they communicate exclusively by exchanging messages; as a consequence, the issues related to lock-based synchronisation and mutual exclusion – as found in thread-based concurrency – are completely avoided. In addition, an asynchronous communication style better captures the way in which events occur and are perceived in the physical world [3]; anyhow, synchronicity (sometimes suitable when programming) can be supported as a particular case [2].

Given the appropriateness of actors for modelling distributed systems, it comes naturally to consider them when approaching the development of particular kinds of modern distributed systems, such as large-scale situated systems and those found in the IoT scenario [16]. Here, the *environment* abstraction becomes prominent and paves the path to *context-awareness*, namely, the ability of distinguishing situations depending on context, which is a peculiarity of any "intelligent" behaviour and is often linked to a *locality* principle, i.e., an entity is mostly directly affected by its immediate (logical or physical) surroundings (which effectively represents its context of operation). In this frame, we can introduce a notion of *situated actor* as the bridging abstraction that adds support for *situatedness* on top of plain actors. That is, a situated actor is an actor that has a given position in an environment or generally in space-time—position often inherited by the hosting or associated physical node. Concretely, such actors can be the software interface to a sensor, an actuator, a processor, or generally a computational *device* immersed in some environment, such as the urban area of a smart city, the elevator of a smart building, a room in a smart house, or an edge part of a smart appliance. In other words, after the work in [19,34], a situated actor can be seen as an *avatar* for a physical device, and most specifically, what we can call a *space-aware avatar*.

Starting from this viewpoint, we focus on how actors could be used to implement complex decentralised behaviours, possibly involving a very-large scale set of devices (and hence actors), as those found, for example, in contexts such as crowd engineering, smart mobility, swarms of drones, environment monitoring, and so on. In principle, this would require a design of the actor system which takes into account discipline, best practices, well-known messaging [30] and structural/behavioural/reactive design patterns. However, when the logic to be expressed involves multiple concerns along different dimensions and abstraction levels, the development and maintenance processes might turn out to be very complicated and costly. There are, in fact, certain system-level properties and algorithms that are difficult to implement when reasoning in terms of individual actors and conversation patterns between actors.

What abstractions could be added to the standard actor model for addressing issues ranging from system-level adaptivity and resiliency to decentralised computation design? How could we build actor-based applications in terms of the *composition* of primitive services (e.g., reusing a crowd estimation service to develop both driving congestion-aware navigation and dispersal advice)? Following the principle of separation of concerns, we could address each problem with the more appropriate paradigm, yet importantly, recovering compatibility between the different views so as to provide a coherent framework for building complex adaptive systems.

3   Case Study: Problem Statement

To better present the goal of the approach proposed in this paper, we introduce a case study that will be used throughout.

Consider a mass event such as an exhibition or a concert. Suppose the event application is deployed and running in background on the smartphones of a large part of the participants, and that the location technology (e.g., the GPS on the phones) is accurate enough to estimate the order of magnitude of distances between nearby devices. Multiple services could be provided, including detection of dangerous crowd, anticipation of congestions, dispersal advice, evacuation plans, rendez-vous for groups of friends, steering to points of interest, and so on. Thus, let's consider a case study where the collection of devices has altogether to monitor – in a distributed way – the "dynamic" density of people, and react to dangerous density levels popping an alert up in each relevant smartphone. Most specifically, the service to implement could be informally expressed as follows:

(i) *only devices that did not fail for at least t_{fail} seconds are considered,*
(ii) *partition the whole network in areas of radius r,*
(iii) *sense the mean density of people D_{mean} in any such area,*
(iv) *and when D_{mean} is greater than D_{alert}, execute some actuation A for t_{act} seconds.*

The key question is: how can we *effectively engineer* such an application? The problem phrasing explicitly refers to spatial, temporal, and situation elements, hence, it would be great to specify the program logic using the same abstractions of the high-level problem description, taking a declarative stance. Ideally, we would like to leverage spatio-temporal building blocks to compose aggregate functionality into a modular solution. At the same time, the language we use should be pragmatic, intercepting static errors (e.g. concerning typing) at compile-time, guaranteeing resiliency properties of the solution, and enabling smooth reuse of existing programming structures and behaviours.

Also, critically, we would like to program such system in a way that is largely independent of the details of the underlying (networking) infrastructure. In other words, the concrete way in which interactions happen should be a platform issue, not affecting the program one writes. If an opportunistic ad-hoc network is in place, coordination may unfold by having devices exchanging messages directly with their reachable neighbours; this decentralised, peer-to-peer mode is important for scalability and for scenarios where a basic communication infrastructure is not available—as in very dense mass events. On the other hand, if the system includes one or more servers or gateways for access to the cloud, interactions and computations can be mediated by infrastructural and platform services. Taking it to a step further, one may even envision a scenario where the execution platform could also be able to transparently and dynamically adapt the system execution strategy to *(i)* the infrastructural support available, and *(ii)* the desired quality of service.

Our goal is to implement this alerting service by an aggregation of actors running on all smartphones, interacting with the actors providing other services, e.g., to receive information sensed locally (for instance, position and estimated distances from sources), and to communicate alert events to the actors managing smartphone screen.

4   Aggregate Computing

We note that services as those described in Sect. 3, as well as many other applications involving a multitude of spatially situated devices, can be best *described* (most specifically, *declaratively specified*) in terms of global, system-level properties and behaviours carried out by groups of interrelated computational elements. In other words, it is often convenient to abstract over the individual computing device and assume a more holistic stance where the "machine that computes", and hence, the machine to be programmed, is made by the (potentially large) set of devices, seen as a unique "body". Once this idea is accepted, we could start thinking about what conceptual tools we could use, what assumptions our model could be based on, and what execution platforms could be needed to address our macro specifications.

Aggregate programming [6] is an emerging paradigm that dismisses the traditional device-centric viewpoint in favour of an aggregate viewpoint where the programmable entity is the entire set of devices (also read as *actors*) that make up the system—i.e., the whole *computational fabric* mixed into the environment. Thus, by shifting the focus from the behaviour of individual actors to global patterns and evolving system structures (top-down design), the approach unburdens the programmer from the need to solve the generally intractable *bottom-up emergence engineering* problem.

The unifying abstraction that allows moving downwards (design) and upwards (execution) the micro/macro layers is that of *computational field* [4,7,18] (or *field* for short), which brings the concept of force field from physics into computer science. In a field ϕ, each space-time event (s,t) is mapped to a computational value $\phi(s,t)$ as computed by the device $\delta_{s,t}$ there located—or the closest to it [8]. The basic operations that are necessary to express interesting field-based computations include (i) functions mapping fields event-wise, (ii) causal transformations allowing to evolve fields while carrying on state (taking into account at each event what was the result at the event's predecessor in time), (iii) observation primitives for updating events in relation to other events in the field according to a *neighbouring relationship* in space, and (iv) domain restriction operations to isolate computations to specific portions of the fields. With such a notion at hand, fully formalised in [31], "aggregate programs" take the form of functional descriptions of field-to-field transformations over time, and one can use the compositional model of functional programming to scale with complexity, and to bottom-up preserve properties of interest (e.g., self-stabilisation [11] or device location independence [32]).

We say that a field is a distributed, diffused, or global data structure because its value is given by, or emerges from, the aggregate of the values taken from an entire set of situated devices. Of course, a correspondence between the physical system and its logical representation as a field must be defined. Usually, the field directly represents the spatial situation of a deployed system, so that each networked device has a position in space, and the neighbouring relation between devices corresponds to proximity. Typically, euclidean distance with a certain threshold is used, but the neighbourhood does not strictly needs to be defined in spatial terms, nor it requires to be uniform or statically specified (fixed); the notion can be logical and ad-hoc. This notion is indeed very important: together with sensors, it concurs to define what the context is for a given element.

The execution model of aggregate computing involves partially-synchronous devices computing at discrete rounds of execution their local piece of the global program and then broadcasting to their neighbourhood the result, which we call the *export*. However, it should be stressed that we can abstract from how the interactions are actually carried out in a concrete system implementation; that is, the model is conveniently neighbour-driven, albeit its actual embodiment could involve a central coordinator or even a dynamic, hybrid infrastructure [33].

It comes natural to implement one such system using actor-based technology. In fact, an actor can logically wrap an individual device and assume a behaviour in which it iteratively accepts incoming messages from other devices and environmental events (as perceived by sensors), self-dispatches the execution of its locally compiled aggregate program, and informs its neighbour actors of the result of its computation. We shall use the term *actor aggregate* to identify the set of actors participating in an aggregate computation, that is, the actors involved in the creation of a computational field. More information about implementing aggregate computing with actors is provided in Sect. 5.1, where a concrete Scala/Akka framework is outlined.

Though useful, the key point of the paper is not just that aggregate computing systems can be implemented as actor systems: what is really crucial is that these two models can be fruitfully *integrated* (see Fig. 1) so that each concern of distributed systems can be tackled at the right abstraction level and with the right tool.

5   Aggregate Computing with SCAFI

SCAFI (SCAla with computational FIelds) [10] is a framework that brings aggregate computing into the Scala programming language [22] and thus enables the specification of distributed and collective behaviours according to an aggregate programming style.

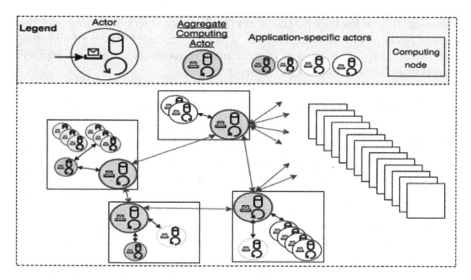

Fig. 1. Graphical representation of a generic actor-based system where application-specific actors integrate with aggregate actors so as to exploit the ability of aggregate computing to express resilient adaptive coordination strategies. (Color figure online)

Note that in order to use this paradigm in practice, multiple ingredients are needed. First, the programmer needs a way – i.e., a *language* – to express aggregate computations, and there must be some *(virtual) machine* able to execute these program specifications locally in each device. Second, a distributed *system* has to be concretely specified and configured, and its runtime execution has to be supported by a *platform*. SCAFI supports all these tasks by equipping developers with a Scala-internal domain-specific language (DSL) based on the field calculus, together with an associated interpreter, and a framework upon which aggregate simulations and systems can be described and run.

Importantly, SCAFI originated with the intention of providing an integrated environment for programming aggregate systems in a modern, mainstream language. In fact, it was proposed as a type-safe and practical alternative to the dynamically typed, external DSL PROTELIS [24].

The choice to target the Scala programming language stems from both technical and practical motivations. On one hand, Scala provides a powerful static type system with type inference, an effective integration of functional and object-oriented paradigms, and advanced features that come handy for library development, also enabling the creation of fluent, DSL-flavoured APIs. That is, Scala allows us to define a standard API and thanks to both particular language constructs (e.g., by-name arguments) and syntactic sugar (e.g., curly braces can replace parentheses in method calls if a single parameter is expected), it is possible to make it appear as an "embedded" language.

On the other hand, Scala is gaining popularity especially for what concerns the development of distributed systems. The use of Akka [1] as the implementation technology for the SCAFI platform is a direct consequence of the choice of Scala as our host language, as well as a reasonable trade-off affording flexibility of design decisions and programming convenience in terms of exposed features from lower-level platform layers.

5.1 Actor-Based Aggregate Computing Platform

SCAFI comes with an actor-based distributed framework, developed in Scala/Akka, that supports both the construction and the execution of concrete aggregate systems. Though implemented with actors, it provides a convenient object-oriented façade for the configuration and management of both individual devices and whole collective applications. It also provides access to the underlying actor-based functionality, for maximum flexibility and control.

In this framework, multiple entities of the domain are modelled as actors. Sensors are essentially actors producing (a stream of) values. Conversely, actuators are actors that consume the values they are fed with, possibly with side effects. Most notably, devices become actors whose behaviour performs, at each execution round, some or all of the following duties: *(i) perception of the local context*, by reading sensors and collecting messages received from other devices; *(ii) execution of the local program obtained out of the aggregate program*, taking the local context as input and yielding both a local result and an export representing the computation just executed as output, *(iii) propagation of the export to the neighbourhood*, and *(iv) execution of actions in the local context*, by triggering actuators.

The notion of a device is a key abstraction of the aggregate computing model. However, it should be noted that the execution of computations and the awareness of neighbourhood can be moved outside the devices. In fact, the devices can ultimately be assimilated to the means by which the system perceives and acts upon specific portions of the (logical or physical) world; in other words, they are representatives of contexts of interest. Nevertheless, it is often useful to distribute as much functionality as possible to the devices, so as to leverage the locality principle and drive collective computations on a peer-to-peer interaction basis. In some cases, still, it may be necessary (or convenient) to centralise some processing or knowledge, or even to adapt the execution strategy according to the available infrastructure [33].

The instantiation of a device involves, in turn, three macro-operations:

1. `PlatformConfigurator.setupPlatform()`: creates the infrastructural support for the current physical node and yields a `PlatformFacade` instance wrapping over the newly launched Akka `ActorSystem`.
2. `PlatformFacade.newAggregateApplication()`: activates a particular application for the current physical node and yields a `SystemFacade` instance wrapping over the corresponding `AggregateApplicationActor`. Notice that one may want to run multiple applications on the same platform node.
3. `SystemFacade.newDevice()`: locally creates a logical node for the given application and yields a `DeviceManager` instance wrapping over the corresponding `DeviceActor`.

The actual implementation and behaviour of the above methods and actors depend on the chosen platform style and settings. Currently, two main platform styles are supported: (i) *peer-to-peer*, for fully decentralised systems where devices directly interact with each other, and (ii) *server-based*, for systems in which there is a central entity responsible for mediating device interactions and/or computations; the server might also keep a representation of the topology of the system, thus leveraging spatial features for the management of the neighbouring relationship. Critically, note that aggregate programs we shall consider in next section are completely independent of which platform (and hence, underlying communication technology) is actually used. Figure 2 shows the minimal code necessary to configure and set up a single device.

```
// STEP 1: CHOOSE INCARNATION
import scafi.incarnations.{ BasicActorP2P => Platform }
import Platform.{AggregateProgram,Settings,PlatformConfig}

// STEP 2: DEFINE AGGREGATE PROGRAM SCHEMA
class Program extends AggregateProgram with CrowdAPI {
  // Specify a "dangerous density" aggregate computation
  override def main(): Any = dangerousDensity()
}

// STEP 3: PLATFORM SETUP
val settings = Settings()
val platform = PlatformConfig.setupPlatform(settings)

// STEP 4: NODE SETUP
val sys = platform.newAggregateApplication()
val dm = sys.newDevice(id = Utils.newId(), program = Program,
                        neighbours = Utils.discoverNbrs())
val devActor = dm.actorRef // get underlying actor
```

Fig. 2. SCAFI code to locally configure the actor of an aggregate application

The essential steps include *(i)* the selection of the kind of platform support to use, *(ii)* the specification of the aggregate computation to run, *(iii)* the instantiation of the basic middleware infrastructure, and *(iv)* the creation of the device actor. Once a reference to the device actor is obtained, it can be used for interaction with standard actor-based functionality, of course depending on the services provided by the device actor implementation; in SCAFI, for example, device actors are observable and provide template methods for simple extension.

As pointed out in Sect. 4, an aggregate computing system can be seen, in a larger system, as the specific subsystem that provides advanced capabilities of robust coordination and collective computation, all with resilient adaptation to changes. In particular, actor aggregates can integrate with application-specific actors; this idea is graphically represented in Fig. 1, where blue actors form an aggregate. This integration can be achieved in multiple ways: the application actors can publish values to device actors by working as sensors, or they can interact with the aggregate platform to fine-tune the neighbouring relation; conversely, the aggregate computing actors can send messages to application actors when certain contextual conditions are met (e.g., pushing alerts to specific regulator actors when a dangerous situation is perceived)—this could be implemented by encoding the message dispatching logic directly in the aggregate program, by using "boundary" actuators, by registering application actors as observers of device actors, or by extending device actors to work as streams.

5.2 Basic Syntax and Semantics

The syntax and typing of the language are concisely represented by the interface (Scala `trait`) shown in Fig. 3, to be inherited by any module specifying aggregate behaviour.

Note that in Scala the return type comes at the end of a method signature; methods can be generic (with type parameters specified in square brackets); $T_i \Rightarrow T_o$ is a function type; $\Rightarrow T$ is a call-by-name parameter passed unevaluated to the function (essentially, syntactic sugar over a 0-ary function); methods can be defined to accept multiple parameter lists, and when these are single-arity, then can be specified with round or curly brackets at the call site. Critically, in the SCAFI DSL the field calculus constructs are rendered as Scala methods and hence inherit the features, the typing rules, and the syntactical constraints of Scala code.

```
trait Constructs {
  def rep[A](init: A)(fun: (A) => A): A
  def nbr[A](expr: => A): A
  def foldhood[A](init: => A)(acc: (A,A)=>A)(expr: => A): A
  def branch[A](cond: => Boolean)(th: => A)(el: => A): A
  def sense[A](name: LSNS): A
  def nbrvar[A](name: NSNS): A
  def aggregate[A](f: => A): A
}
```

Fig. 3. The Scala trait that any aggregate program has to inherit from.

When describing, reasoning about, or designing systems with the field calculus constructs, a twofold interpretation is possible for them. On the one hand, an operator can be seen as working on whole fields, in a sort of *global viewpoint* that also corresponds to the natural semantics of the language. On the other hand, the same operator can be considered in the context of a single device and the event at which it is executed; this is the *local viewpoint* from which the operational semantics unfolds [12]. These two perspectives are complementary and both concur to a full understanding of the model.

Aggregate Programs. An aggregate program consists of a set of function definitions and a body of expressions. In SCAFI, it materialises into the definition of a "main method" of a class implementing the `Constructs` trait. The execution of an aggregate program is given by an iterative, partially synchronous "cumulative execution" of the local programs (which have the same structure and result of the aggregate program) running at the devices that comprise the system. Thus, the result emerging from an aggregate program is the field of the results achieved by executing it on each device.

Simple Fields. The most trivial program is a constant expression. For example,

```
"Hello, " + "World"
```

locally evaluates to the `"Hello, World"` string in every device, whereas globally it produces a uniform constant field that holds that value at any point—as obtained by concatenating the two constant fields `"Hello,"` and `"World"`, pointwise. Constant fields may be useful for expressing system parameters. Fields that are constant but not uniform could be produced by leveraging built-in or user-defined functions that behave diversely from device to device, such as:

```
mid()
```

which returns the identifier of the executing device, collectively contributing to the field of device identifiers—and similarly for any other built-in wrapping a local sensor as seen below.

Dynamic Fields. The `rep` operator supports the construction of fields that evolve over time, by repeatedly applying (on a round-by-round basis) a 1-ary function `fun` that maps the previous value (initially, `init`) to the new one. It enables to carry state along, from computation to computation, and use it to determine the next state. In the following example, `rep` is used for counting the number of computation rounds performed by devices since the beginning of computation:

```
// Initially 0; state is incremented at each round
rep(0){ _+1 } // or equivalently: rep(0)( x => x+1 )
```

Note that in Scala, lambdas can be succinctly defined by using underscores "_" for denoting successive parameters. The frequency at which devices compute rounds can vary over time and from device to device, hence, in general, the resulting field will be heterogeneous in time and space. See [8] for details about field convergence.

Interaction: Communication and Observation. Another common operation is the one used to make values of a field depend on others occurring in the neighbourhood. For the purpose, there is the `nbr` construct, which supports device interaction by means of communications carried out by broadcasting the result of evaluating `expr` from the executing device to the corresponding neighbourhood. At each device, an `nbr` expression evaluates to a map from neighbours to the (lately received) result of evaluating `expr` at their side, effectively working as a primitive for neighbourhood observation. In the global viewpoint, a field of fields is generated, where the domain of the inner fields is the neighbourhood set for the corresponding points. Construct `nbr` has to be nested inside a `foldhood` operation, which is used to reduce the neighbour map of `expr` to a single value by accumulating on the values according to an aggregator function `acc` with identity `init`; on top of it, various specialised aggregations can be defined (e.g., `minHood` or `sumHood`). For example, the following expression

```
foldhood(0)(_+_){ nbr{1} }
```

computes the number of neighbours at each device; it works by evaluating the `nbr` expression in the context of the very current device (by actually executing the body of `nbr`) and of all its neighbours (by reading the corresponding value that has been recently communicated) and then folding over the resulting structure as you would expect from functional programming.

Similarly, in the following code we associate to each device the minimum number of computation rounds found in its neighbourhood:

```
foldhood(Int.MaxValue)(min(_,_)){ nbr{ rep(0){ _+1 } } }
```

Context-Sensitiveness and Sensors. Every aggregate computation is locally executed against a context which includes *(i)* the export describing the previous computation (construct `rep`), *(ii)* messages received from neighbours (construct `nbr`), and *(iii)* a set of values perceived from the (physical or software) environment. Sensing is the main mechanism for extracting such values from the environment, effectively enabling context-sensitive behaviours; in practice, it is carried out by querying sensors. In the aggregate computing model there are two kinds of sensors: local sensors and neighbouring sensors.

Expression `sense[T](name)` retrieves a value of type T from a local sensor identified by **name**. For instance, expression

```
sense[Double]("temperature")
// Generic type for 'sense' is instantiated to 'Double'
```

returns, in any device, a **Double** value from the **temperature** sensor, which contributes to the construction of a global field of temperature readings. At this level, the manner in which sensors are defined and accessed is not specified, i.e., it is an implementation detail handled at the platform level; pragmatically, this could resolve into a sensor actor "publishing" on a particular device actor, or into the simple association of a function to a (sensor) name.

Construct `nbrvar` provides another perception feature. It is very similar to `nbr`, but instead of inspecting neighbours for an expression, it locally perceives some information concerning neighbours—a sort of "environmental probe". This operator yields a field mapping each neighbour to some value, which has to be reduced pointwise by a `foldhood` operation as for the case of `nbr`. A commonly used environmental sensor is the one that, for each node, provides an estimate of the distance from neighbours, e.g., used as follows to retrieve the distance of the more distant neighbour:

```
// Compute the maximum distance from neighbours
foldhood(Double.MinValue)(max(_,_)){ // Also: maxHood {...}
  nbrvar[Double](NBR_RANGE_NAME)
}
```

Field Domain Restrictions. We have seen that interaction with `nbr` is based on a notion of neighbourhood, which is defined through some physical or platform-dependent proximity relation. However, it is often useful to further regulate admissible interactions on the basis of local conditions that depend on how the computation evolved. For example, it might make sense to differentiate the algorithm carried out by devices that have recently joined the system from the behaviour of devices in a fully operating mode. In other words, it is frequently needed to define separate branches of computation that are dynamically joined by subgroups of devices. Such a feature, called *domain restriction*, is supported by the `branch` construct, which works by splitting the domain of devices into two completely isolated parts (`th` and `el`) according to a boolean field `cond` expressing some condition. Hence, the result of a `branch` expression is actually a field partitioned into two sub-fields. As an example, let's use `branch` to create a partition based on the value read from a local sensor:

```
branch(sense[Boolean]("flag")){
  compute(...)     // sub-computation
}{
  Double.MaxValue // not computing
}
```

The isolation property of field partitions requires that devices belonging to different domains are not allowed to interact. This is enforced by the execution engine, according to the operational semantics of the field calculus, through an *alignment* process. Essentially, an aggregate computation can be represented as a tree where the nodes are domain split points, and it turns out that such a structure is exactly the *export* of the computation, that is, the object that is broadcasted from any device to the corresponding neighbourhood. Then, two devices are aligned when they take the same path in the tree, i.e., when they follow the same sub-computation or partition or subfield. This works, in practice, by keeping track of the "computation path" taken by the executing device and then retaining, at any step, only the neighbour exports matching up. From this description, it should be clear that, in general, *(i)* the computation path and hence the alignment between two devices can vary from round to round, and *(ii)* the alignment can be partial (i.e., can extend to a particular split point, and cannot be retrieved once lost—there is currently no primitive for domain joins).

Functions. In SCAFI, there are two distinct kinds of function. First of all, there are "normal" Scala functions, which serve as units for encapsulating behaviour or algorithmic logic. For example, it is possible to define a version of `foldHood` that does not consider the device itself, or to wrap over the reading of a particular sensor with a terser linguistic item:

```
def foldhoodMinus[A](init: =>A)(acc: (A,A)=>A)(ex: =>A):A=
  foldhood(init)(acc)(mux(mid()==nbr(mid())){init}{ex})

def isSource = sense[Boolean]("source")
```

where `mux` is a purely functional multiplexer.

Second, SCAFI provides first-class aggregate functions – as defined by the higher-order version of the field calculus [12] – which have an extended semantics: they not only work as abstractions, but also as units for alignment. In other words, an aggregate function creates a computation in a domain that is identified by the function itself, so that two devices are structurally aligned only when they execute the same aggregate function. In practice, functions that have to work on whole fields should be defined by wrapping the function body with construct `aggregate`. This feature is so general that aggregate functions can be used to express the `branch` operator:

```
def branch[A](cond: => Boolean)(th: => A)(el: => A): A =
  (if(cond){
    () => aggregate{ th }
  } else {
    () => aggregate{ el }
  })()
```

Devices running distinct aggregate functions (e.g., those returned by the *then* and *else* parts of the `if` above) constitute different sub-domains and thus they are not allowed to interact via `nbr`.

As defined in detail in [12], higher-order functions are especially key to make aggregate computations open to injection of new code at run-time: special sensors can produce lambdas representing new code, which can be spread around and be executed remotely by a group of devices which then form a team carrying on a new aggregate program[2].

5.3   Composition and Building Blocks

In the previous subsection, the key constructs of the field calculus have been introduced: they represent the basic "moves" for expressing field-based computations. They are somewhat low-level, but the good news is that they can be combined into more meaningful patterns, for aggregate computing is designed to make any behaviour *compose* with one another functionally, and to do so at multiple levels. Thanks to this property, it is possible to envision a stack of aggregate functionality [6], i.e., layers of libraries and APIs for collective adaptive computation—from more general to more application-specific ones.

---

[2] Injection of new code clearly raises security concerns which we do not address here: we simply assume that all the devices participating to the same aggregate application can be trusted.

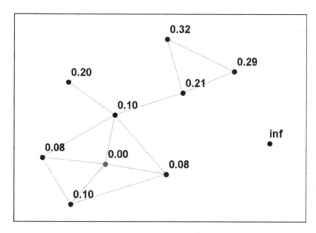

Fig. 4. Snapshot of a stabilised gradient field from a simulation in SCAFI. The bold dots represent devices (nodes). The gray lines represent connections according to the neighbouring relation. The labels above the nodes show a string representation of the result of the last computation (i.e., the root of the computation export) at the corresponding device. The red node is the source device from which the gradient is calculated. (Color figure online)

For example, one of the most common patterns is the *gradient* [14], which computes the field of the minimum estimated distances from given source points (see Fig. 4):

```
def nbrRange = nbrvar[Double](NBR_RANGE_NAME)

def gradient(source: Boolean): Double =
  rep(Double.PositiveInfinity){ distance =>
    mux(source) {
      0.0
    } {
      minHood { nbr{distance} + nbrRange }
    }
}
```

Initially, we don't know if a path from some device to a source device exists, so an infinite distance is assumed. Source devices are obviously at a null distance from themselves. Instead, the other devices select the shortest path among those passing from the neighbourhood. The minimum distance computed is retained from round to round using `rep`.

Gradient-Cast. Multiple types of aggregations can be performed along a distance-gradient. In fact, it comes handy to define a generalised operator G as a gradient algorithm parameterised upon the `metric` for calculating increments (i.e., distances), which can carry some value of `field` from the source outward, with the logic `acc` by which such value gets evolved while ascending the gradient:

```
def G[V:OrderingFoldable](src:Boolean, field:V, acc:V=>V, metric: =>Double): V =
  rep((Double.MaxValue,field)){ case (distance,value) =>
    mux(src) {
      (0.0, field)    // ..on sources
    } {
      minHoodMinus { // minHood except myself
        (nbr{ distance } + metric, acc( nbr{ value }))
      }
    }
  }._2 // yielding the resulting field of values
```

The context bound `V:OrderingFoldable` statically enforces that the instantiated generic type `V` has an implicit `OrderingFoldable[V]` typeclass instance in scope, which provides a definition of methods `top():V`, `bottom():V`, and `compare(V,V):Int`. These constraints on `V` ensure that `minHoodMinus` can work out the minimum value for tuples `(distance,value)`, where we also assume that in the scope of the definition of `G` there are implicit `OrderingFoldables` for both `Doubles` and 2-element tuples of `OrderingFoldables`.

Upon `G`, it is straightforward, for example, to implement a basic `hopGradient` (where a distance is the number of hops from a node to another) and a `broadcast` function that simply propagates a value from source points to the rest of the network:

```
def hopGradientByG(src: Boolean): Int =
  G[Int](src, 0, acc = _+1, metric = 1)

def broadcast[V:OrderingFoldable](source: Boolean, field: V): V =
  G[V](source, field, acc = x=>x, metric = nbrRange)
```

Converge-Cast. Essentially, `G` allows for an information flow from source devices to their global surroundings—a sort of propagation or diffusion of values. The dual operation involves an information flow directed from a global area towards specific collection points, which can be used to perform distributed sensing. This is supported by the generalised operator `C`, which **accumulates** values along the `potential` field, starting with `local` at the sources where `potential` is maximum and aggregating while descending the chain of parents, ultimately converging to the points where `potential` is minimum.

```
def C[V:OrderingFoldable](potential: V, acc: (V,V)=>V, local: V, Null: V): V = {
  rep(local){ v =>
    acc(local, foldhood(Null)(acc){
      mux(nbr(findParent(potential)) == mid()){
        nbr(v)
      } {
        nbr(Null)
      }
    })
  }
}

def findParent[V:OrderingFoldable](potential: V): ID = {
  mux(implicitly[OrderingFoldable[V]].compare(minHood{ nbr(potential) },
```

```
                                             potential)<0 ){
    minHood{ nbr{ (potential, mid()) } }._2
  }{
    Int.MaxValue
  }
}
```

To better visualise how the algorithm works, let's consider a 3×3 grid of devices with unitary distance between rows and columns, neighbouring relation on adjacent rows and columns (i.e., Manhattan distance), and device 3 at the 2nd row and 1st column with the "source" sensor set to true. The following expression:

```
def p = distanceTo(isSource) // potential

(p, mid()+"->"+findParent(p), C[Double](p, _+_, 1, 0.0))
```

evaluates to

```
/* (1, 0->3,  3)    (2, 1->0, 2)    (3, 2->1, 1)
   (0, 3->.., 9)    (1, 4->3, 4)    (2, 5->4, 2)
   (1, 6->3,  1)    (2, 7->4, 1)    (3, 8->5, 1) */
```

as, for example, the source device (where the potential field is 0) folds (with a sum) on the aggregated values coming from the top, bottom, and right devices; conversely, "edge" devices (with no "parent") at distance 3 from the source emit the local value 1.

Sparse-Choice. The generic operator S enables to select devices sparsely in such a way that the network gets partitioned into "areas of responsibility". In other words, it carries out a leader election process (see Fig. 5), where grain is the mean distance between two leaders—according to a notion of distance expressed by metric. It could be implemented as follows:

```
def S(grain: Double, metric: Double): Boolean =
  breakUsingUids(randomUid, grain, metric)
```

where randomUid generates a random field of unique identifiers:

```
def randomUid: (Double,ID) =
  rep((Math.random()), mid()) { v => (v._1, mid()) }
```

which is in turn exploited to break the network symmetry:

```
def breakUsingUids(uid: (Double,ID), grain: Double, metric: => Double): Boolean =
  uid == rep(uid) { lead:(Double,ID) =>
    val acc = (_:Double)+metric
    distanceCompetition(G[Double](uid==lead,0,acc,metric),
                        lead, uid, grain, metric)
  }
```

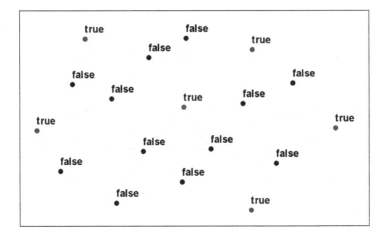

Fig. 5. Stabilised field in a SCAFI simulation for S. The red nodes are those which compute **true**, i.e., the elected leaders. (Color figure online)

by means of a competition for leadership between devices defined as:

```
def distanceCompetition(d: Double,
                        lead: (Double,ID),
                        uid: (Double,ID),
                        grain: Double,
                        metric: => Double) = {
  val inf:(Double,ID) = (Double.PositiveInfinity, uid._2)
  mux(d > grain){ uid }{
    mux(d >= (0.5*grain)){ inf }{
      minHood {
        mux(nbr{d}+metric >= 0.5*grain){
          nbr{inf}
        }{
          nbr{lead}
        }
      }
    }
  }
}
```

Time-Decay. The T operator can be used to express time-related patterns, providing a convenient abstraction over **rep** construct. It works by decreasing the `initial` field with a `decay` function until a `floor` value is reached:

```
def T[V:Numeric](initial: V, floor: V, decay: V=>V): V = {
  val ev = implicitly[Numeric[V]] // getting a Numeric[V] object from the context
  rep(initial){ v =>
    ev.min(initial, ev.max(floor, decay(v)))
  }
}
```

Upon T, the implementation of a `timer` function is straightforward:

```
def timer[V](initial: V): V = {
  val ev = implicitly[Numeric[V]] // getting a Numeric[V] object from the context
  T(initial, ev.zero, (t:V)=>ev.minus(t, ev.one))
} // Decreases 'initial' by 1 at each round, until 0
```

In turn, `timer` supports the definition of a `limitedMemory` function that computes `value` for `timeout` and then returns `expValue` after expiration, effectively realising a finite-time memory:

```
def limitedMemory[V,T](value: V, expValue: V, timeout: T): (V,T) = {
  val ev = implicitly[Numeric[V]] // getting a Numeric[V] object from the context
  val t = timer[T](timeout)
  (mux(ev.gt(t, ev.zero)){value}{expValue}, t)
}
```

Note that the above definition of `timer` depends on the frequency of operation of a given device. If one desires a notion of temporariness that is based on physical time, it could be implemented as follows:

```
def timer(dur: Duration): Long = {
  val ct = System.nanoTime() // Current time
  val et = ct + dur.toNanos   // Time-to-expire (bootstrap)

  rep((et, dur.toNanos)) { case (expTime,remaining) =>
    mux(remaining<=0) { (et,0) }{ (expTime, expTime - ct) }
  }._2 // Selects the component expressing remaining time
}
```

where the state about both the expiration time and the remaining time is retained across rounds via `rep`. A simulation for `timer` is shown in Fig. 6.

6   Case Study: Implementation

We now consider the crowd density monitoring scenario outlined in Sect. 3, and present the aggregate program implementation (Sect. 6.1) and then the actor platform configuration (Sect. 6.2).

6.1   Aggregate Program Implementation

Using SCAFI, an aggregate program expressing the desired functionality can be encoded as shown in Fig. 7. See Fig. 8 for a set of snapshots taken from the corresponding SCAFI simulation[3].

The algorithm uses a `rep` to keep track of the last time when an alert was triggered. Then, the crowd density estimation process starts, considering only the devices that did not fail for at least a timeframe `t_fail`. The latter point

---

[3] The simulation is publicly available at the following repository: https://bitbucket. org/metaphori/demo-aggregate-agere16.

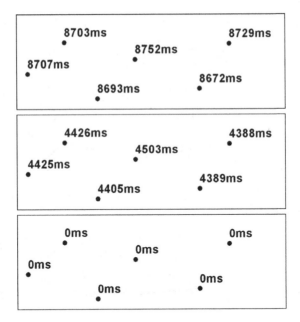

Fig. 6. Snapshots of a SCAFI simulation for `timer`; the third one depicts the stabilised field.

is achieved with a functional block `recentlyTrue` which can be implemented as follows:

```
def recentlyTrue(dur: Duration, cond: => Boolean): Boolean =
  rep(false){ happenedRecently =>
    branch(cond){ true } { branch(!happenedRecently){ false }{ timer(dur) > 0 } }
  }
```

which returns `true` while `cond` is `true` or while the timer has not yet elapsed since `cond` flipped from `true` to `false`. In this process, the space is split into monitoring areas where the collectors of the mean density are located at a mean distance of `meanDist` (which is the double of the `radius`). If the mean density is above threshold `D_alert`, then an alert is issued. The mean density is calculated using `average`, a building block which is implemented as follows:

```
def summarise(sink: Boolean,
              acc: (Double,Double)=>Double,
              local: Double,
              Null: Double): Double =
  broadcast(sink, C(distanceTo(sink), acc, local, Null))

def average(sink: Boolean, value: Double): Double =
  summarise(sink, (a,b)=>{a+b}, value, 0.0) / summarise(sink, (a,b)=>a+b, 1, 0.0)
```

where `summarise` works by first collecting the mean density at the `sink` and then propagating that value to the entire area (notice that `broadcast` refers

```
object CrowdSensingProgram extends AggregateProgram with BuildingBlocks {
  /* Parameters */
  val t_fail = (1 minute)      // Time w/o failures
  val t_act = (5 seconds)      // Time for actuation
  val D_alert = 10.0           // Mean people density threshold
  val radius = 20              // Radius of monitoring areas
  val meanDist = radius*2      // Mean distance between area leaders

  /* Program result types */
  trait Result
  case object Ok extends Result
  case object Alert extends Result
  case object FailedRecently extends Result

  trait IsActing
  case object Acts extends IsActing
  case object Idle extends IsActing

  /* Core logic */
  def main = rep( (Ok,Idle) ){ case (lastStatus, wasActing) =>
    val isWorking = recentlyTrue(t_act, lastStatus==Alert)
    val isActing = branch (isWorking) { act(); Acts } { Idle }

    (branch(withoutFailuresSince(t_fail)) {
      val areaLeader = S(grain = meanDist, metric = nbrRange)
      val D_mean = average(areaLeader, senseLocalDensity())

      // Branching working devices sensing high and low density
      branch(D_mean > D_alert){ Alert } { Ok }
    }{ // Branch of devices that have failed recently
      FailedRecently
    },
    isActing)
  }

  /* Functions */
  def senseLocalDensity() = foldhood(0)(_+_){ nbr(1) }
  def withoutFailuresSince(d: Duration) = !recentlyTrue(d, sense("failure"))
  def act[T](): Unit = { /* act in some way */ }

  /* Utility functions */
  def now = System.nanoTime()
  def never = Long.MaxValue
}
```

Fig. 7. Aggregate program in SCAFI for the crowd sensing case study.

to a "spatial broadcast" building block in the algorithm and not to an actual communication act).

6.2 Linking Aggregate Computing Actors with Other System Actors

Once we came up with an aggregate program that realises our intended algorithm, this can be deployed to device actors, which will make it executing. Then, using the ideas introduced in Sects. 4 and 5.1, the aggregate application can be mixed as a subsystem into a larger application, where the aggregate computing actors can coordinate and exchange information with other actors by standard message passing.

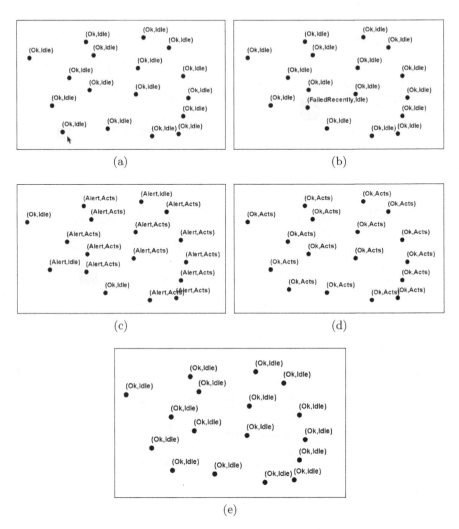

Fig. 8. Simulation of the case study in SCAFI. Snapshot (a) shows the starting network; the selected device is set to encounter a failure. In snapshot (b) the same device is moved in a crowded region. Once the device gets reconsidered for the density algorithm, as of snapshot (c), the threshold is exceeded and an alert is spread. The device is then moved out to restore a legal density, so that the devices in snapshot (d) are not alarmed anymore but still continue to act for some time, until reaching snapshot (e).

```
// PRIOR STEPS AS FROM SECTION 5
// STEP 4: NODE SETUP
val sys = platform.newAggregateApplication()
val dm = sys.newDevice(id = Utils.newId(),
                       program = CrowdSensingProgram,
                       neighbours = Utils.discoverNbrs())
val devActor = dm.actorRef // get underlying actor

// Retrieve underlying actor-system
val actorSys = sys.actorSystem
// Retrieve reference to application-specific actor on another ActorSystem
val appActor = actorSys.context.actorFor("akka://AnotherSubsystem/user/SomeActor")
// Create a preprocessing actor that notifies 'appActor' only when value changes
val preprocessor = actorSys.actorOf(Props(classOf[PreprocessorActor], appActor))
// Tell 'devActor' to communicate its outputs to 'preprocessor'
devActor ! NotifyComputationResultTo(preprocessor)

// Provide a sensor value to 'devActor'
devActor ! SensorValue("temp", 27.celsius)
```

That is, by carefully exposing the underlying actor implementation, we endow aggregate systems with message-passing interfaces through which it is possible to adjust, steer and enact a modularised spatio-temporal computation/coordination logic—engineered with proper tools.

7   Discussion

This paper proposes an approach to the development of collective adaptive systems – e.g., as conceived in domains such as pervasive computing, IoT, or CPS – that is centered around two main ingredients: aggregate computing and actors.

Effectively engineering solutions in these scenarios is remarkably difficult, for many issues have to be dealt with in a coherent and organised fashion; in software engineering, this general challenge is usually approached incrementally by filling the abstraction gap between business requirements and technological equipment with well-engineered layers of abstractions, more likely implemented by different specialists. In other words, the problem of building end-to-end solutions is usually split in two parts: (i) the development of a platform or middleware and, on top, (ii) the construction of applications.

Specifically, the aggregate computing platform (described in Subsect. 5.1) is what supports the definition as well as the runtime operation of aggregate applications. However, complex applications often consist of different kinds of services, which may be best developed with different tools. Aggregate computing, in particular, is designed to effectively engineer the self-adaptive, self-organising behaviour of a collection of situated computing devices. The key message, hence, is that the aggregate framework can be regarded as a specialised tool for effectively capturing particular needs at the application or even middleware-level, typically centered around expressing complex coordination in space-time.

On the other hands, actors have already been considered for both platform and application development in settings such as the IoT [16,20]. Similarly, establishing an aggregate platform on top of actors appears to be congenial [33] and to promote a number of ideas related to adaptation of system execution. Indeed, the operational and network semantics of the field calculus [31], by abstracting and accounting for asynchronicity and round-by-round evolution, are well-suited to be rendered within the message-oriented and macro-step traits of the actor model. Furthermore, we argue that defining actor boundaries around aggregate computing middleware and application services paves the way to an effective integration of this framework in other platforms and more diversified applications. More concretely, for instance, field computations can be regarded as coordination events to be dispatched to actor-based handlers with glue or functional responsibilities. The idea of aggregate actors and their signified role in complex software systems may plausibly contribute, in a seamless way, to the coordination and adaptation needs encountered in pervasive computing and IoT domains.

8   Related Works

An extensive survey of approaches and languages for programming aggregates of devices has been presented in [5]. In such work, four groups of approaches and their representatives – device abstraction languages (e.g., NetLogo, TOTA), pattern languages (e.g., GPL, OSL), information movement languages (e.g., TinyDB, Regiment), and general purpose spatial languages (e.g., MGS, field calculus) – are analysed with respect to a reference example involving all the essential space-time operations. In the rest of this section, we focus instead on specific aspects or similarities arising from approaches in different domains.

Our execution model, described in Sect. 4, might resemble a variant of the Bulk Synchronous Parallel (BSP) model [27]. In fact, aggregate computations could be carried out in a BSP-fashion. However, usually our notion of round is not global as the BSP superstep, but local to devices, and no barrier synchronisation is enforced. In fact, while BSP is a model for "precise" parallel programming also allowing accurate performance estimation, the field calculus is primarily aimed at programming distributed systems that "approximate" an ideal continuous computation. Though application-dependent, the requirements on the algorithmic actuation for complex self-organising systems such as those targeted by aggregate programming are usually less strict. In other words, the two approaches have different goals and basic assumptions. Self-stabilisation and consistency results in the field calculus are key to give meaning of global snapshots of a computational field—the interested reader can refer to [8,32] for a deeper treatment.

The idea of computing in a global-fashion is not a prerogative of distributed programming. For instance, consider Diderot [25], a BSP-inspired parallel computing DSL for building image analysis and visualisation algorithms, e.g., in biomedical scenarios. Interestingly, it explicitly refers to spatial computation patterns; for example, it provides support for continuous tensor field manipulation, spatially-local communication via explicit neighbouring queries, and global communication as flow of information. In a language perspective, Diderot adopts an imperative style; conversely, aggregate programming relies on a functional approach, which is instrumental for achieving the compositionality of collective behaviours. Also, the demarcation arguments for BSP are still valid here, with the additional fact that Diderot is very specific in scope, mainly addressing the mathematical and parallel needs of image data processing. Nevertheless, a more detailed comparison will be conducted in the future to study additional constructs for the field calculus.

Also, the use of spatial abstractions and agent-based approaches for programming WSNs and MANETs is not new [5]. For example, SpatialViews [21] is a high-level programming model where a MANET is abstracted into *spatial views*, i.e., virtual networks of situated service provider nodes, that can be iterated on; operationally, this is achieved via migratory execution. SpatialViews works by programmatically visiting nodes and requesting services on them, in a kind of procedural orientation; again, there is a difference in abstraction, since aggregate computing aims to program an ensemble declaratively by means of space-time computation patterns. Secondly, the ability to scale with complexity via multiple spatial views and nested iterators can be contrasted to the functional compositionality which is arguably the most prominent feature of our approach.

Even though this paper has focussed on the plain Actor model, there are a number of extensions or variations to "standard actors" that could help for dealing with spatially-situated systems of mobile devices. The identification of the key features of an extended Actor model acting as the base upon which erecting an aggregate computing layer may be a useful future work. In this context, related works to be considered include, for instance, ActorSpace [9], which provides a scoped, attribute-based mechanism that uses destination patterns for broadcasting messages to an abstract group of receivers; in particular, we could leverage this feature for implementing neighbourhood communication. Another language for programming MANETs, AmbientTalk [29], uses automatic buffering of outgoing messages for providing resilience against transient network partitions, as well as an *ambient acquaintance* mechanism for the discovery of services in nearby devices.

In the context of pervasive computing, IoT, and CPSs, several works have considered or developed extensions to actor-like models and languages in order to provide convenient design [13] and programming [26] abstractions, support the development of middleware software and platforms [20], or address peculiar problems in those scenarios (e.g., interoperability [17], dynamic functionality allocation [23,28], and so on). For instance, ELIoT [26] is a development platform for IoT applications that provides a custom runtime fitting embedded devices as well as a dialect of the Erlang language where actor support is extended for IoT scenarios, with features including selection of diverse communication guarantees, mechanisms for remote code execution, and additional addressing schemes (e.g., for broadcasts). Calvin [23] is a platform for IoT systems that uses migratable actors for logically describing applications and enabling flexible deployment and runtime management. In [15], performance issues in IoT applications are tackled by statically defining effective actor system deployments through a cost-based method. In [28], the problem of resilient dynamic partitioning of pervasive applications has been tackled by defining these as actor systems with elastic bindings and strategies that enable the spreading of functionality actors across different devices (stretching) as well as the reverse operation (retraction), depending on the context. In the vision of swarmlets [17], actor-based accessors wrapping heterogeneous sensors, actuators, and services are proposed as a mechanism for composing functionality into well-defined components, despite technological diversity. The on-going work on aggregate computing, especially on the platform-side, does share some of the points of these efforts: the adoption of actors as a basis for the middleware layer [10] and to promote the integration of complex applications (as suggested in this paper); the opportunity for remote deployment of code at runtime [12]; actor migration as a way to transfer functionality to convenient loci and hence even adapt the system execution in a context-aware fashion [33].

9   Conclusion

In this paper, we have advanced the idea of considering aggregate computing as a layer for programming complex adaptive systems that builds on and integrates with situated actors. We have also shown how the SCAFI toolchain supports the specification of field-based aggregate computations and the construction of concrete actor-based aggregate systems. Ultimately, the case study puts into practice the field calculus constructs and building blocks by addressing a complex distributed sensing scenario.

This paper represents the first step towards the definition of a conceptual and pragmatical integration of the aggregate computing model and the actor model. This combination is proposed as a way to tackle the complexity of nowadays distributed computing scenarios (such as the IoT and CASs), where there is high need to both harness and exploit the pervasive computing cyberspace with applications exhibiting adaptation and resiliency.

Interesting future work can be envisioned to corroborate the idea along multiple directions. Extensions of the plain actor model can be taken into consideration to both support the implementation of the aggregate computing platform as well as to investigate further connections and opportunities to enrich the proposed integration; examples may include extensions to support specialised communication patterns (such as broadcasts to logical neighbourhoods), a lifecycle-oriented structuring of rounds, as well as a partitioning and relocation semantics. Among the open challenges, achieving self-adaptation of system execution – based on capabilities and trade-offs between localised computation, energy consumption, and communication overhead – is of particular relevance, spanning multi-layer architectures connecting the edge to the cloud through the fog computing, and may be approached through re-wiring and mobility of functionality actors; a related key challenge is about how to effectively support safe and efficient strategies for adaptive actor-based application partitioning [28]. Finally, we expect the idea of this paper will be better substantiated by the development of real-life applications in the context of pervasive computing and

IoT; in particular, this may contribute to a deeper investigation on the use of aggregate computing components in large heterogeneous systems (emphasising the coordination and integration role of computational fields), to reveal further technical and conceptual issues and opportunities, and to provide insights by both a design and methodological perspective.

References

1. Akka. http://akka.io. Accessed 1 Feb 2017
2. Agha, G.: Actors: A Model of Concurrent Computation in Distributed Systems. MIT Press, Cambridge (1986)
3. Armstrong, J.: Programming Erlang: Software for a Concurrent World. Pragmatic Bookshelf, Raleigh (2007)
4. Beal, J., Bachrach, J.: Infrastructure for engineered emergence in sensor/actuator networks. IEEE Intell. Syst. **21**, 10–19 (2006)
5. Beal, J., Dulman, S., Usbeck, K., Viroli, M., Correll, N.: Organizing the aggregate: languages for spatial computing. CoRR, abs/1202.5509 (2012)
6. Beal, J., Pianini, D., Viroli, M.: Aggregate programming for the Internet of Things. IEEE Comput. **48**(9), 22–30 (2015)
7. Beal, J., Viroli, M.: Space–time programming. Phil. Trans. R. Soc. Lond. A Math. Phys. Eng. Sci. **373**(2046) (2015). https://doi.org/10.1098/rsta.2014.0220
8. Beal, J., Viroli, M., Pianini, D., Damiani, F.: Self-adaptation to device distribution changes. In: Cabri, G., Picard, G., Suri, N. (eds.) 10th IEEE International Conference on Self-Adaptive and Self-Organizing Systems, SASO 2016, Augsburg, Germany, 12–16 September 2016, pp. 60–69 (2016). Best paper of IEEE SASO 2016
9. Callsen, C.J., Agha, G.: Open heterogeneous computing in actorspace. J. Parallel Distrib. Comput. **21**(3), 289–300 (1994)
10. Casadei, R., Viroli, M.: Towards aggregate programming in Scala. In: First Workshop on Programming Models and Languages for Distributed Computing, PMLDC 2016, pp. 5:1–5:7. ACM, New York (2016)
11. Damiani, F., Viroli, M.: Type-based self-stabilisation for computational fields. Log. Methods Comput. Sci. **11**(4), 1–53 (2015)
12. Damiani, F., Viroli, M., Pianini, D., Beal, J.: Code mobility meets self-organisation: a higher-order calculus of computational fields. In: Graf, S., Viswanathan, M. (eds.) FORTE 2015. LNCS, vol. 9039, pp. 113–128. Springer, Cham (2015). https://doi.org/10.1007/978-3-319-19195-9_8
13. Derler, B.P., Lee, E.A., Vincentelli, A.S.: Modeling cyber physical systems. Proc. IEEE **100**(1), 13–28 (2012)
14. Fernandez-Marquez, J.L., Serugendo, G.D.M., Montagna, S., Viroli, M., Arcos, J.L.: Description and composition of bio-inspired design patterns: a complete overview. Nat. Comput. **12**(1), 43–67 (2013)
15. Haubenwaller, A.M., Vandikas, K.: Computations on the edge in the Internet of Things. Procedia Comput. Sci. **52**, 29–34 (2015)
16. Hiesgen, R., Charousset, D., Schmidt, T.C.: Embedded actors - towards distributed programming in the IoT. In: 2014 IEEE Fourth International Conference on Consumer Electronics Berlin (ICCE-Berlin), pp. 371–375. IEEE (2014)
17. Latronico, E., Lee, E.A., Lohstroh, M., Shaver, C., Wasicek, A., Weber, M.: A vision of swarmlets. IEEE Internet Comput. **19**(2), 20–28 (2015)

18. Mamei, M., Zambonelli, F.: Programming pervasive and mobile computing applications: the TOTA approach. ACM Trans. Softw. Eng. Methodol. **18**(4), 1–56 (2009)
19. Mrissa, M., Médini, L., Jamont, J.-P., Le Sommer, N., Laplace, J.: An avatar architecture for the web of things. IEEE Internet Comput. **19**(2), 30–38 (2015)
20. Ngu, A.H., Gutierrez, M., Metsis, V., Nepal, S., Sheng, Q.Z.: IoT middleware: a survey on issues and enabling technologies. IEEE Internet Things J. **4**(1), 1–20 (2017)
21. Ni, Y., Kremer, U., Stere, A., Iftode, L.: Programming ad-hoc networks of mobile and resource-constrained devices. ACM SIGPLAN Not. **40**(6), 249–260 (2005)
22. Odersky, M., et al.: An overview of the Scala programming language. Technical report (2004)
23. Persson, P., Angelsmark, O.: Calvin-merging cloud and IoT. Procedia Comput. Sci. **52**, 210–217 (2015)
24. Pianini, D., Viroli, M., Beal, J.: Protelis: practical aggregate programming. In: Proceedings of ACM SAC 2015, Salamanca, Spain, pp. 1846–1853. ACM (2015)
25. Reppy, J., Samuels, L.: Bulk-synchronous communication mechanisms in Diderot (2015)
26. Sivieri, A., Mottola, L., Cugola, G.: Building Internet of Things software with ELIoT. Comput. Commun. **89**, 141–153 (2016)
27. Valiant, L.G.: A bridging model for parallel computation. Commun. ACM **33**(8), 103–111 (1990)
28. Vallejos, J., Gonzalez Boix, E., Bainomugisha, E., Costanza, P., De Meuter, W., Tanter, É.: Towards resilient partitioning of pervasive computing services. In: Proceedings of the 3rd Workshop on Software Engineering for Pervasive Services (SEPS 2008), pp. 15–20, January 2008
29. Van Cutsem, T., et al.: AmbientTalk: programming responsive mobile peer-to-peer applications with actors. Comput. Lang. Syst. Struct. **40**(3), 112–136 (2014)
30. Vernon, V.: Reactive Messaging Patterns with the Actor Model: Applications and Integration in Scala and Akka, 1st edn. Addison-Wesley Professional, Boston (2015)
31. Viroli, M., Audrito, G., Damiani, F., Pianini, D., Beal, J.: A higher-order calculus of computational fields. CoRR, abs/1610.08116 (2016)
32. Viroli, M., Beal, J., Damiani, F., Pianini, D.: Efficient engineering of complex self-organising systems by self-stabilising fields. In: IEEE Self-Adaptive and Self-Organizing Systems 2015, pp. 81–90. IEEE, September 2015
33. Viroli, M., Casadei, R., Pianini, D.: On execution platforms for large-scale aggregate computing. In: Workshop on Collective Adaptation in Very Large Scale Ubicomp: Towards a Superorganism of Wearables, Ubicomp 2016. ACM, New York (2016)
34. Zambonelli, F.: Key abstractions for IoT-oriented software engineering. IEEE Softw. **34**(1), 38–45 (2017)

Actors and Programming – Selected Issues

Pluggable Scheduling for the Reactor Programming Model

Aleksandar Prokopec[(✉)]

Oracle Labs, Zürich, Switzerland
aleksandar.prokopec@gmail.com

Abstract. The reactor model is a foundational programming model for distributed computing, whose focus is modularizing and composing computations and message protocols. Previous work on reactors dealt mainly with the programming model and its composability properties, but did not show how to schedule computations in reactor-based programs. In this paper, we propose a pluggable scheduling algorithm for the reactor model. The algorithm is customizable with user-defined scheduling policies. We define and prove safety and progress properties. We compare our implementation against the Akka actor framework, and show up to $3\times$ performance improvements on standard actor benchmarks.

1 Introduction

The recently proposed reactor model [3, 26, 31] uncovered a new route to composable distributed computing. Instead of composing message protocols across multiple actors, the reactor model advocates protocol composition within a single unit of concurrency called a reactor. This composition is achieved by exposing multiple typed first-class event streams instead of a static `receive` statement.

The original reactor model proposal [31] dealt only with the programming model, but did not discuss the underlying implementation. The existence of multiple event streams within a single reactor poses a scheduling problem that differs from scheduling in the standard actor model, in which each actor has a single mailbox. In the reactor model, the fundamental constraint is the following: events from different event streams must be scheduled fairly, but serially for any two event streams that belong to the same reactor.

The goal of this paper is twofold. First, we propose a scheduler for the reactor model, identify its properties and show correctness. Second, we make the scheduler pluggable, allowing clients to implement custom scheduling policies.

There are several reasons why a scheduler should be pluggable. First, it is expensive and time consuming to develop an optimal scheduler. A more prudent plan is to develop a system with a sub-optimal scheduler, and then (let clients) improve it incrementally when concrete requirements arise.

Second, not every scheduler is a perfect fit for every situation. A scheduler can be Pareto-optimal, meaning that there is no other scheduler that is equal

© Springer Nature Switzerland AG 2018
A. Ricci and P. Haller (Eds.): Programming with Actors, LNCS 10789, pp. 125–154, 2018.
https://doi.org/10.1007/978-3-030-00302-9_5

or better on all workloads. However, there may exist another scheduler that is better on one particular workload, but worse on some other workloads.

For example, in the Ping-Pong benchmark [15], a message is likely to arrive soon, and it helps to keep a (re)actor activated even when there are no pending messages to handle. However, in the Thread Ring benchmark, the same heuristic wastes processor time, as it is in most cases unlikely that a message will arrive soon. In these cases, users should be able to decide which scheduling policy is more appropriate for their workload, or implement adaptive schedulers that can dynamically adjust themselves to the conditions in the program.

Third, certain scheduling policies are application-specific and rely on explicit domain knowledge. For example, if a reactor needs a special system-wide resource (such as a GPU, a DSP or a temperature sensor reading), then the scheduler needs to negotiate the availability of the resource with the OS. A generic scheduler cannot do this, and this warrants a user-defined scheduling policy, which embeds such domain-specific knowledge into the scheduling mechanism.

This paper brings forth the following contributions:

- Detailed description and implementation of a scheduling algorithm for the reactor programming model (Sect. 3).
- A list of safety- and progress-related properties that a reactor scheduler must satisfy. We analyze the proposed scheduling algorithm, and show that it satisfies these properties under specific assumptions on the user-defined scheduling policy (Sects. 2.1 and 3.3).
- A pluggable mechanism for user-defined scheduling policies, which can embed application-specific knowledge (Sect. 4).
- An overview of optimization techniques used in our implementation, which was added to this extended version of the original paper [24] (Sect. 5).
- A performance comparison on the Savina benchmark suite [15] with the widely adopted Akka actor framework. We show that our reactor implementation outperforms Akka on 6 out of 8 benchmarks by a factor of $1.1 - 3.3\times$, and otherwise has comparable performance (Sect. 6).

This work focuses on scheduling reactors in a single reactor system, on a single shared-memory machine. Scheduling reactor execution in a fault-tolerant distributed setting is not the goal. That problem is based on an entirely different set of assumptions (such as faults, preemptions, network delay, lack of shared memory), and consequently results in different abstractions. In practice, this is the task of the cluster manager [14,38], and not the reactor scheduler. However, effective single-machine scheduling is likely a prerequisite for efficient distributed computations, since it ensures a better utilization of each machine.

This paper is an extended version of the previous work on pluggable scheduling for the reactor programming model [24]. In this version, we present an overview of optimization techniques that were used to improve the performance of our scheduler: explicit work stealing, lazy task scheduling, reanimation threads, message arrival speculation and actor class profiling (Sect. 5).

Code examples are written in Scala [20], a statically compiled language, primarily targetting the JVM. Syntax is similar to Java, but more concise. Variables and final variables are defined with keywords `var` and `val`, respectively, and methods with the `def` keyword, as in Python. Type annotations come after a `:` following an identifier, similar to Pascal. Function objects are declared with a list of parameters, followed by `=>` and a body. Partial functions are declared as a list of `case` statements, and are defined for the values matched by at least one of the cases. Traits and the `with` keyword are equivalents of Java interfaces and `implements`. Type parameters are enclosed in square brackets, `[]`. Operators, such as `!`, are normal methods with symbolic names. Critical sections are delimited with a `synchronized` block.

We start by describing the reactor model in more detail in Sect. 2, and we then show the proposed scheduling algorithm in Sect. 3.

2   Reactor Model

The reactor programming model [31] is a generalization of the standard actor model [2,4]. There are three major differences between these models. First, the reactor model exposes multiple first-class event streams instead of a static `receive` statement. Second, in the reactor model, a computation can wait for events from multiple event streams simultaneously, whereas an actor can be suspended on a single `receive` statement at a time. Third, targets of message sends are typed channels instead of untyped actor references[1]. As argued before [31], these three fundamental differences allow modularity and composition of message protocols within a single reactor, a feature that was previously not possible with actors alone. For example, reactor model allows defining best-effort and reliable broadcasts, failure detectors [10,18] and CRDTs [34], and exposing them as reusable components, that can be either embedded into a reactor, or further composed into more complex components.

In the reactor model, the principal unit of concurrency is called a *reactor*. Analogous to how an actor can process at most a single message at once, a reactor can process at most a single event at any point in time. This *serializability* property is one of the major strengths of (re)actors, as it allows users to access local state without synchronization.

Consider a reactor that counts how many events it received. The following code snippet declares a reactor template `AnalysisReactor` that tracks how many string events it received. Field `numEvents` is part of the reactor's state:

```
class AnalysisReactor extends Reactor[String] {
  var numEvents = 0 }
```

Defining a reactor template does not yet start a reactor instance. Before we see how to do that, we need to define how the reactor receives events. Entities that allow handling incoming events are called *event streams*. Every reactor gets a default event stream called `main.events` when it is created. To receive an

---

[1] In Erlang, actor references are called process IDs.

event, users need to pass an event handler to the stream's onEvent method. We extend the body of the previous reactor template with a call to onEvent:

```
main.events.onEvent { x => numEvents += 1 }
```

Generally, an event stream has the type Events[T], indicating that it delivers events of type T. In our case, main.events has the type Events[String], because we declared a reactor of type Reactor[String].

Unlike processes in the π-calculus [19], where a process can block until a message arrives on a channel, or join calculus [8], where a process can decide to block until another process sends a matching message, a reactor is not limited to receiving events on a single event stream. During its lifetime, a reactor can receive from any number of event streams. Effectively, a reactor has multiple synchronous control flows. Concretely, apart from the main event stream, every reactor has a system event stream called sysEvents that delivers lifecycle events – for example, when the scheduler assigns execution time to the current reactor, or the reactor terminates. We can react to a subset of system events by passing a partial function to onMatch method of the event stream. In the following, we expand the earlier reactor template with a variable numSch, and count the number of times the reactor was assigned execution time. We expect that each time the reactor is scheduled, it handles several events. When the reactor terminates, we print the average number of events handled each time it got scheduled:

```
var numSch = 0
sysEvents.onMatch {
  case Scheduled => numSch += 1
  case Stopped => print(numEvents / numSch) }
```

Every event stream has a corresponding *channel*. A channel is the writing end of the event stream. It has the type Channel[T], where T corresponds to the event stream type. Whereas an event stream can be used only by the reactor that owns it, a channel can be shared with any other reactor. The basic operation on a channel is an event send !. In the following, we extend the reactor template to send a message to the main channel when the reactor starts:

```
sysEvents.onMatch { case Started => main.channel ! "started" }
```

To create additional channels and event streams, a reactor can use the open statement. Given the type of events, say Int for integers, the open statement returns a fresh pair of a channel and the corresponding event stream:

```
val (numberEvents, numberChannel) = open[Int]
```

To create a running reactor instance from a template, we call the spawn method of the reactor system. Spawning a reactor returns its main channel:

```
val ch: Channel[String] = system.spawn(Proto[AnalysisReactor])
```

Proto is a wrapper around the specific reactor class, used to set properties such as the textual name of the reactor, or its scheduling policy.

We claimed earlier that reactors generalize actors. To validate this, we encode an Akka-style [1] actor using a reactor from the Reactors.IO framework [3].

The reactor receives events of type `Any`, which is the top type in Scala. Any event x from the main event stream is forwarded to the partial function `receive` if the partial function is defined for it. Otherwise, the event is discarded.

```
abstract class AkkaActor extends Reactor[Any] {
  def receive: PartialFunction[Any, Unit]
  main.events.onEvent { x =>
    if (receive.isDefinedAt(x)) receive(c)
  } }
```

Exact formal semantics of the reactor model can be found in related work [31]. In a nutshell, the reactor model consists of the following components:

- **Defining and starting computations:** reactor templates that define reactors, and the spawn method used to start them.
- **Receiving events:** event streams and the onEvent method, used to subscribe to incoming events and eventually handle them.
- **Sending events:** channels and the ! operator, used to asynchronously send events to other reactors.
- **Modularising protocols:** the open method, used to create supplementary channels in the current reactor[2].

The main difference with the actors is that there are multiple event streams in each reactor, and events can be delivered on any of them. Before examining the proposed scheduling algorithm, we examine its essential properties.

2.1 Properties of a Reactor Scheduler

We now explore important properties that a reactor scheduler should satisfy. In what follows, we say that an event is *delivered* if it is enqueued on an event queue. We say that a reactor is *activated* when it becomes scheduled to execute and process some of its delivered events. We say that an event is *handled* when the event handlers from corresponding event streams get invoked for that event.

Serializability states that a reactor at any point in time runs at most one of its event handlers. Processing events serially, in sequence, prevents data races that would otherwise result from simultaneously manipulating reactor state, and obviates the need for user-level synchronization. Importantly, serializability applies to events received on all event streams belonging to the same reactor – at most one handler across all event streams may be active at a time.

Fairness states that if an event is delivered to the reactor on some event stream, then the corresponding event handler is eventually invoked, unless the

---

[2] It was shown that encoding multiple protocols in the actor model using a single actor is possible, but made easier with custom protocol description languages [37]. Conversely, protocol modularisation can also be achieved by encapsulating groups of actors, each of which handles one aspect of the protocol. A custom architecture description language was made to facilitate this type of encapsulation [5]. One goal of the reactor model is to allow modularisation in the core model, without relying on another language layer.

event stream gets sealed by user code[3]. An important assumption that we make is that no reactor executes an infinite loop, i.e. the handling of every event consists of a finite number of steps.

Although fairness ensures that delivered events are eventually handled, a stronger guarantee is sometimes more useful. Whenever possible, a scheduler should avoid a scenario in which a set of events delivered to one event stream grows indefinitely[4]. This can, for example, occur in a multiple producer, single consumer setting. Fairness only ensures that the single consumer is eventually scheduled, but does not prevent its event queue from growing indefinitely. To be fair, a scheduler must ensure that some event streams get processed more often than others. We formulate *bounded delivery time fairness* as follows – for any two events x and y, such that x is the d_x-th event delivered globally and y is d_y-th, and x is the h_x-th event handled globally and y is h_y-th, difference $h_x - h_y$ must be bound by $d_x - d_y + C$, where C is a constant. This is essentially a global relaxed FIFO condition.

Aside from being fairly executed, reactors must be able to exploit parallelism in the system. A reactor scheduling system is *scalable* if it meets the following conditions. First, event handling must not contend with concurrent event delivery. Second, event delivery time must be $O(1)$ when there are P events delivered concurrently on any subset of event streams. Third, event delivery time must be $O(1)$ irrespective of the number of event streams E in the system.

The scheduling sytem must be *efficient* – the absolute execution time spent in scheduling must be negligible, or be amortized by the execution time of user code. This property is checked with an empirical evaluation.

The last important concern is *pluggability*. Clients that possess domain knowledge must be able to apply this knowledge to a custom scheduler to make the system more efficient. Pluggability allows manually controlling when a specific reactor is executed, and how much execution time it gets.

Some of these properties, such as serializability, ensure that a program never violates semantics of the reactor model. We refer to them as *safety* properties, as they guarantee that nothing bad happens. Other properties, such as fairness, bounded delivery time fairness and scalability, improve *progress* of a reactor-based program. Their absence can in worst case prevent the program from completing, but does not violate semantics or cause incorrect behavior. As we will see in Sect. 3, the proposed pluggable scheduling system enforces safety properties. Progress properties are good-to-have, but not essential for all programs.

---

[3] Users can do this explicitly in the reactor programming model, in which case the undelivered events are dropped. It is unclear to us how to achieve this using automatic GC, since there always exists a reference from the onEvent callback to the event stream object.

[4] This is not always possible – there exist programs in which the number of events grows over time. For example, if every reactor upon receiving an event sends out two events in response, then the overall number of messages in the program grows exponentially over time. However, if there exist an execution schedule in which the number of messages in the program at any given point is bounded, then the scheduler should use that execution schedule.

For such properties, the scheduling system establishes a well-defined foundation, and delegates the decision of fulfilling them to other components.

3   Scheduling Algorithm

In this section, we describe the proposed pluggable scheduling algorithm. We start by describing the internals of our reactor system implementation, and then show the algorithm itself. Finally, we prove that the algorithm satisfies serializability and fairness, and, under specific assumptions, can also achieve bounded delivery time fairness.

3.1   Reactor System Internals

An *event queue* contains a set of delivered, but not yet processed events for a particular event stream. Since events must be handled serially within a reactor, an event queue serves as a buffer between the reactor and the senders. An event queue is an equivalent of an actor mailbox.

In the following, we show the EventQueue trait. Method enqueue atomically enqueues an event to the event queue and returns the event queue size. It can be called by any number of threads concurrently. Method dequeue atomically removes an event, emits it on an event stream events, and returns the number of remaining elements at the point when the event was removed. Method dequeue is quiescently consistent [13] – it can be called by at most a single thread at a time. When dequeue emits the event on the associated event stream, control transfers from the scheduler to the event handlers installed by the user code.

```
trait EventQueue[T] {
  def enqueue(x: T): Int
  def dequeue(): Int
  def events: Events[T]
  def size: Int }
```

A connector of type Connector[T] is a wrapper that binds an event stream, a channel and an event queue together. Calling open creates a new connector.

Different reactors have different textual names, used to retrieve their channels. The set of all possible names comprises the *namespace* of the reactor system. At any point in time, at most a single reactor can have any single name.

When created, every reactor is assigned a unique numeric ID. The set of all possible UIDs forms the *UID space*. During the entire lifetime of the system, every UID can be assigned to at most one reactor, and cannot be reused.

A *reactor system* is an entity that contains a set of reactors, the scheduling system, and a single namespace and UID space. Usually, there is a single reactor system per process, but users can create additional reactor systems if necessary. Configuration properties such as pickling and network resources are set when creating the reactor system. A *prototype*, represented with the Proto[T] type, is a configurable wrapper around the reactor template. It allows configuring the textual name and the scheduling policies of the reactor instance, and is passed as an argument to spawn. Immediately before the reactor instance starts, the reactor system creates a *frame* object of type `Frame`, used to hold internal reactor state – reactor name, UID, scheduling policy, connectors, lifecycle state and information on whether the respective reactor is currently executing.

A reactor's scheduling policy is captured in a `Scheduler` object. Method `initSchedule` is called once when the reactor is created, and `schedule` is called every time a reactor is activated. Method `newPendingQueue` creates a queue with a list of active connectors, and allows the scheduler to express a queuing policy.

```
trait Scheduler {
  def initSchedule(f: Frame): Unit
  def schedule(f: Frame): Unit
  def newPendingQueue(): Queue[Connector[_]] }
```

Queue exposes standard queue operations enqueue and dequeue. Note that its implementation and queuing policy are different than that of an event queue. A *pending queue* stores *event queues*, and the two are **separate entities**.

As we will see in the next section, user-defined `Scheduler` objects allow fine-tuning how the scheduling system works.

3.2 Scheduling Algorithm Implementation

From a high-level standpoint, the algorithm works as follows. When a reactor needs to execute, the `active` field in its frame is set to `true`, and the scheduler is notified. The reactor then gets execution time. It repetitively removes an event queue from the pending queue, and calls `dequeue` on the event queue until either the scheduler tells it to stop, in which case a non-empty event queue is placed back to the pending queue, or the event queue becomes empty, in which case the pending queue is polled for the next event queue.

There are two ways that a reactor can get execution time. First is when a reactor instance is created with spawn, and the second is when an event is delivered to a reactor. In both cases, the reactor is activated and sent for execution.

We first consider the spawn operation, shown in Fig. 1. The method starts by reserving a UID in line 4, and the reactor name in line 5. It then creates a `Frame` object in line 6. In lines 8 through 11, frame is marked as not activated, reference to the scheduler specified in the prototype is copied, the lifecycle state is set to New, and a connector table is created. In line 12, the scheduler's `newPendingQueue` method returns the queue data structure that will hold non-empty event queues. The scheduler is asked to set a custom state object in the frame's `schedulerState` field. This is done in the call to `initSchedule` in line 13, and the default connector is allocated in line 14.

At this point, the frame is completely initialized and may begin execution. A call to `activate` in line 15 activates the frame. This method acquires the frame's lock in line 23, and checks if the frame is already active in line 24. If not, the `active` field is set to `true` in line 25. If the field `active` was set, the scheduler's `schedule` method is called in line 27. This indicates that there is a

```
1  def spawn[T](
2    system: ReactorSystem, proto: Proto[T]
3  ): Channel[T] = {
4    val uid = system.reserveId()
5    val uname = system.acquire(proto.name)
6    val f = new Frame(uid, uname, proto, system)
7    try {
8      f.active = false
9      f.scheduler = proto.scheduler
10     f.lifecycle = New
11     f.connectors = new Map[String, Connector[_]]
12     f.pending = f.scheduler.newPendingQueue()
13     f.scheduler.initSchedule(f)
14     f.main = open(f, "main", f.queueFactory)
15     activate(f)
16   } catch { case t: Throwable =>
17     system.release(uname)
18     throw t }
19   f.main.channel }
20
21 def activate(f: Frame) {
22   var run = false
23   f.monitor.synchronized {
24     if (!f.active) {
25       f.active = true
26       run = true } }
27   if (run) f.scheduler.schedule(f) }
```

Fig. 1. Reactor creation

newly activated frame that should be scheduled on some thread. The scheduler
should give the reactor execution time at the earliest opportunity.

When the scheduler assigns execution time on some thread, that thread must
call the execute method shown in Fig. 2. This method starts the reactor's event
loop, and has several stages. First, it prepares the reactor context – it asserts that
the frame is active in line 2, and optionally sets thread-local state (not shown in
the code). Then, it calls lifecycleAndProcessBatch to continue executing
the reactor's lifecycle. After the lifecycle method completes, either exceptionally
or normally, execute checks if the reactor should continue executing or not.
Line 8 tests if there are any pending event queues with unprocessed events and
the reactor did not terminate. If so, the reactor is rescheduled, and otherwise its
active field is set to false.

The lifecycleAndProcessBatch method uses the auxiliary methods
checkNew and checkStopped to treat newly created and stopped reactors
differently. Method checkNew is called before event processing starts, and it
atomically changes the state from New to Running. If the state changes to
running, it means that this is the first time that the reactor was run, so the
checkNew method needs to run the reactor constructor. It is important to run
the constructor asynchronously, and not in the spawn method, to ensure non-
blocking semantics. The constructor is run in line 17 with a call to the prototype's
create method.

```
1  def execute(f: Frame) {
2    assert(f.active)
3    assert(f.isolationCount.compareAndSet(0, 1))
4    try lifecycleAndProcessBatch(f)
5    finally {
6      var repeat = false
7      f.monitor.synchronized {
8        if (!f.pending.isEmpty && f.lifecycle != Stopped) repeat = true
9        else f.active = false }
10       f.isolationCount.set(0)
11       if (repeat) f.scheduler.schedule(this) } }
12
13 def checkNew(f: Frame) {
14   var isNew = false
15   f.monitor.synchronized {
16     if (f.lifecycle == New) { f.lifecycle = Running; isNew = true } }
17   if (isNew) f.reactor = proto.create() }
18
19 def checkStopped(f: Frame, forced: Boolean) {
20   var stop = false
21   f.monitor.synchronized {
22     val isRunning = f.lifecycle == Running
23     val mustStop = f.pending.isEmpty && f.connectors.length == 0
24     if (isRunning && (forced || mustStop)) {
25       f.lifecycle = Stopped; stop = true } }
26   if (stop) f.system.release(name) }
27
28 def lifecycleAndProcessBatch(f: Frame) {
29   try { checkNew(f); processEvents(f) }
30   catch { case t: Throwable => checkStopped(f, true) }
31   finally checkStopped(f, false) }
32
33 def processEvents(f: Frame) {
34   f.schedulerState.onBatchStart(this)
35   val c = popPending(f); if (c != null) drain(c) }
36
37 def popPending(f: Frame): Connector[_] = f.monitor.synchronized {
38   if (f.pending.nonEmpty) f.pending.dequeue() else null }
39
40 @tailrec def drain(c: Connector[_]) {
41   val remaining = c.queue.dequeue()
42   if (f.schedulerState.onBatchEvent(c)) {
43     if (remaining > 0 && !c.isSealed) drain(c)
44     else {
45       val nc = popPending(f); if (nc != null) drain(nc) }
46   } else if (remaining > 0 && !c.isSealed)
47     f.monitor.synchronized { f.pending.enqueue(c) } }
```

Fig. 2. Reactor loop

The checkStopped method similarly checks for termination, and is called
after handling the events. A reactor must terminate if it is in the Running
state, its pending queue is empty, and there are no more live connectors. If the
forced argument is set to true, it means that user code threw an exception,
and the reactor must be terminated regardless of its execution state. When the
state is atomically changed to Stopped, the reactor name is released in line 26.

In practice, all these methods emit lifecycle events on the system event stream, but we omit them from Fig. 2 for brevity.

At this point, the reactor can start handling the delivered events. The method lifecycleAndProcessBatch first calls the method processEvents, which in line 34 notifies the scheduler that a batch of events is about to be handled. The processEvents method then calls popPending to dequeue a non-empty connector. If a reactor just started, it is likely that no events were yet delivered, and popPending returns null. In this case, processEvents simply returns. If there is a non-empty connector, processEvents calls the drain.

The drain method calls dequeue on the event queue in line 41. This releases an event on the corresponding event stream, and enters user code. After the event handlers process the event, dequeue returns the number of remaining events at the point in time when the event was removed. The drain method then asks the scheduler if it should continue executing events in line 42. If the scheduler decides that additional events should be batched, drain checks if the event queue is non-empty, and calls itself tail-recursively in line 43, with the same connector. If the current event queue is empty, drain attempts to pop the next non-empty connector if there is one, and calls itself recursively in line 45. If the scheduler denies processing additional events, the drain method puts the non-empty event queue back to the pending queue in line 47.

Using the onBatchEvent method, the scheduler can decide how many events to handle. Usually, a scheduler will handle a batch of events, to amortize the cost of setting up the reactor context, as explained in Sect. 6.1.

```
1  def send[T](c: Connector[T], x: T) {
2    val f = c.frame
3    val size = c.queue.enqueue(x)
4    var run = false
5    if (size == 1) f.monitor.synchronized {
6      f.pending.enqueue(c)
7      if (!f.active) {
8        f.active = true
9        run = true
10     }
11   }
12   if (run) f.scheduler.schedule(this) }
```

Fig. 3. Event send

A reactor is also activated when an event is delivered on one of its event streams. This is done by the send method in Fig. 3, which first enqueues the event on the respective event queue in line 3. If the event queue size after calling enqueue is exactly 1, it means that the corresponding event stream was previously dormant, and it became active when the event was enqueued. In this case, the reactor's lock is acquired in line 5, and the event queue is placed on the pending queue in line 6. If the reactor was not previously active, its active field is set to true, and the reactor is scheduled for execution in line 12. The execute method from Fig. 2 is eventually invoked on some thread.

Note that the implementation of the schedule method must be synchronized, since multiple concurrent reactors can call send at the same time. We will show several implementations of the schedule method in Sect. 4.

3.3 Analysis of the Scheduling Algorithm

Having seen the scheduling algorithm, we state several claims about its properties. We prove that the algorithm is safe with respect to the serializability property. For space reasons, we skip other safety properties such as exactly-once delivery. We then prove fairness and bounded delivery time fairness, with specific assumptions about the Scheduler implementation.

Theorem 1 (Safety). *Assume that schedule executes the reactor exactly once. At any point in time, for a specific reactor, there exists at most a single event handler that is executing.*

Proof. No thread is initially running execute. The first call to schedule occurs in the activate method in Fig. 1, and the second schedule occurs in the send method in line 12 in Fig. 3. If either activate or send calls schedule, then the active field was previously false and was atomically set to true by the same thread. No other thread calls schedule until execute reaches line 11 in Fig. 2.

The execute method calls schedule in line 11 only if active was not set from true to false. It follows that, for a specific reactor, there is always at most one thread that left the active field in the true state, and that thread calls schedule. By assumption, execute is called only once for every schedule call, and execute calls dequeue for every event only once, so it follows that there is at most a single event handler executing at any time[5].   □

Lemma 1 (Deactivation). *The reactor's pending queue never contains an event queue that is empty.*

Proof. We show this inductively – the claim is initially true, and no operation violates it. The pending queue is initially empty. The send method puts only non-empty event queues to the pending list. Events are only dequeued by the drain method from Fig. 2, and this method never puts an empty event queue back to the pending list. By Theorem 1, no other thread can interfere by concurrently executing drain.   □

Lemma 2 (Activation). *A non-empty event queue is either on the reactors's pending queue, or is put on the pending queue after a finite number of steps.*

Proof. An event is delivered to the event stream in line 3 of the send method shown in Fig. 3. If, in line 3, enqueue returns a size greater than 1, then there is another thread T for which enqueue previously returned 1. Between the point

---

[5] In fact, check in line 3 of Fig. 2 ensures this even if schedule calls execute from multiple threads.

in time t_0 when enqueue returned 1 for that other thread T, and the point in time t_1 when T puts the queue on the pending list, no other thread can drain that event queue, because that event queue is not yet on the pending list. By contradiction, assume that the event queue *is* on the pending list between t_0 and t_1. That would only be possible if, between t_0 and t_1, enqueue returned 1 for some other thread in line 3, which would imply that the event queue size became 0 between t_0 and t_1. That would be a contradiction, because the event queue can only be dequeued after being placed on the pending list, and, by Lemma 1, the event queue was not on the pending list at time t_0.

Now, consider the thread for which enqueue returns size 1 in line 3 of Fig. 3. That thread puts the event queue to the pending list after a finite number of steps. Next, consider the thread that calls popPending. If the event queue is non-empty when that thread subsequently calls dequeue in line 41, the event queue is put back to the pending queue by the same thread after a finite number of steps. By Lemma 1, the queue cannot become empty before this happens. □

Theorem 2 (Fairness). *Assume that schedule eventually executes the specified reactor, and that every event queue added to the pending list gets removed after calling dequeue on the pending list sufficiently many times. Then, if an event gets delivered to an event stream belonging to some reactor, that event is eventually handled by an event handler.*

Proof. By Lemma 2, a non-empty event queue is on the pending queue, or will be after a finite number of steps. By assumption, every reactor is eventually executed, and every event queue on the pending queue is eventually dequeued. For each such event queue, at least one event is handled. Consequently, every event is eventually handled.   □

Achieving bounded delivery time fairness is deferred to the pluggable Scheduler object. Accordingly, the proof of the bounded delivery time fairness makes heavy assumptions on the Scheduler implementation.

Theorem 3 (Bounded delivery time fairness). *Let $\mathbb{S}$ be the set of reactors for which schedule was called. Assume that the scheduler always executes the reactor from $\mathbb{S}$ with the least recent event ξ, that the dequeue call on the pending queue of the respective reactor returns the event queue that contains ξ, and that onBatchEvent returns true if the argument connector contains the most recent event in the system. Then, the scheduling is fair with respect to the previous definition.*

Proof. Under the given assumptions, dequeue call in line 41 always returns the oldest event in the system. Therefore, scheduling is fair for the constant $C = 1$ in the bounded delivery time fairness definition from Sect. 2.1.   □

4   Scheduling Policies

In this section, we go over several implementations of the Scheduler trait. There are several ways in which a Scheduler governs the scheduling policy. First, it decides when to execute frames submitted with the schedule

method. Second, it decides how long a scheduled reactor should execute with
schedulerState. Third, it decides which event stream to flush with the
newPendingQueue method.

The schedulerState objects expose the onBatchStart and
onBatchEvent methods. The former is called when a reactor starts handling a
batch of events, and the latter is called after handling each event of that batch.
Most schedulers use some variant of the DefaultState, which handles up to
BATCH_SIZE events during one scheduled frame execution.

```
class DefaultState extends State {
  private var batch = 0
  def onBatchStart() { batch = BATCH_SIZE }
  def onBatchEvent(c: Connector[_]) = {
    batch -= 1; return batch > 0 } }
```

The newPendingQueue method decides on the queuing policy of the active
event queues. Unless specified otherwise, the pending queue implements the
FIFO policy, as that trivially achieves the fairness property – at least one event
is eventually scheduled from each event queue.

Thread pool scheduler. Task schedulers, such as the Fork/Join pool [17] from
the JDK, are designed to multiplex a set of tasks across a set of worker threads.
It is useful to reuse the effort put into task schedulers when implementing a
reactor scheduler. In the following, we show the ExecutorScheduler, which
uses a JDK Executor to schedule reactor frames:

```
class ExecutorScheduler(val e: Executor)
extends Scheduler {
  def initSchedule(f: Frame) =
    f.schedulerState = new DefaultState with Runnable {
      def run() = execute(f) }
  def schedule(f: Frame) = executor.execute(f.schedulerState) }
```

The initSchedule method, called when the reactor starts, creates a
default state with the JDK Runnable interface mixed in, so the scheduler state
is simultaneously used as a *task*. When run by a task scheduler, this task object
calls the execute method from Fig. 2. Method schedule passes this task to
the Executor, delegating the decision of when to run the reactor to a task-based
scheduler.

Dedicated thread or process scheduler. In some cases, we want to give a
specific reactor a higher priority by assigning it a dedicated thread or a process.
Here, the decision of when to run is delegated to the underlying OS. Such a reactor need not process events in batches, and can simply flush all its event streams
until they are empty, as shown in the following scheduler state implementation:

```
class DedicatedState extends State {
  def onBatchStart() {}
  def onBatchEvent(c: Connector) = true }
```

The ThreadScheduler uses an auxiliary method loop, which calls
execute from Fig. 2, and then waits inside a monitor until the reactor terminates or there is a pending event queue. The loop ends when the reactor
terminates.

```
def loop(f: Frame) = do {
  execute(f)
  f.monitor.synchronized {
    while (!hasStopped(f) && !hasPending(f)) f.monitor.wait()
  }
} while (!hasStopped(f))
```

When the reactor starts, the `ThreadScheduler` creates a `DedicatedState` object with a thread that calls `loop`. The thread is started in `schedule` the first time that the reactor is supposed to run, triggered by the spawn in Fig. 1.

```
class ThreadScheduler extends Scheduler {
  def initSchedule(f: Frame) =
    f.schedulerState = new DedicatedState {
      val thread = new Thread {
        override def run() = loop(f) } }
  def schedule(f: Frame) =
    f.monitor.synchronized {
      if (!f.schedulerState.thread.isStarted)
        f.schedulerState.thread.start()
      f.monitor.notify() } }
```

The dedicated thread is subsequently notified whenever, during event delivery, the `schedule` method gets called from the `send` method from Fig. 3.

Piggyback scheduler. Normal programs are started by executing the `main` function on the main thread of the program. A reactor-based program has no notion of a main thread. It is therefore convenient to *piggyback* the existing main thread to one of the reactors in the program. This is the task of the following `PiggybackScheduler` implementation:

```
class PiggybackScheduler extends Scheduler {
  def initSchedule(f: Frame) {}
  def schedule(f: Frame) =
    if (f.schedulerState == null) {
      f.schedulerState = new DedicatedState
      loop(f)
    } else f.monitor.synchronized {
      f.monitor.notify()
    } }
```

The first time `schedule` is called by the `spawn` method, the piggyback scheduler executes the event loop, thus blocking the current thread. Subsequently, `schedule` calls in the `send` method notify the thread that there are new events.

Scheduler with bounded delivery time fairness. The `Scheduler` implementations shown so far satisfy the fairness property, but they do not necessarily have bounded time delivery. An OS kernel or a task scheduler can satisfy bounded delivery time fairness across a set of threads or tasks. However, neither has information about the number and age of events delivered to different reactors, and cannot give more time to reactors whose load is higher.

In the following, we show a scheduler that is fair according to the definition from Sect. 2.1. We use an event queue factory that assigns a timestamp to an event when it gets enqueued. The event queue itself respects the FIFO policy. The timestamp of the oldest event can be obtained by calling `headTime` on the queue. We define a pair of helper methods that return the numeric priority of a connector and a reactor frame:

```
def cpriority(c: Connector[_]) = -1 * c.queue.headTime
def fpriority(f: Frame) = cpriority(f.pending.head)
```

The `pending` list implementation is a priority queue that sorts the event queues using `cpriority`. The fair scheduler maintains another priority queue `tasks` for the set of activated reactor frames, based on `fpriority`. When a reactor is started, its event queue factory is replaced by a timestamping queue factory. The scheduler state uses the same connector as long as its priority is higher than the priority of the other activated frames, and other connectors of the current frame. The `schedule` method enqueues a frame to the `tasks` queue, and a separate thread dequeues and executes frames.

```
class BoundedDeliveryTimeFairScheduler extends Scheduler {
  private val tasks = new PriorityQueue[Frame](fpriority) {
  def newPendingQueue() = new PriorityQueue[Connector[_]](cpriority)
  def initSchedule(f: Frame) {
    f.queueFactory = new TimestampQueueFactory(f.queueFactory)
    f.schedulerState = new State {
      def onBatchStart() {}
      def onBatchEvent(c: Connector[_]) =
        cpriority(c) > fpriority(tasks.head) &&
        cpriority(c) > cpriority(f.pending.head)
    } }
  def schedule(f: Frame) = tasks.enqueue(f)
  startThread { while(true) execute(tasks.dequeue()) } }
```

This is a proof-of-concept implementation of a fair scheduler, which is neither scalable (because it is single-threaded) nor efficient (because $C = 1$). In practice, it is useful to relax this requirement to some degree to achieve higher performance.

Timer scheduler. Real-time computations, such as interactive graphics rendering, must be scheduled at regular intervals. The following implementation is based on the `java.util.Timer`, and it periodically schedules reactor execution.

```
class TimerScheduler(period: Long) extends Scheduler {
  val timer = new java.util.Timer
  def initSchedule(f: Frame) {
    f.schedulerState = new DefaultState
    val task = new java.util.TimerTask {
      def run() {
        if (hasStopped(f)) this.cancel()
        else execute(f) } }
    timer.schedule(task, period, period) }
  def schedule(f: Frame) {} }
```

The `initSchedule` method creates a new `TimerTask` that periodically executes the frame, or cancels itself if the reactor has terminated.

Resource scheduler. In some cases, a reactor must be scheduled only when a specific resource is available. A resource can be an external hardware sensor, an embedded coprocessor, or a general purpose GPU.

```
class ResourceScheduler extends Scheduler {
  def initSchedule(f: Frame) { f.schedulerState = new DefaultState }
  def schedule(f: Frame) { OS.requestResource(() => execute(f)) } }
```

When `schedule` gets called, `ResourceScheduler` requests an OS resource and passes a callback that executes the frame once the resource becomes available.

5 Scheduler Optimizations

The previous sections described the scheduling algorithm, with the emphasis on making it pluggable. The design is sufficient for making the scheduling generic, but we did not explain how we achieve high throughput. In this section, we go over several techniques that we used to improve the performance of the default scheduler implementation in the Reactors framework. The main goal in these techniques is to reduce the amount of time spent in the scheduler compared to the amount of time spent in application code.

5.1 Explicit Work Stealing

In a typical task-based work stealing scheduler [6], there is a set of worker threads, usually corresponding to the number of processors. Each worker thread has an associated work stealing queue. When the program creates a new concurrent task of execution in some thread, it places that task onto the work stealing queue. A task is removed from the queue either after the current task of the corresponding worker thread completes, or when another worker runs out of tasks on its own queue and *steals* the task from a queue of its peer.

There are several overheads associated with work stealing. First, a task object needs to be created and placed on the queue. Second, inactive worker threads need to be notified that there is work available for them. Third, a previously inactive worker thread must scan the work queues of other threads, and steal an available task. The overhead of having to wait can be reduced by having the active worker thread steal back the tasks it previously submitted as early as possible. Some task-based work stealing schedulers expose the API that allows the client code to explicitly start the work stealing process [17].

In our implementation, the worker thread dequeues the previously submitted tasks immediately after completing event handling. This allows executing a different reactor frame on the active worker thread before context switching the current frame. After the line 35 of the code in Figure 2, the worker calls a special method `stealSchedule`, shown in Fig. 4, which dequeues and runs frame tasks.

Piggybacking the worker thread can only have a single level of nesting. To ensure this, each worker thread keeps a `state` field that initially

```
 1 def stealSchedule() {
 2   if (state == STEAL_SCHEDULE) {
 3     return
 4   }
 5   state = STEAL_SCHEDULE
 6   try {
 7     var loopsLeft = STEAL_SCHEDULE_COUNT
 8     while (loopsLeft > 0) {
 9       val executedSomething = pollWorkQueueAndRunFrame()
10       if (executedSomething) {
11         loopsLeft -= 1
12       } else {
13         loopsLeft = 0
14       }
15     }
16   } finally {
17     state = ASLEEP
18   }
19 }
```

Fig. 4. Worker thread piggybacking

has the value AWAKE, but switches to STEAL_SCHEDULE upon entering the stealSchedule method. Recursive calls to stealSchedule check this field and immediately return. The method then attempts to poll pending tasks up to STEAL_SCHEDULE_COUNT times.

This optimization is usually only beneficial if the time spent in the polling method pollWorkQueueAndRunFrame is short, since the scheduler spends useless cycles and slows the overall execution otherwise. For this reason, we only poll the local queue of the current worker thread in our implementation.

5.2 Lazy Task Scheduling

The optimization in Sect. 5.1 improves throughput by reducing the context switch pauses, but does not eliminate the cost of creating task objects. Compared to starting a thread, spawning a task is much more lightweight, but creating a task and pushing it onto a work stealing queue is still relatively expensive.

In this section, we describe an optimization that drastically reduces the number of tasks in some benchmarks. The optimization is based on the following observation: in most (re)actor programs, an execution of an event handler is relatively short (in fact, this is a recommendation in many frameworks, since monopolizing the worker threads with long event handlers can lead to message overflows). Furthermore, the longer the execution of an event handler is, the more likely it is that it will send messages to other reactors. This means that the time between sending two messages from a single event handler, and the time between sending a message and exiting from an event handler, are both usually short. Sending a message potentially results in scheduling a reactor frame, as shown in Fig. 3, which results in creating a task object. Consequently, postponing the task creation until the next schedule call or until the completion of the event handler usually does not have a negative performance impact.

```
1 val miniQueue = new AtomicReference[Frame](null)
2
3 @tailrec final def schedule(frame: Frame) {
4   val oldFrame = miniQueue.get
5   if (oldFrame eq null) {
6     if (!miniQueue.compareAndSet(oldFrame, frame)) {
7       schedule(frame)
8     }
9   } else {
10    if (!miniQueue.compareAndSet(oldFrame, null)) {
11      schedule(frame)
12    } else {
13      val task = createTaskFor(oldFrame)
14      pushToWorkQueue(task)
15    }
16  }
17 }
```

Fig. 5. Lazy scheduling of frame task objects

To exploit the previous observation, we augment each worker thread with an additional one-element queue, which we call a *mini-queue*, and use it to store reactor frames that were activated, but whose scheduling was lazily postponed. Initially, when a reactor frame gets execution time on some worker thread, the mini-queue is empty, i.e. set to null. When the reactor sends a message, and that message requires scheduling the reactor frame, the reactor frame is instead atomically placed on the mini-queue. If another reactor frame needs to be scheduled, the old reactor is first atomically removed, and then corresponding task object gets created and pushed to the work queue. This is shown in Fig. 5.

The code in Fig. 4 is similarly adjusted to check not only for pending work on the work stealing queue, but also flush the state of the mini-queue.

5.3   Reanimation Thread

The optimization from Sect. 5.2 trades latency for higher throughput. While in most cases, the decrease in latency is not observable, it is possible to write a program in which an event handler sends one message, but then does not return control to the scheduler for a long time. In these cases, an activated frame gets temporarily stuck on the mini-queue, and it cannot be stolen by other worker threads, since it is not on the work stealing queue.

To prevent this scenario, our implementation uses an additional non-worker thread, called a *reanimation thread*, that is usually in the sleep state, but occasionally wakes up and scans the mini-queues of the worker threads. When the reanimation thread finds a non-empty mini-queue, it atomically removes the frame and executes it. This is shown in Fig. 6.

When it is unlikely that there are any benefits from scanning the mini-queues, the reanimation thread should spend the least amount of CPU time possible. For this reason, after the reanimation thread inspects all the worker threads, it adjusts its sleep period to a new value that depends on the previous value, the

```
1  class ReanimationThread extends Thread {
2    setDaemon(true)
3
4    def run() {
5      var sleepPeriod = 0
6      while(true) {
7        Thread.sleep(sleepPeriod)
8        var count = 0
9        for (worker <- workers) {
10         val f = worker.miniQueue.get
11         if (f != null && worker.miniQueue.compareAndSet(f, null)) {
12           execute(f)
13           count += 1
14         }
15       }
16       sleepPeriod = adjust(sleepPeriod, count, workers.length)
17     }
18   }
19 }
```

Fig. 6. Reanimation thread implementation

number of removed frames and the total number of workers, as specified by the following equation:

$$adjust(period, count, workers) = 2 \cdot period \cdot \frac{workers - count}{workers} \qquad (1)$$

In the above equation, if the *count* is low, then the new period value is increased by up to 2×. On the other hand, if the *count* is high, the period is rapidly decreased. The net effect is that when the reanimation thread helps almost all workers, the period is almost immediately reduced to a minimum value, and otherwise slowly decays towards the maximum value. When the benefit of flushing mini-queues is small, this approach reduces the overall CPU time spent by the reanimation thread. The new period is clamped between some minimum and maximum value, which is in our case between 1 ms and 200 ms.

5.4   Message Arrival Speculation

After a reactor executes an event handler, it normally undergoes a context switch and returns the control to the scheduler. In applications in which pairs of reactors exchange values, a message frequently arrives to the reactor shortly after it had begun its context switch. In these cases, it pays off to speculate on the arrival of the message and delay the context switch. This speculation is based on the bet that the message arrival time is lower than the time required for the context switch. To estimate the message arrival time, each reactor does sampling – a reactor occasionally spins before its context switch and counts the number of messages that arrived during spinning. The sampling frequency must be low to avoid slowing down the program. After accumulating a set of samples, the reactor decides whether to regularly spin before the context switch, or not.

Importantly, message arrival speculation is dynamic – it is only applied if the scheduler detects that it is likely to improve performance. If during the sampling period, a reactor does not notice any benefits from delaying the context switch, then it will not apply speculative spinning.

Concretely, a reactor decides to speculate that a message will arrive as follows. Define the time period δ as the ration between the context switch delay d and the total time required to do the context switch c (which is estimated experimentally, by sending messages to a reactor with an empty event handler). The reactor decides to delay context switches by a relative delay δ if and only if the percentage of arrivals $\hat{p}$ during sampling satisfies:

$$\delta \leq \hat{p} \qquad (2)$$

The intuition behind this is that delaying the context switch potentially slows down the program. To make up for this slowdown, the relative delay must be smaller than the percentage of cases in which it accurately predicted that a message will arrive, avoiding the full context switch. The reactor must pick the optimal value for δ, so it collects a sample for a range of values δ_i and $\hat{p}_i$, and picks the one for which the following expression is minimized:

$$\delta_i - \hat{p}_i \qquad (3)$$

After deciding on the context switch delay, the reactor continues sampling the delay benefits, and repetitively revisits the speculation decision after collecting new sample sets. This way, if message arrival pattern changes during the execution, the reactor adjust the context switch delay.

In Fig. 7, we show the performance of two benchmarks from the Savina suite [15] for which message arrival speculation is particularly effective. In the *Fork*

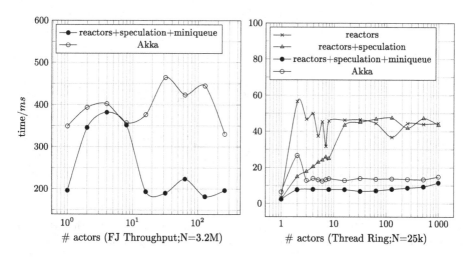

Fig. 7. Impact of the parallelism level on different benchmarks with message arrival speculation enabled (running time vs. number of reactors)

Join Throughput benchmark, a reactor allocates K other reactors, and sends each of them a message in a round-robin manner. The performance improvement on the *Fork Join Throughput* benchmark is high when K is above 8, which is the number of processors on the test machine. The reason is that when there is a higher number of reactors, speculative spinning allows messages to pile up at some of the reactors, so when the reactor gets scheduled, the batch of messages it can process is larger. For K below 8, performance becomes close to that of the Akka framework. The *Thread Ring* benchmark allocates R reactors that pass a token around in a ring pattern. Here, the situation is reversed – it only makes sense to spin and wait for the next message if each reactor can be pinned to a processor (which is true if the ring size R is small). Otherwise, spinning delays the assignment of a processor to inactive reactors, and slows down the program overall. We show the performance of Reactors compared to Akka, when speculative spinning is disabled, when it is enabled, and when we additionally apply the lazy task scheduling optimization (mini-queue).

For other benchmarks, message arrival speculation does not yield any benefits. Nevertheless, it is important to ensure that the sampling overhead does not compromise overall performance, so the sampling frequency φ is initially kept at a low value, in our case 0.2%. The downside of doing this is that it takes a long time to collect a sample set when speculation *is* beneficial. To retain the best of both worlds, a reactor adapts the sampling frequency according to the belief that arrival speculation helps. When and if a reactor notices an arrival of a message (but before it has gathered a full sample needed for its speculation decision), it adaptively increases the sampling frequency. A reactor is allowed to do this, since sampling is itself a context switch delay – a higher sampling frequency is therefore not detrimental when context switch delays help.

In Fig. 8, we show some of the benchmarks on which speculation does not help, namely *Thread Ring* (with $R \gg \#processors$), *Streaming Ping-Pong*, *Big* and *Fibonacci*. We plot the running time of the benchmark with respect to the initial sampling frequency φ_0. Based on these benchmarks, we decided to keep φ_0 at the value 0.2%.

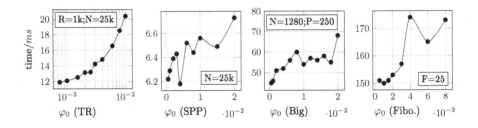

Fig. 8. Impact of different sampling frequencies on performance for benchmarks that do not benefit from speculation (running time vs. sampling frequency)

A theoretical model of the message arrival speculation optimization was described recently, along with a more in-depth performance analysis [25]. For more information, we refer the readers to related work.

5.5   Class-Based Reactor Profiling

Speculation described in Sect. 5.4 works well only if the lifetime of a reactor is sufficiently long to gather a sample that estimates the benefits of delaying context switches. In many applications, the average lifetime of a reactor is shorter than that, so reactors do not manage to effectively estimate speculation benefits. This is true even if a reactor adaptively adjusts the sampling frequency as described in Sect. 5.4. To accomodate these cases, our implementation periodically profiles the stable sampling frequency with respect to the class of the reactor. This information is stored in a per-class histogram, and used as the initial sampling frequency when a reactor gets created. This way, the information about the ideal sampling rate gets shared among reactors of the same type, and applications with short reactor lifetimes can also benefit from speculation. In our implementation, the lifetime of the sampling frequency profile is specific to a single execution of a program.

When profiling numeric values such as the sampling frequency, the more recent information must be given a higher importance. The intuition is that the applications are going through phases, and the optimal values may change over time. We use the following expression to update the sampling frequency:

$$record(oldRate, newRate) = 0.8 \cdot oldRate + 0.2 \cdot newRate \qquad (4)$$

By using the expression (4), the more recent profiling information quickly starts dominating, and the old value tends to decay and become less important over time. Every profiled value is continuously interpolated in this way.

6   Evaluation

We used standard actor benchmarks from the Savina suite [15] to test the performance of our scheduler (code online [3]) against the industry-standard Akka framework [1]. We used established evaluation methodologies [9,22]. Benchmarks were done on a quad-core 2.8 GHz Intel i7-4900MQ processor with 32 GB of RAM, and the results are shown in Fig. 9.

Ping-Pong. In this benchmark, one (re)actor sends a preallocated *ping* message to another (re)actor, which then responds with a *pong* message. This is repeated N times. This benchmark is designed to test how fast the scheduling system exchanges the context between two (re)actors, when it is likely that they each will be reactivated soon after deactivation. Our reactor implementation is around 1.6× faster when compared to Akka.

Streaming Ping-Pong. The Akka project [1] often uses an alternative form of the Ping-Pong benchmark in which the first actor starts by sending W *ping*

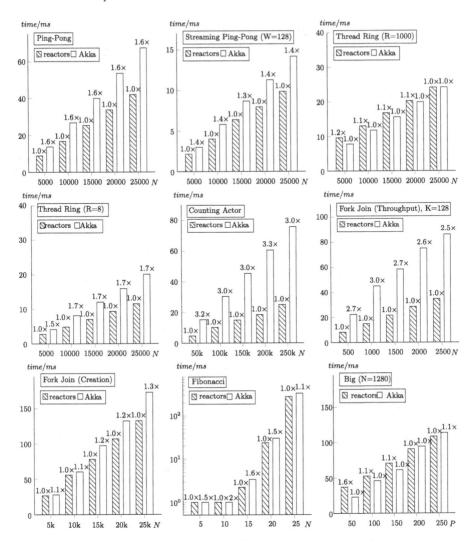

Fig. 9. Running time on standard actor benchmarks (lower is better)

messages, instead of a single one. Whereas in the Ping-Pong benchmark each actor waits for the reply before sending the next message, in Streaming Ping-Pong, the two actors keep a sliding window of messages and usually do not yield control to the scheduler. Our reactor system is $1.3 - 1.4\times$ faster than Akka.

Thread Ring. Here, R (re)actors are arranged in a ring, and each waits for a message before sending it to the next (re)actor in the ring. The program ends after the message is forwarded N times. When R is much larger than the processor count, the benchmark tests context switching when it is unlikely that a (re)actor will be reactivated soon after deactivation. When $R = 1000$, depending

on N, our system is in some cases as fast as Akka, and sometimes up to 1.2×
slower. For $R = 8$, our system is up to 1.7× faster compared to Akka.

Counting Actor. A producer actor sends N numbers to a counter actor. The
counter actor accumulates the sum of the numbers, and terminates. The benchmark is somewhat similar to Streaming Ping-Pong, but also evaluates the efficiency of allocating messages. Reactors have typed channels that can specialize
on the message type, and can avoid boxing. In our implementation, we rely on the
type specialization optimization in Scala [7] that avoids boxing primitive types
such as integers. For this (scheduler-unrelated) reason, our implementation is
around 3× faster than Akka.

Fork Join (Throughput). A single (re)actor allocates K (re)actors that count
incoming messages, and sends them N messages in a round-robin manner. The
benchmark evaluates messaging throughput, and quality of batching messages.
Our system is $2.5 - 3.0×$ faster than Akka.

Fork Join (Creation). Benchmark creates N (re)actors, and sends a message
to each of them. After a (re)actor receives a message, it terminates. This benchmark tests actor creation performance. Depending on N, our system is as fast
as Akka, and sometimes up to 1.3× faster.

Fibonacci. This benchmark computes Fibonacci numbers recursively, where
each recursive call creates a (re)actor that sends the result to its parent. For
sizes $N < 2$, leaf actors send 1 immediately after creation. This benchmark tests
dynamic actor creation performance. Results are shown in logarithmic scale in
Fig. 9. Our system is $1.1 - 2.0×$ faster than Akka, depending on N.

Big. This benchmark creates a large set of (re)actors N, each sending P pings
to P randomly chosen (re)actors, awaiting a reply for each ping. The benchmark
tests many-to-many message passing. Depending on P, our system is in some
cases $1.1 - 1.6×$ slower than Akka, and in some cases 1.1× faster than Akka.

6.1   Effect of Batch Size on Performance

In benchmarks that have high average message count per actor, exchanging
contexts between actors frequently can be detrimental. Each context switch
requires relatively expensive state checks from Fig. 2, and a call to the `schedule`
method. Amortizing these costs by handling multiple events in one scheduling
batch greatly increases performance.

As argued in Sect. 2.1, batch size must be bound to ensure bounded delivery
time – large batch sizes have a negative effect of delaying execution of other reactors. Batching must amortize context switch costs, but also prevent starvation.

In Fig. 10, we show a selection of benchmarks where batch size affects the
benchmark running time. In Streaming Ping-Pong and Counting Actor, the
inflection point is around batch size 5, but performance converges above 40. We
show the Fork Join Throughput benchmark for different choices of the number
of reactors K. We leave out out-of-scale points below batch size 10 for $K = 128$.

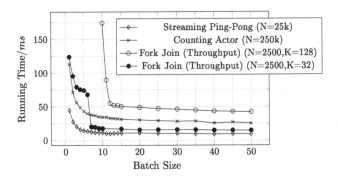

Fig. 10. Dependence of the running time on the batch size for benchmarks with a high message load (lower is better)

For $K = 32$, we can see a steep jump around 7. Here, the batch size is just large enough to give inactive reactors sufficient time to fill their event queues. By the time a reactor is reactivated, it has sufficiently many pending events to benefit from batching. Based on these benchmarks, we keep the BATCH_SIZE constant from Sect. 4, at value 50.

6.2   Event Stream Scalability

The last thing to show is that the system scales with the number of event streams per reactor. In Fig. 11, we show our custom *Roundabout benchmark*, in which the roundabout actor receives N messages on K different event streams. The running time remains almost constant while increasing the number of event streams – the gentle upward slope is a consequence of decreasing cache-locality.

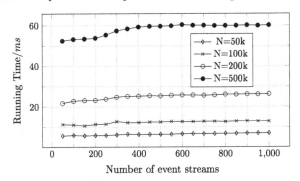

Fig. 11. Roundabout Benchmark (Lower is Better)

7   Related Work

The actor programming model was proposed by Agha [4], and has gone through many variants since then. One of the most notable applications of the actor model is the Erlang programming language [2]. On the JVM, Scala Actors attempted to mimic the Erlang model [11] – since JVM does not have continuations, semantics of the Erlang-style `receive` statement could not be completely imitated. Akka is a widely adopted actor-based framework [1], which takes a step away from the Erlang model in that it supports only a single top-level `receive` statement. Kilim [36] is another JVM actor framework that takes a more sophisticated approach by exposing the `@pausable` annotation, used to mark and transform methods that potentially suspend. The Reactors.IO framework exposes event streams as first-class objects. The advantage of first-class streams is that suspendable computations can be chained as a sequence of callbacks [3,28,31].

Selector model is an actor model variant with multiple mailboxes [15]. In this model, there are multiple guarded mailboxes that the actor can programmatically activate or deactivate. Although the abstract selector model allows a dynamic number of mailboxes, the current selector implementation requires specifying the number of mailboxes before the selector starts [16]. The scheduling algorithm is based on the multi-level queue scheduling [35], used to separate mailboxes into priority levels. This separation does not necessarily ensure fairness, so authors mention LRU round-robin scheduling as necessary future work.

The Kilim framework introduced the concept of *scheduler hopping*. Here, an actor can programmatically change the scheduling policy during the lifetime of an actor. Neither Akka, nor Reactors.IO allow changing the policy after actor creation. We believe that it is easy to add scheduler hopping to Reactors.IO.

Most actor schedulers are built on top of a task scheduler, such as the Fork/Join framework [17]. Depending on the task scheduler implementation, this approach ensures fairness. However, bounded delivery time fairness, as defined in Sect. 2.1, is not necessarily ensured – giving all actors equal execution times can cause starvation when the message-load is non-uniform. We have not yet found programs where this is problematic, and the prebundled schedulers in Reactors are not fair. On the other hand, it is common to have schedulers that extend the Fork/Join task scheduler with domain-specific knowledge, and this was done for actor systems [1], asynchronous programming frameworks [12], streaming frameworks [29], and for data-parallel collections [27,30].

Many frameworks use pluggability to defer some scheduling decisions to the client. For example, message scheduling in Akka [1] uses the underlying task scheduler to assign equal execution chunks to actors, but this does not guarantee message handling bounded delivery time fairness. It is the client's job to implement a fair *dispatcher* if that is necessary. Aside from custom dispatchers, both Akka and Reactors allow users to inject their own message queue implementations. This is advantageous in use-cases such as message persistence, for which more efficient queue data structures exist [23,32]. Parallel actor monitors [33] for the AmbientTalk language [21] expose a user API that can optionally enable parallelism within an actor. Ensuring scalability is thus deferred to the client-side. The Mesos cluster runtime [14] has a very thin scheduler based on *resource offers*, which does not even guarantee fairness. This may be an indication that programs where fairness is an issue are in practice rare, and can be dealt on a case-by-case basis. At the same time, pluggable schedulers are useful, as they allow clients to deal with pathological edge cases when they occur.

8   Conclusion

We described a scheduler algorithm for the reactor programming model, and presented its implementation. We showed that the scheduler satisfies safety properties such as handling at most one message in a reactor at a time, and also guarantees fairness and bounded delivery time fairness with specific guarantees from the scheduling policy. Scheduling policies are pluggable – in addition to the default policies shown in Sect. 4, users can define their own custom policies. We empirically showed that the scheduler is scalable and efficient by comparing our implementation against the industry-standard Akka framework, on the Savina actor benchmark suite.

An interesting area of future work is scheduling reactor programs that additionally use heterogeneous resources of the host system, such as GPUs, DSPs and external sensors. Achieving scalability and good performance in such non-uniform computations is more challenging, but also potentially more rewarding. We believe that our pluggable scheduler infrastructure is well suited for this task.

References

1. Akka Documentation (2015). http://akka.io/docs/
2. Erlang/OTP documentation (2015). http://www.erlang.org/
3. Reactors, IO Website (2016). https://reactors.io
4. Agha, G.: Actors: A Model of Concurrent Computation in Distributed Systems. MIT Press, Cambridge (1986)
5. Astley, M., Agha, G.A.: Customization and composition of distributed objects: middleware abstractions for policy management. In: Proceedings of the 6th ACM SIGSOFT International Symposium on Foundations of Software Engineering, SIGSOFT 1998/FSE-6, pp. 1–9. ACM, New York (1998). http://doi.acm.org/10.1145/288195.288206
6. Blumofe, R.D., Leiserson, C.E.: Scheduling multithreaded computations by work stealing. J. ACM **46**(5), 720–748 (1999). http://doi.acm.org/10.1145/324133.324234
7. Dragos, I., Odersky, M.: Compiling generics through user-directed type specialization. In: Proceedings of the 4th Workshop on the Implementation, Compilation, Optimization of Object-Oriented Languages and Programming Systems, ICOOOLPS 2009, pp. 42–47. ACM, New York (2009). http://doi.acm.org/10.1145/1565824.1565830
8. Fournet, C., Gonthier, G.: The Join Calculus: a Language for Distributed Mobile Programming, September 2000. https://www.microsoft.com/en-us/research/publication/join-calculus-language-distributed-mobile-programming/
9. Georges, A., Buytaert, D., Eeckhout, L.: Statistically rigorous java performance evaluation. SIGPLAN Not. **42**(10), 57–76 (2007). http://doi.acm.org/10.1145/1297105.1297033

10. Guerraoui, R., Rodrigues, L.: Introduction to Reliable Distributed Programming. Springer, Heidelberg (2006). https://doi.org/10.1007/978-3-642-15260-3
11. Haller, P., Odersky, M.: Event-based programming without inversion of control. In: Lightfoot, D.E., Szyperski, C. (eds.) JMLC 2006. LNCS, vol. 4228, pp. 4–22. Springer, Heidelberg (2006). https://doi.org/10.1007/11860990_2
12. Haller, P., Prokopec, A., Miller, H., Klang, V., Kuhn, R., Jovanovic, V.: Scala Improvement Proposal: Futures and Promises (SIP-14) (2012). http://docs.scala-lang.org/sips/pending/futures-promises.html
13. Herlihy, M., Shavit, N.: The Art of Multiprocessor Programming. Morgan Kaufmann Publishers Inc., San Francisco (2008)
14. Hindman, B., et al.: Mesos: a platform for fine-grained resource sharing in the data center. In: Proceedings of the 8th USENIX Conference on Networked Systems Design and Implementation, NSDI 2011, pp. 295–308. USENIX Association, Berkeley (2011). http://dl.acm.org/citation.cfm?id=1972457.1972488
15. Imam, S.M., Sarkar, V.: Savina - an actor benchmark suite: enabling empirical evaluation of actor libraries. In: Proceedings of the 4th International Workshop on Programming Based on Actors Agents and Decentralized Control, AGERE! 2014, pp. 67–80. ACM, New York (2014). http://doi.acm.org/10.1145/2687357.2687368
16. Imam, S.M., Sarkar, V.: Selectors: actors with multiple guarded mailboxes. In: Proceedings of the 4th International Workshop on Programming Based on Actors Agents and Decentralized Control, AGERE! 2014, pp. 1–14. ACM, New York (2014). http://doi.acm.org/10.1145/2687357.2687360
17. Lea, D.: A Java fork/Join framework. In: Proceedings of the ACM 2000 Conference on Java Grande, JAVA 2000, pp. 36–43. ACM, New York (2000). http://doi.acm.org/10.1145/337449.337465
18. Lynch, N.A.: Distributed Algorithms. MK Publishers Inc., San Francisco (1996)
19. Milner, R., Parrow, J., Walker, D.: A calculus of mobile processes. I. Inf. Comput. **100**(1), 1–40 (1992). https://doi.org/10.1016/0890-5401(92)90008-4
20. Odersky, M., al.: An Overview of the Scala Programming Language. Technical report IC/2004/64, EPFL Lausanne, Switzerland (2004)
21. Pinte, K., Lombide Carreton, A., Gonzalez Boix, E., De Meuter, W.: Ambient clouds: reactive asynchronous collections for mobile ad hoc network applications. In: Dowling, J., Taïani, F. (eds.) DAIS 2013. LNCS, vol. 7891, pp. 85–98. Springer, Heidelberg (2013). https://doi.org/10.1007/978-3-642-38541-4_7
22. Prokopec, A.: ScalaMeter Website (2014). http://scalameter.github.io
23. Prokopec, A.: Snapqueue: lock-free queue with constant time snapshots. In: Proceedings of the 6th ACM SIGPLAN Symposium on Scala, Scala 2015, Portland, OR, USA, 15–17 June 2015, pp. 1–12 (2015). http://doi.acm.org/10.1145/2774975.2774976
24. Prokopec, A.: Pluggable scheduling for the reactor programming model. In: Proceedings of the 6th International Workshop on Programming Based on Actors, Agents, and Decentralized Control, AGERE 2016, pp. 41–50. ACM, New York (2016). http://doi.acm.org/10.1145/3001886.3001891
25. Prokopec, A.: Accelerating by idling: how speculative delays improve performance of message-oriented systems. In: Rivera, F.F., Pena, T.F., Cabaleiro, J.C. (eds.) Euro-Par 2017. LNCS, vol. 10417, pp. 177–191. Springer, Cham (2017). https://doi.org/10.1007/978-3-319-64203-1_13
26. Prokopec, A.: Encoding the building blocks of communication. In: accepted at Onward 2017, to appear (2017)

27. Prokopec, A., Bagwell, P., Rompf, T., Odersky, M.: A generic parallel collection framework. In: Jeannot, E., Namyst, R., Roman, J. (eds.) Euro-Par 2011. LNCS, vol. 6853, pp. 136–147. Springer, Heidelberg (2011). https://doi.org/10.1007/978-3-642-23397-5_14

28. Prokopec, A., Haller, P., Odersky, M.: Containers and aggregates, mutators and isolates for reactive programming. In: Fifth Annual Scala Workshop, SCALA 2014, pp. 51–61. ACM (2014). http://doi.acm.org/10.1145/2637647.2637656

29. Prokopec, A., Miller, H., Schlatter, T., Haller, P., Odersky, M.: FlowPools: a lock-free deterministic concurrent dataflow abstraction. In: Kasahara, H., Kimura, K. (eds.) LCPC 2012. LNCS, vol. 7760, pp. 158–173. Springer, Heidelberg (2013). https://doi.org/10.1007/978-3-642-37658-0_11

30. Prokopec, A., Odersky, M.: Near optimal work-stealing tree scheduler for highly irregular data-parallel workloads. In: Caşcaval, C., Montesinos, P. (eds.) LCPC 2013. LNCS, vol. 8664, pp. 55–86. Springer, Cham (2014). https://doi.org/10.1007/978-3-319-09967-5_4

31. Prokopec, A., Odersky, M.: Isolates, channels, and event streams for composable distributed programming. In: 2015 ACM International Symposium on New Ideas, New Paradigms, and Reflections on Programming and Software (Onward!), Onward! 2015, pp. 171–182. ACM, New York (2015). http://doi.acm.org/10.1145/2814228.2814245

32. Prokopec, A., Odersky, M.: Conc-trees for functional and parallel programming. In: Shen, X., Mueller, F., Tuck, J. (eds.) LCPC 2015. LNCS, vol. 9519, pp. 254–268. Springer, Cham (2016). https://doi.org/10.1007/978-3-319-29778-1_16

33. Scholliers, C., Tanter, E., De Meuter, W.: Parallel actor monitors: disentangling task-level parallelism from data partitioning in the actor model. Sci. Comput. Program. **80**, 52–64 (2014). Feb

34. Shapiro, M., Preguiça, N., Baquero, C., Zawirski, M.: A Comprehensive Study of Convergent and Commutative Replicated Data Types. Research Report RR-7506, January 2011. https://hal.inria.fr/inria-00555588

35. Silberschatz, A., Galvin, P.B., Gagne, G.: Operating System Concepts, 8th edn. Wiley Publishing (2008)

36. Srinivasan, S., Mycroft, A.: Kilim: Isolation-typed actors for java. In: Vitek, J. (ed.) ECOOP 2008. LNCS, vol. 5142, pp. 104–128. Springer, Heidelberg (2008). https://doi.org/10.1007/978-3-540-70592-5_6

37. Sturman, D.C., Agha, G.A.: A protocol description language for customizing failure semantics. In: Proceedings of IEEE 13th Symposium on Reliable Distributed Systems, pp. 148–157, October 1994

38. Verma, A., Pedrosa, L., Korupolu, M.R., Oppenheimer, D., Tune, E., Wilkes, J.: Large-scale cluster management at Google with borg. In: Proceedings of the European Conference on Computer Systems (EuroSys), Bordeaux, France (2015)

A Study of Concurrency Bugs
and Advanced Development Support
for Actor-based Programs

Carmen Torres Lopez[1], Stefan Marr[3], Elisa Gonzalez Boix[1(✉)],
and Hanspeter Mössenböck[2]

[1] Vrije Universiteit Brussel, Pleinlaan 2, 1050 Brussel, Belgium
{ctorresl,egonzale}@vub.be
[2] Johannes Kepler University, Linz, Austria
hanspeter.moessenboeck@jku.at
[3] University of Kent, Canterbury, UK
s.marr@kent.ac.uk

Abstract. The actor model is an attractive foundation for developing concurrent applications because actors are isolated concurrent entities that communicate through asynchronous messages and do not share state. Thereby, they avoid concurrency bugs such as data races, but are not immune to concurrency bugs in general.

This study taxonomizes concurrency bugs in actor-based programs reported in literature. Furthermore, it analyzes the bugs to identify the patterns causing them as well as their observable behavior. Based on this taxonomy, we further analyze the literature and find that current approaches to static analysis and testing focus on communication deadlocks and message protocol violations. However, they do not provide solutions to identify livelocks and behavioral deadlocks.

The insights obtained in this study can be used to improve debugging support for actor-based programs with new debugging techniques to identify the root cause of complex concurrency bugs.

Keywords: Actor model · Concurrency · Bugs · Survey

1 Introduction

With the widespread use of multicore systems, even in everyday phones, concurrent programming has become mainstream. However, concurrent programming is known to be hard and error-prone. Unlike traditional sequential programs, concurrent programs often exhibit *non-deterministic* behavior which makes it difficult to reason about their behavior. Many bugs involving concurrent entities, e.g. processes, threads, actors [3], manifest themselves only in rare execution traces. Identifying and analyzing concurrency bugs is thus an arduous task, perhaps even an art.

© Springer Nature Switzerland AG 2018
A. Ricci and P. Haller (Eds.): Programming with Actors, LNCS 10789, pp. 155–185, 2018.
https://doi.org/10.1007/978-3-030-00302-9_6

When studying techniques to support the development of complex concurrent programs, our first research question is what types of concurrency bugs appear in such programs. The answer to this question depends on the concurrency model in which the program is written. Most existing studies about concurrency bugs focus on thread-based concurrency [1, 2, 6, 10, 37, 39, 43, 56].

The established frame of reference, however, does not directly apply to other concurrency models which are not based on a shared memory model such as the actor model, communicating sequential processes (CSP), etc. In this paper we study concurrency bugs in message passing concurrent software, in particular, in actor-based programs.

The actor model is attractive for concurrent programming because it avoids by design some concurrency bugs associated with thread-based programs. Since actors do not share mutable state, programs cannot exhibit memory-level *race conditions* such as data races. In addition to that, deadlocks can be avoided if communication between actors is solely based on asynchronous message passing. However, this does not mean that programs are inherently free from concurrency issues.

This paper surveys concurrency bugs in the literature on actor-based programs and aims to answer three research questions: (1) which kind of concurrency bugs can be avoided by the actor model and its variants, (2) what kind of patterns cause concurrency bugs in actor programs, and (3) what is the observable behavior in the programs that have these bugs?

To provide a common frame of reference to distinguish different types of concurrency bugs that appear in actor-based programs, we propose a taxonomy of concurrency bugs in actor-based programs (in Sect. 3). The taxonomy aims to establish a conceptual framework for concurrency bugs that facilitates communication amongst researchers. It is also meant to help practitioners in developing, testing, debugging, or even statically analyzing programs to identify the root cause of concurrency bugs by offering more information about the types of bugs and their observable properties.

Based on our taxonomy of bugs, we analyze actor literature that reports concurrency bugs and map them to the proposed classification. Furthermore, we identify which types of bugs have been addressed in literature so far, and which types have been studied less.

The contributions of this paper are:

- A systematic study of concurrency bugs in actor-based programs based on a literature review. To the best of our knowledge it is the first taxonomy of bugs in the context of actor-based concurrent software.
- An analysis of the patterns and observable behaviors of concurrency bugs found in different actor-based programs.
- A review of the state of the art in static analysis, testing, debugging, and visualization of actor-based programs to identify open research issues.

2   Terminology and Background Information

Before we delve into the classification of concurrency bugs in actor-based programs, we discuss the terminology used in this paper and the basic concepts on actor-based programs and concurrency issues.

Since the actor model was first proposed by Hewitt et al. [30], several variations of it emerged. Based on De Koster et al. [21], we distinguish three variants in addition to the classic actor model: *active objects* (e.g. ABCL [58], AmbientTalk/1 [22]), *processes* (e.g. Erlang [4], Scala) and *communicating event-loops* (e.g. E [41], AmbientTalk/2 [57], JavaScript). In all these variants, concurrency is introduced by actors. All actors communicate with one another by means of *messages*. Messages are stored in a *mailbox*. Each actor has a thread of execution, which perpetually processes one message at a time from the mailbox. The processing of one message by an actor defines a *turn*. Each actor has a *behavior* associated that defines how the actor processes messages. The set of messages that an actor knows how to process in a certain turn denotes the *interface* of the actor's behavior. Actors can store state which can only be accessed or mutated by the actor itself. In other words, actors have exclusive access to their mutable state.

A *concurrency bug* is a failure related to the interactions among different concurrent entities of a system. Following Avizienis's terminology [7], a *failure* is an event that occurs when the services provided by a system deviate from the ones it was designed for. The discrepancy between the observed behavior and the theoretically correct behavior of a system is called an *error*. Hence, an error is an event that may lead to a failure. Finally, a *fault* is an incorrect step in a program which causes an error (e.g. the cause of a message transmission error in a distributed system may be a broken network cable). A fault is said to be *active* when it causes an error, and *dormant* when is present in a system but has not yet manifested itself as an error. Throughout this paper, we use the terms concurrency bug and issue interchangeably.

Although actors were originally designed to be used in open distributed environments, they can be used on a single machine, e.g. in multicore programming. This paper analyses concurrency bugs that appear in actor-based programs used in either concurrent or distributed systems. However, bugs that are only observable in distributed systems (e.g. due to network failures) are out of the scope of this paper.

3   Classification of Concurrency Bugs in Actor-based Programs

While there is a large number of studies for concurrency bugs in thread-based programs, there are only few studies on bugs in the context of message passing programs. Zhang et al. [59] study bug patterns, manifestation conditions, and bug fixes in three open source applications that use message passing. In this

Table 1. Taxonomy of concurrency bugs

Concurrency Model	Category of Concurrency Bugs		Bug Definition
Threads	Lack of Progress	Deadlock	condition in a system where two or more threads are blocked forever waiting for another thread to do something [45]
		Livelock	condition in which two or more threads while not blocked cannot make further progress [43]
	Race Condition	Data race	special case of race condition that occurs when two threads access the same data and at least one of them writes the data [1]
		Bad interleaving (also know as high-level data race [6], atomicity violation [1])	occurs when the program exposes an inconsistent intermediate state due to the overlapping execution of two threads [45]
		Order violation	occurs when the expected order of execution of at least two memory accesses is not respected [1]
Actors	Lack of Progress	Communication deadlock	condition in a system where two or more actors are blocked forever waiting for each other to do something
		Behavioral deadlock	condition in a system when two or more actors are not blocked but wait on each other for a message to be able to progress, i.e. the message to complete the next step is never sent
		Livelock	condition similar to a deadlock in which two or more actors are not able to make progress but they continuously change their state
	Message Protocol Violation	Message order violation	condition in which the order of exchanging messages of two or more actors is not consistent with the intended *protocol* of an actor
		Bad message interleaving	occurs when a message is processed between two messages which are intended to be processed one after the other
		Memory inconsistency	occurs when different actors have inconsistent views of shared resources. The effects of the turn that modifies a conceptually shared resource, may not be visible to other actors which also alter the same resource

context, literature typically uses general terms to refer a certain issue, for example ordering problems [38]. For actor-based programs however, there is so far no established terminology for concurrency bugs.

This section introduces a taxonomy of concurrency bugs for the actor model derived from bugs reported in literature and from our own experience with actor languages. Table 1 first summarizes the well-known terminology for thread-based programs from literature, and then introduces our proposed terminology for concurrent bugs in actor-based programs. Our overall categorization starts out from the distinction of shared-memory concurrency bugs in literature, which classifies bugs in two general categories: lack of progress issues and race conditions.

Depending on the guarantees provided by a specific actor model, programs may be subject to different concurrency bugs. Therefore, not all concurrency bugs are applicable to all actor variants. In the rest of the section we define each type of bug, and detail in which variants it cannot be present.

3.1 Lack of Progress Issues

Two different kinds of conditions can lead to a lack of progress in an actor-based program: deadlocks and livelocks. However, these issues manifest themselves differently in actor-based programs compared to thread-based programs.

Communication Deadlock. A communication deadlock is a condition in a system where two or more actors are blocked forever waiting for each other to do something. This condition is similar to traditional deadlocks known from thread-based programs. We base the terminology on the work of [15] in Erlang concurrency bugs.

Communication deadlocks can *only* occur in variants of the actor model that feature a blocking `receive` operation. This is common in variants of the actor model based on processes. Examples of such actor systems include Erlang and the Scala Actors framework [29]. A communication deadlock manifests itself when an actor only has messages in its inbox that cannot be received with the currently active `receive` statement. Listing 1.1 shows a communication deadlock example in Erlang [15]. The *fault* is in line 12, where the pong process is blocked because it is waiting for a message that is never sent by the ping process. Instead the ping process returns ok.

```
1 play() ->
2   Ping = spawn(fun ping/0),
3   spawn(fun() -> pong(Ping) end).
4
5 ping() ->
6   receive
7     pong_msg -> ok
8   end.
9
10 pong(Ping) ->
11   Ping ! pong_msg,
12   receive
13     ping_msg -> ok
14   end.
```

Listing 1.1. Communication deadlock example in Erlang (from [15]). Line 12 has a blocking **receive** causing the pong process to deadlock because the expected message is never sent.

Behavioral Deadlock. A behavioral deadlock happens when two or more actors *conceptually* wait for each other because the message to complete the next step in an algorithm is never sent. In this case, no actor is necessarily suspended or otherwise unable to receive messages. We call this situation a behavioral deadlock, because the mutual waiting prevents local progress. However, these actors might still process messages from other actors. Since actors do not actually block, detecting behavioral deadlocks can be harder than detecting deadlocks in thread-based programs.

We illustrate a behavioral deadlock in an implementation of the dining philosophers concurrency problem written in Newspeak [9] which is shown in Listing 1.2. The behavioral deadlock has the effect that some philosophers cannot eat (as they never acquire two consecutive forks), preventing global progress. Line 12 shows that the left fork has the same value as the id of the philosopher, but for the right fork the program computes its value. For example, philosopher 1 will eat with fork 1 and 2 and so on. The *error* occurs when the philosopher puts down its forks: the right fork gets a wrong value (line 22) because the implementation swapped numForks and leftForkId variables. This programming mistake is the *fault* that causes fork 2 and 4 to be always taken. Consequently, there is no global progress since philosopher 2 and 4 never eat and philosopher 1 and 3 eat only once. Philosopher 5 can always eat showing local progress, however.

```
1  class PhilosopherActor new: id rounds: rounds
2      counter: aCounter arbitrator: arbitrator = (
3    (* ... *)
4    public start = (
5      arbitrator <-: pickUpForks: self id: id.
6    )
7  )
8  class ArbitratorActor new: numForks resolver: resolver = (
9    (* ... *)
10   public pickUpForks: philosopher id: leftForkId = (
11     | rightForkId |
12     rightForkId := 1 + (leftForkId % numForks).
13     ((forks at: leftForkId) or: [forks at: rightForkId])
14       ifTrue:  [ philosopher <-: denied ]
15       ifFalse: [
16         forks at: leftForkId  put: true.
17         forks at: rightForkId put: true.
18         philosopher <-: eat ]
19   )
20   public putDownForks: leftForkId = (
21     | rightForkId |
22     rightForkId := 1 + (numForks % leftForkId).
23     forks at: leftForkId  put: false.
24     forks at: rightForkId put: false.
25   )
26 )
```

Listing 1.2. Behavioral deadlock example of a dining philosopher implementation. Line 22 calculates rightForkId incorrectly, preventing the philosophers from eating.

In contrast to communication deadlocks, all variants of actor models can suffer from behavioral deadlocks. One cause for such deadlocks are *flexible interfaces* [21], because when an actor limits the set of messages it accepts, the overall system can reach a state where actors mutually wait for messages being sent, without allowing any progress. On the other hand, if an actor implements two or more interfaces, it could be that only one of them is deadlocked, allowing some progress with respect to interactions with other actors.

Livelock. A program is in a livelock when an actor or a group of actors can make local progress, but the program is not 'able to make global progress. For example, actors can change their state receiving and executing messages, but the overall execution of the program stalls and cannot be finished.

An example for a livelock is given in Listing 1.3. It shows the sleeping barber problem [23] implemented in Newspeak [9]. The waiting room, the barber, and the customers are implemented as actors. The concurrency issue in this example is caused by a *fault* in line 7. Instead of receiving the next customer from the collection of customers waitingCustomers, the barber always receives the same first customer. Both actors, room and barber are not blocked. The barber asks for the next customer to the room (line 20) and the room sends the customer to the barber to do the haircut (line 8). But, as the customer that is sent is always the same, there is no global progress.

```
1  class WaitingRoomActor new: capacity barber: anActor = (
2    (* ... *)
3    public next = (
4      waitingCustomers size > 0
5      ifTrue: [
6        | customer |
7        customer := waitingCustomers first.
8        barber <-: enter: customer in: self ]
9      ifFalse: [
10       barber <-: wait.
11       barberAsleep := true ]
12   )
13 )
14 class BarberActor new: resolver = (
15   (* ... *)
16   public enter: customer in: room = (
17     customer <-: start.
18     busyWait: (random next: avHaircutRate) + 10.
19     customer <-: done.
20     room <-: next
21   )
22 )
```

Listing 1.3. Livelock in a sleeping barber implementation. Line 7 reads always the same customer, but does not remove it from the list, preventing global progress.

3.2   Message Protocol Violations

As shown in Table 1, thread-based programs commonly suffer from three sorts
of low-level race conditions: data races, bad interleavings (also know as high-
level data race [6], atomicity violation [1]), and order violations. Actors, on the
other hand, cannot suffer from those low-level race conditions since they have
exclusive access to their state and messages are processed serially. Nevertheless,
all actor-based programs can have race conditions related to the order in which
messages are processed. We consider these race conditions to be at a *high-level*
to distinguish them from the low-level memory access race conditions that occur
in thread-based programs.

High-level race conditions in actor based-programs can be observed when
two or more actors exchange messages that are not consistent with the intended
protocol of the application. Therefore, we refer to them more specifically as *message protocol violations*. We identified three types of message protocol violations,
which are described in the remainder of this subsection: *message order violations,
bad message interleavings*, and *memory inconsistencies*.

Message order violation. A message order violation appears when the order
in which two or more actors exchange messages is not consistent with the
intended *protocol* of the actor. This includes messages that are received out
of order or in unexpected interleavings. They are typically caused by actors only
supporting a subset of all possible message sequences.

Message order violations are common for instance in JavaScript. In a con-
temporary browser, each script runs inside one single-threaded event-loop per
page. After the initial parsing and interpretation of <script> tags, the event-
loop processes incoming events related to page lifecycle events, UI events, timer
events, XRS responses, etc. The order in which corresponding event handlers
are executed is non-deterministic, e.g., because of user actions or I/O timing,
which can give rise to an unexpected ordering of messages that is not handled
correctly by the program. Listing 1.4 extracted from [46] shows an example of
such a message order violation. The *fault* occurs in line 2, in this case because
of an interleaving between the execution of the user action onclick and the
HTML parsing.

The code in Listing 1.4 defines an input tag for a button in an HTML
page (line 2), and two scripts: one declaring two variables (init and y)
and the behavior of function f which is executed when the button is clicked
(line 4–line 12), and a second script which updates the variables init and y.
Since the parsing of the input tag and the execution of the scripts happen in
different turns of the event-loop, a violation in the order of messages execution
can occur. For instance, if the button is clicked before the first script runs, the
function f is not yet declared, causing the JavaScript interpreter to crash.

Note that message order violations in JavaScript only affect a *single* actor,
because a JavaScript program runs in a *single* event-loop, which processes all
types of events. General message order violations can also involve more than two
actors.

```
1   <html><body>
2     <input type="button" id="b1" onclick="javascript:f()">
3     ... <!-- many elements -->
4     <script>
5     function f() {
6       if (init)
7         alert(y.g);
8       else
9         alert("not ready");
10    }
11      var init = false, y = null;
12    </script>
13      ...
14    <script>
15      y = { g: 42 };
16      init = true;
17    </script>
18  </body></html>
19
```

Listing 1.4. Message order violation within a single event-loop in JavaScript (from [46]). On line 2, the onclick event can be triggered by the user before the function f is parsed and made available, causing an error.

Bad message interleaving. We define a *bad message interleaving* as the condition when a message is processed between two messages which are expected to be processed one after the other, causing some misbehavior of the application or even a crash.

In the original actor model, when an actor sends a message to a recipient actor, the message is placed in a mailbox and is guaranteed to be eventually delivered by the actor system. All messages are thus expected to be delivered in the order in which the sender actor sent them. However, there are two sources of bad interleavings. First, messages from different senders may be interleaved in between messages from one sender. In other words, even if the actor model enforces that messages from a sender actor are received in a FIFO order, messages from different sender actors may occur between them. The second source of bad interleavings of messages occurs in variants of the actor model which do not guarantee in-order delivery of the messages. This can be found in actor models used to build distributed systems, like Scala or ActorFoundry [35] in which communication between actors is not enforced to work in a FIFO manner.

Listing 1.5 shows an example of bad message interleavings in ActorFoundry (extracted from [35]). The listing shows an example of bad message interleaving in a network communication between two actors, Server and Client. In line 10, the Client sends an asynchronous message to the Server to store the value 1. In line 11, the Client does a call, which waits for a result, to retrieve the value from the Server. The *fault* is triggered by line 13, because it can happen that the Server processes the set message between the two get messages. Consequently, the values of v1 and v2 will be inconsistent.

Note that in the context of JavaScript, bad message interleavings can also occur within a single event-loop if programs can receive notifications for external

```
1  class Server extends Actor {
2    int value = 0;
3    @message void set(int v)  { value = v; }
4    @message int  get()       { return value; }
5  }
6  class Client extends Actor {
7    ActorName server;
8    Client(ActorName s) { server = s; }
9    @message void start() {
10     send(server, "set", 1);
11     int v1 = call(server, "get");
12     int v2 = call(server, "get");
13     assert v1 == v2;
14   }
15 }
```

Listing 1.5. Bad message interleaving example in ActorFoundry (from [35]). The
Server actor can interleave the messages set and get send by the Client. If that
is the case v1 will a value that differs from v2.

events, e.g. events from the network, from timers or from sensors. Such issues
have been previously reported by [31].

Memory inconsistency. A memory inconsistency is a condition in which different actors have inconsistent views of shared resources. This can be caused
because the effects of the turn that modifies a *conceptually shared resource*
may not be visible to other actors which also alter the same resource. Previous research on Erlang has collected such kinds of problems [24,32,33].

Listing 1.6 shows a modified fragment of an Erlang program used by
D'Osualdo et al. [24] to verify the property of mutual exclusion in actors. The
program (originally introduced by Huch [32]) spawns one database process and
several client processes. The purpose of the program is to save information in a
database, which acts as a conceptually shared resource by different client actors.
The database consists of a map of key-value tuples. When a client process sends
an allocate message to the database, the database checks if the key exists
already (line 8). If the value does not exist (line 25) then it is saved. The free
message in the client computes the value to be saved (line 10) and then the
client process sends the tuple to the database. If a second process does lookup
before the first value is saved, the lookup function will fail due to the key not
having been inserted yet. The *fault* occurs in line 19, when the database process
receives the key and value to be stored. Another client that has a different value
with the same key can save it. Thus, the value sent by the first process will be
overwritten by the value of another client process. To fix this error, the message
pattern should be declared inside a receive statement after line 10 to save the
value sent by the client and avoid other processes making a lookup.

```
1  main() ->
2      DB = spawn(fun()->dataBase(#{})end),
3      spawnmany(fun()->client(DB) end).
4
5  dataBase(M) ->
6    receive
7        {allocate,Key,P} ->
8            case lookup(Key,M) of
9                fail ->
10                   P!free,
11                   dataBase(M);
12               succ ->
13                   P!allocated,
14                   dataBase(M)
15           end;
16       {lookup,Key,P} ->
17           P!lookup(Key,M),
18           dataBase(M);
19       {value,Key,V} ->
20           dataBase(maps:put(Key,V, M))
21   end.
22
23 lookup(K,M) ->
24   case maps:find(K,M) of
25       error -> fail;
26       _V      -> succ
27   end.
```

Listing 1.6. Memory inconsistency example in Erlang (based on [24, 32]). Line 19 shows a message pattern that allows different processes to store different values for the same key.

3.3   Comparison with Existing Terminology in Actor Literature

As pointed out in the introduction, the goal of establishing a taxonomy is to provide a common vocabulary for concurrency bugs in actor-based programs. In what follows we relate our terminology to the one presented in other efforts tackling concurrency bugs for actor-based programs.

Bad message interleavings have been denoted as *ordering problems* by Lauterburg et al. [35] and Long et al. [38] and as *atomicity violation* by Zheng et al. [60] and Hong et al. [31]. We consider ordering problems to be too coarse-grained terminology. We decided to use the term bad message interleaving to avoid confusion with atomicity violations in thread-based concurrent programs due to low-level memory accesses errors.

Message order violations have been collected under many different names in literature: *data races* by Petrov et al. [44], *harmful races* by Raychev et al. [46], *order violations* by Hong et al. [31], and *message ordering bugs* by Tasharofi et al. [55]. We consider message order violations to be a descriptive name while avoiding confusion with low-level data races present in thread-based programs.

Memory inconsistency problems have been denoted as *race conditions* by Hughes and Bolinder [33]. D'Osualdo et al. [24] tackled this problem by proving a correctness property referred to as "mutual exclusion".

In literature, the term *orphan messages* [17] refers to messages that an actor sends but that the receiver actor(s) will never handle. Rather than a kind of concurrency bug, we consider orphan messages as an observable property of an actor system which may be a symptom of a concurrency bug like communication deadlocks or message ordering violations. We use this terminology in the next section when we classify concurrency bugs reported in literature with our taxonomy. Orphan messages can for example be present in actor languages that allow flexible interfaces such as Erlang, the Scala Actors framework and the Akka library [21]. An actor may change the set of messages it accepts after another actor has already sent a message which can only be received by an interface which is no longer supported.

4   Concurrency Bugs in Actor-based Programs

In this section, we review various concurrency bugs reported in literature, and classify them according to the taxonomy introduced in Sect. 3. The goal is twofold: (1) to classify concurrency bugs collected in prior research in the bug categories according to our taxonomy and (2) to identify bug patterns and observable behaviors that appear in programs exhibiting a particular concurrency bug. The latter is useful to design mechanisms for testing, verification, static analysis, or debugging of such concurrency issues.

Table 3 shows the catalog of analyzed concurrency bugs collected from literature. In the first column we categorized these bugs according to the taxonomy presented in Table 1. For each bug scenario we describe the bug pattern as a generalized description of the fault by identifying the actions that trigger the error. In the remainder, we highlight the identified bug patterns in italic. We also describe the observable behavior of the program that has the concurrency issue, i.e. the failure.

4.1   Lack of Progress Issues

To the best of our knowledge, the literature reports on communication deadlocks mostly in the context of Erlang programs. Bug-4 in Table 3 is an example of a communication deadlock collected by Christakis and Sagonas [15], which corresponds to the example depicted in Listing 1.1. Christakis and Sagonas distinguish two causes for communication deadlocks in Erlang programs:

- *receive-statement with no messages* i.e. empty mailbox,
- *receive with the wrong kind* i.e. the messages of the mailbox are different to the ones expected by the receive statement.

We classify these conditions as bug patterns for orphan messages, which can lead to communication deadlocks in Erlang.

Christakis and Sagonas [14] mention also other conditions that can cause mailbox overflows or potentially indicate logical errors. Such conditions include *no matching receive*, i.e. the process does not have any receive clause matching a message in its mailbox, or *receive-statement with unnecessary patterns*, i.e. the `receive` statement contains patterns that are never used.

Bug-9 is similar in kind to bug-4. Bug-9 was identified by Gotovos et al. [28] when implementing a test program in Erlang which has a server process that receives and replies to messages inside a loop. The server process blocks indefinitely because it waits for a message that is never sent. They also identify it as problematic, *when a message is sent to an already finished process*, which is exhibited by bug-10. This can happen due to two possible situations. First, if a client process sends a message to an already finished server process, the client process will throw an exception. Second, if the server process exits without replying after the message was received, the client process will block waiting for a reply that is never sent. We categorize bug-4, bug-9, and bug-10 as communication deadlocks and the observable behaviors as orphan messages.

D'Osualdo et al. [24] identified three other bug patterns leading to abnormal process termination in Erlang programs, which might cause deadlocks: *sending a message to a non-pid value, applying a function with the wrong arity* and *spawning a non-functional value*. These bug patterns could result in a communication deadlock or in a message order violation if the termination notification is not handled correctly.

Aronis and Sagonas [5] studied built-ins operations that can cause races in Erlang programs. Because the studied built-ins can access memory that is shared by processes, races can be observed in form of different outputs. Their classification on observable interferences of Erlang/OTP built-ins can help to diagnose communication deadlocks, message order violations, and memory inconsistencies.

4.2   Message Protocol Violations

Message order violation. In Erlang, updating certain resources such as the global name registry requires careful coordination to avoid concurrency issues. For example, we categorize bug-1 as a message order violation, which as a result makes a race on the global process registry visible [13]. The bug is caused because two processes try to register processes for the same global name more than once, which is done with non-atomic operations. For correctness, these processes would need to coordinate with each other.

Bug-11 reported by Christakis et al. [12] is another example of a message order violation exhibited when a *spawned process terminates before the parent process registers its process id*. The application expects the parent process to register the id of the spawned process before the spawned process is finalized, but as the execution of `spawn` and `register` functions are not atomic, an unexpected termination can cause a message order violation.

Zheng et al. [60] studied concurrency issues that can appear in JavaScript programs. In their example, which corresponds to bug-14, two events are executed but the application cannot return the responses in time, e.g. *the second message is executed with the value of the first message*. They argue that the cause of this issue can be the network latency and the delay in managing the responses by the JavaScript engine. If the events operate on the same data, it can lead to inconsistencies e.g. deleting an object of a previous event. We consider this kind of race as a message order violation, because the order of the messages is not consistent with the protocol of the web application.

In the context of JavaScript, Petrov et al. [44] identified 4 different message order violations. An *interleaving between the execution of a script and the event for rendering an input text box* is shown in bug-17, which can lead to inconsistencies when saving the text a user entered. Also problematic is the potential *interleaving of creating an HTML element and executing a script that uses the element* shown in bug-18. If the HTML element has not yet been created, it will cause an exception. Moreover, bug-19 corresponds to the scenario where *executing a function can race with is definition*. This can happen when the function is invoked first because the HTML loads faster, and the script where it is declared is only loaded later. For example in bug-20, *the onload event of an HTML element is triggered before the code is loaded*, which causes the event handler to never run correctly.

Raychev et al. [46] detected similar race conditions to the one of Petrov et al. [44], which we categorize as message order violations. Their bug example is depicted in Listing 1.4 and corresponds to bug-16. Hong et al. [31] also collected message ordering violations in three different existing websites. One of its examples shows a scenario where *a user input invokes a function before it is defined*. This last example is detailed in bug-23. From all these collected bugs, we conclude that a common issue in JavaScript programs is the *bad interleaving of two events in an unexpected order*.

Tasharofi et al. [55] identified twelve bugs in five Scala projects using the Akka actor library, which we categorize as message ordering problems. Bug-13 gives details of one of these bugs. The study found two bug patterns in Scala and Akka programs that can cause concurrency bugs in actors. First, *when changing the order of two receives in a single actor (consecutive or not)*, which can provoke a message order violation. Second, *when an actor sends a message to another actor which does not have the suitable receive for that message*. This last issue corresponds to an orphan message, and can also lead to other misbehaviors such as communication deadlocks.

Bad message interleaving. Bug-12 corresponds to the example of bad message interleaving collected by Lauterburg et al. [35] which was shown in Listing 1.5. The bug pattern occurs when *an actor executes a third message between two consecutive messages due to the actor model implementation being not FIFO*.

Zheng et al. [60] also identified bad message interleavings such as the one exhibited in bug-15. The bug pattern corresponds to the *use of a variable not initialized by other methods before it was defined*. This delay of receiving a response can be caused by a busy network and leads to an exception in the application. Hong et al. [31] also observed bad message interleavings in JavaScript programs. Bug-21 shows a pattern in which a variable is undefined because *after a user has uploaded a file to a workspace, the user changes the workspace before the file has been completely uploaded.* In the case of bug-22, a variable is `null` because an *event handler updates the DOM between two inputs events that manipulate the same DOM element.*

Memory inconsistency. To the best of our knowledge, memory inconsistency issues have only been reported in the context of Erlang programs. Christakis and Sagonas [13] shows an example of high-level races between processes using the Erlang Term Storage in bug-2. In this case the error is due to *inserting and lookup in tables that have public access,* thus it is possible that two or more processes try to read and write from them simultaneously. A second example detailed in bug-3, shows a similar issue that can happen when accessing tables of the Mnesia database. The cause is due to the *use of reading and writing operations that can cause race conditions.* We categorize both issues as memory inconsistency problems.

Hughes and Bolinder [33] detected four bugs corresponding to memory inconsistencies in *dets,* the disk storage back end used in the Erlang database Mnesia. Bug-5 refers to *insert operations that run in parallel* instead of being queued in a single queue. They can cause inconsistent return values or even exceptions. The observable behavior of bug-6 corresponds to an inconsistency of visualizing the dets content. This issue can occur when *reopening a file that is already open and executing insert and get_contents operations in parallel.* Bug-7 and bug-8 are caused due to failure on integrity checks. Of the four bugs that were found, these two are the ones that can occur with the least probability. Bug-7 is reproduced only in one specific scenario when *running three processes in parallel,* and bug-8 can occur only in those languages implementations that *can keep new and old versions of the server state.*

Huch [32] and D'Osualdo et al. [24] conducted studies to verify mutual exclusion in Erlang programs. Listing 1.6 shows an example. The bug pattern identified corresponds to the *wrong definition of the behavior of the actor,* and the observable property is that two actors can store different values for the same key which leads to inconsistencies, i.e. the actors can share the same resource.

4.3   Actor Variants and Possible Bugs

Based on our review of concurrency bugs above, we summarize which concurrency bugs can occur for each variant of the actor model. Furthermore, we identify the patterns that can cause a concurrency bug and the behavior that can be observed in the programs that have these bugs.

In languages that implement the *process* actor model, e.g. Erlang and Scala, programs can exhibit communication deadlocks because the actor implementation provides blocking operations. A common observable behavior of this concurrency bug are the orphan messages. This means an actor with this issue is blocked, i.e. the process is in a waiting state. These languages can also suffer from message order violations and memory inconsistencies. For message order violations possible bug patterns are the delays in managing responses, or the unsupported interleaving of messages i.e. the actor protocol does not correspond to the executed message interleavings. These can result in a program crash or inconsistent computational results. Memory inconsistencies are typically caused by a wrong message order when accessing shared resources.

Languages such as AmbientTalk or JavaScript that use the *communicating event-loop* model do not provide blocking primitives, and thus, do not suffer from communication deadlocks. However, other lack of progress issues such as behavioral deadlocks and livelocks can occur. Bug patterns for a behavioral deadlock or a livelock are typically mistakes in the sequential code of the actor, or a message that was sent to the wrong actor at the wrong time. The resulting observable behavior can be a wrong program output in which one or more actors do not progress with their computation. Behavioral deadlocks are possible in all variants of actor models. They are one of the most difficult bugs to identify, because actors are not blocked, but do not make any progress. Livelocks are similarly hard to diagnose as behavioral deadlocks.

Similarly to the process actor variant, event-loop based programs can suffer from message order violations and bad message interleavings. Generally, message order violations, bad message interleaving, and memory inconsistencies are race conditions that can happen in all actor-based programs including in programs using the class or *active object* actor model variants.

5   Advanced Development Techniques

This section surveys the current state of the art of techniques that support the development of actor-based programs. The goal is to identify the relevant *subfields of study* and *problems* in the literature. Furthermore, for each of these techniques we analyzed based on the literature how they relate to the bug categories of our taxonomy to identify open issues.

Specifically, we survey techniques for static analysis, testing tools, debuggers, and visualization. Table 2 gives an overview of the categories of bugs that static analysis and testing techniques address. It leaves out debugging and visualization techniques, since they are typically not geared towards a specific set of bugs.

5.1   Static Analysis

The static analysis approaches surveyed in this section include all approaches that identify concurrency issues without executing a program. This includes approaches based on typing, abstract interpretation, symbolic execution, and model checking. The following descriptions are organized by the category of concurrency bugs these approaches address.

Lack of progress issues. In the field of actor languages, Erlang has been subject to extensive studies. Dialyzer is a static analysis tool that uses type inference in addition to type annotations to analyze Erlang code [47]. The static analysis uses information on control flow and data flow to identify problematic usage of Erlang built-in functions that can cause concurrency issues. Dialyzer also has support for detecting message order violations as well as memory inconsistencies [13,48]. Christakis and Sagonas [15] extended Dialyzer to also detect communication deadlocks in Erlang using a technique based on *communication graphs*.

Another branch of work uses type systems to prevent concurrency issues. For actor languages, this includes for instance the work of Colaço et al. [17]. Based on a type system for a primitive actor calculus, they can prevent many situations in which messages would be received but never processed, i.e., so-called orphan messages. However, static analysis cannot detect all possible orphan messages. Therefore, the approach relies on *dynamic type checks* to detect the remaining cases. Similar work was done for Erlang, where orphan messages are also detected based on a type system [19].

Dam and Fredlund [20] proposed an approach using static analysis to verify properties such as the boundedness of mailboxes. The verification of this property can avoid the presence of orphan messages in a program. Their technique applies *local model checking in combination with temporal logic and extensions to the μ-calculus* for basic Erlang systems.

Similarly, Stiévenart et al. [52] used *abstract interpretation* techniques to statically verify the absence of errors in actor-based programs and upper bounds of actor mailboxes. As mentioned before the verification of mailbox bounds can avoid the presence of orphan messages. The proposed technique is based on different mailbox abstractions which allows to preserve the order and multiplicity of the messages. Thus, this verification technique can be useful to avoid message order violations.

Message protocol violation. D'Osualdo et al. [24] also worked on Erlang and used static analysis and *infinite-state model checking*. Their goal is to check specific properties for programs that are expressed with annotations in the code. With this approach, they are able to verify for instance correct mutual exclusion semantics modeled with messages. However, their current approach cannot model arbitrary message order violations, because the used analysis abstracts too coarsely from messages.

Garoche et al. [26] verify safety properties statically for an actor calculus by using *abstract interpretation*. Their work focuses on orphan messages and specific message order violations. Their technique is especially suited for detecting unreadable behavior, detecting unboundedness of resources, and determining whether linearity constraints hold.

Zheng et al. [60] developed a static analysis for JavaScript relying on *call graphs and points-to sets*. The analysis detects bad message interleavings and message order violations. With the properties of JavaScript, one can consider this analysis as a special case for actor systems where only a single actor is analyzed with respect to its reaction to incoming messages. WebRacer [44] is a tool that uses a *memory access model and a notion of happens-before relations* for detecting races at the level of the DOM tree nodes. The detected bugs correspond to bad message interleavings and message order violations in our taxonomy. EventRacer [46] is another tool that aims at finding bad message interleavings or message order violations in JavaScript applications. In this case the authors proposed a race detection algorithm based on *vector clocks*.

5.2 Testing Tools

This section describes work on testing actor based-programs to identify concurrency bugs. Some of the approaches are based on recording the interleaving of messages, the usage of state model checkers, and techniques to analyze message schedules.

Lack of progress issues. Sen and Agha [49] present an approach to detect communication deadlocks in a language closely related to actor semantics. They use a *concolic testing* approach that combines symbolic execution for input data generation with concrete execution to determine branch coverage. The key aspect of their technique is to minimize the number of execution paths that need to be explored while maintaining full coverage.

Concuerror [12] is a systematic testing tool for Erlang that can detect abnormal process termination as well as blocked processes, which might indicate a communication deadlock. To identify these issues, Concuerror *records process interleavings* for test executions and implements a stateless search strategy to explore all interleavings.

Message protocol violation. Claessen et al. [16] use a *test-case-generation approach* based on QuickCheck in combination with a custom user-level scheduler to identify race conditions. The focus is specifically on bad message interleavings and process termination issues. To make their approach intuitive for developers, they visualize problematic traces. Hughes and Bolinder [33] use the same approach and apply it to a key component of the Mnesia database for Erlang. They demonstrate that the system is able to find race conditions at the message level that can occur when interacting with the shared memory primitives used by Mnesia.

Basset [35,36] is an automated testing tool based on Java PathFinder, a *state model checker*, that can discover bad message interleavings in Scala and ActorFoundry programs. Tasharofi et al. [54] improve Basset with a technique to reduce schedules to be explored, which improves the performance of Basset. Their key insight is to exploit the transitivity of message send dependencies to prune the search space for relevant execution schedules. For the Scala-Akka programs there is another testing tool called Bita, which can also detect message order violations. Their proposal is based on a technique called schedule coverage, which analyzes the order of the receive events of an actor [55].

The Setac framework [53] for the Scala Actors framework enables testing for race conditions on actor messages, specifically message order violations. A test case defines *constraints on schedules and assertions* to be verified, while the framework identifies and executes all relevant schedules on the granularity of message processing. The Akka actor framework for Scala also provides a test framework called TestKit.[1] However, it does not seem to provide any sophisticated automatic testing capabilities, which seems to indicate that the current techniques might not yet be ready for adoption in industry.

Cassar and Francalanza [11] investigate how to minimize the overhead of instrumentation to detect race conditions. Instead of relying exclusively on synchronous instrumentation, they use *asynchronous monitoring* in combination with a logic to express correctness constraints on the resulting event traces.

Hong et al. [31] proposed a JavaScript testing framework called WAVE for the same classes of issues mentioned by [44,46]. The framework *generates test cases based on operation sequences.* In case of a concurrency bug, they can observe different results for the generated test cases.

5.3   Debuggers

This section reviews the main features provided by current debuggers for actor-based systems. It includes techniques for both online and postmortem debugging.

Causeway [51] is a postmortem debugger for distributed communicating event-loop programs in E [41]. It focuses on displaying the *causal relation of messages* to enable developers to determine the cause of a bug. Causality is modeled as the partial order of events based on Lamport's happened-before relationship [34]. We consider that this approach can be useful for detecting message protocol violations.

REME-D [27] is an online debugger for distributed communicating event-loop programs written in AmbientTalk [57]. REME-D provides message-oriented debugging techniques such as the *state inspection*, in which the developer can inspect an actor's mailbox and objects, while the actor is suspended. It also supports a catalog of breakpoints, which can be set on asynchronous and future-type messages sent between actors. Like Causeway, REME-D allows inspecting the history of messages that were sent and received when an actor is suspended, also known as *causal link browsing* [27]. Therefore, we consider debugging techniques provided in REME-D to be helpful for detecting message order violations. Also the technique of inspecting the state of the actor can facilitate debugging any lack of progress issues such as behavioral deadlocks and livelocks.

Kómpos [40] is an online debugger for SOMns. For debugging actor-based programs, Kómpos provides a wide set of *message-oriented breakpoints and stepping operations.* For example, Kómpos breakpoints allow developers to inspect the program state before a message is sent or after the message is received, but before it is processed on the receiver side. Moreover, is possible to pause the program execution before a promise is resolved with a value or before the first statement of a callback to that promise is executed, i.e. once the promise has been resolved. Breakpoints to pause on the first and last statement of methods

---

[1] *Akka.io: Testing Actor Systems*, Lightbend Inc., access date: 8 February 2017, http://doc.akka.io/docs/akka/current/scala/testing.html.

Table 2. Overview of the bug categories addressed in literature. A 'p' indicates that a bug category is addressed only partially. Typically, the approaches are limited by, for instance, a too coarse abstraction or a description language not expressive enough to capture all bugs in a category.

	Communi. Deadlock	Behav. Deadlock	LiveLock	Message Or. Violation	Bad Msg. Inter.	Mem. Incon.
Static Analysis						
Christakis and Sagonas [15]	X					
Christakis and Sagonas [13]				X		X
Colaço et al. [17]	p					
Dagnat and Pantel [19]	p					
Dam and Fredlund [20]	p					
Stiévenart et al. [52]	p			p		
D'Osualdo et al. [24]	p			p		p
Garoche et al. [26]	p			p		
Zheng et al. [60]				p	p	
Petrov et al. [44]				X	X	
Raychev et al. [46]				X		
Testing Tools						
Sen and Agha [49]	X					
Claessen et al. [16]					X	
Christakis et al. [12]	X					
Lauterburg et al. [36]					X	
Tasharofi et al. [55]					X	
Tasharofi et al. [53]				p	p	
Tasharofi et al. [54]				p	X	
Hughes and Bolinder [33]				p		X
Hong et al. [31]				X	X	
Cassar and Francalanza [11]				p	p	p

activated by an asynchronous message sent can be also set. Stepping operations can be triggered from the mentioned breakpoint locations. Furthermore, one can continue the actor's execution and pause in the next turn or pause before the execution of the first statement of a callback registered to a promise. This set of debugging operations gives more flexible tools to actor developers to deal with lack of progress issues such as behavioral deadlocks and livelocks. In addition, a specific actor visualization is offered that shows actor turns and messages sends. This can be useful when trying to identify the root cause of a message protocol violation.

In the context of JavaScript, the Chrome DevTools online debugger supports Web Workers,[2] which are actors that communicate with the main actor through message passing. The Chrome debugger allows pausing *workers*. In the case of *shared workers* it also provides mechanisms to inspect, terminate, and set breakpoints.[3] For debugging messages and promises on the event-loop, Chrome also supports *asynchronous stack traces*. This means, it shows the stack at the point a callback was scheduled on the event-loop. Since this works transitively, it allows inferring the point and context of how a callback got executed. We consider that stack information could help finding both message order violation and lack of progress issues.

Erlang also has an online debugger[4] that supports *line, conditional, and function breakpoints*. The Erlang processes can be inspected from a list and for each process a view with its current state as well as its current location in the code can be opened, which allows one to inspect and interact with each process independently. It also supports stepping through processes and inspecting their state. We consider that process inspection information could help finding both message protocol violations and lack of progress issues.

The ScalaIDE also includes facilities for debugging of actor-based programs.[5] It is a classic online debugger with support for stepping, line and conditional breakpoints. Furthermore, one can follow a message send and *stop in the receiving actor*. Additionally, the debugger supports asynchronous stack traces similar to Chrome [25]. We consider these techniques useful for debugging message protocol violations. They can also be used to identify behavioral deadlocks and livelocks when inspecting the state of the receiving actor.

The recently proposed Actoverse debugger [50] enables *reverse debugging* of Akka programs written in Scala. It uses snapshots of the state of actors to enable back-in-time debugging in a postmortem mode. Furthermore, Actoverse provides message-oriented breakpoints and a message timeline that visualizes

---

[2] *Web Workers*, W3C, access date: 14 February 2017, https://www.w3.org/TR/workers/.

[3] http://blog.chromium.org/2012/04/debugging-web-workers-with-chrome.html.

[4] *Debugger*, Ericsson AB, access date: 14 February 2017, http://erlang.org/doc/apps/debugger/debugger_chapter.html.

[5] *Asynchronous Debugger*, ScalaIDE, access date: 14 February 2017, http://scala-ide.org/docs/current-user-doc/features/async-debugger/index.html.

the messages exchanged by actors similar to a sequence diagram. The authors aim to ease finding the cause of message protocol violations in Akka programs.

5.4 Visualization

This section discusses mechanisms and approaches to visualize actor-based systems for debugging. Some of the techniques represent actor communication flow with petri nets. Other techniques detail an actor's state, its mailbox, and the traces of causal messages that are sent and received.

Miriyala et al. [42] proposed the use of *predicate transition nets* for visualizing actors execution. Based on the classic model of actors the proposal focus on the representation of the actor behavior and sent messages. The activation of each transition in the petri net corresponds to a behavior execution. The authors emphasize that the order of net transitions should be represented in the same order as the execution of messages of the actor system. The main idea is that the user interacts with a visual editor for building the execution of an actor system in the petri net.

Coscas et al. [18] present a similar approach in which the predicate transition nets are used to *simulate actors execution in a step by step mode*. When a user fires a specific transition he or she only observes a small part of whole net. The approach also verifies messages that do not match with the ones expected by the actor, i.e. messages that do not match the actor's interface.

The Causeway debugger also visualizes the program's execution based on views for *process order, message order, stack and source code view* [51]. The *process order* view shows all messages executed for each actor in chronological order, e.g. a parent item with asynchronous message sends. The *message order* view shows the causal messages for a message sent, i.e. other messages that have been executed before the message was sent and provoked the send of the message we want to debug. In this view it is also possible to distinguish processes by color, which helps users to visualize when a message flow (known as activation order) corresponds to a different process. The *stack view* shows a partial causality of messages. It is considered partial because the call chain shown in the stack only visualizes the messages that have been executed, it does not show the other possible messages that can cause the invocation of a message (known as happened-before relation). The *source code view* shows the code where the message was sent in the code. Thanks to the synchronization achieved between all the views it is possible to transit through the messages related to the execution of the actor's behavior that led to the bug.

Gonzalez Boix et al. [27] show the actor state in their REME-D debugger. The *actor view* shows messages that are going to be executed in the actor's mailbox. At the same time it is also shown the state of the actor and its objects. This view is useful for the user in order to be able to interact with the objects and messages of the actor that is inspected. One of the main advantages of this online debugger is the possibility of pausing and resuming the actor's execution.

Recently, Beschastnikh et al. [8] developed ShiViz, a visualization tool where developers can visualize logs of distributed applications. The mechanism is based on *representing happens-before relationships of messages* through interactive time-space diagrams. The tool also offers search fields by which messages can be searched in the diagram using keywords. Additionally, it is possible to *find ordering patterns*, which could help to identifying wrong behaviors in an execution.

6   Conclusion and Future Work

To enable research on debugging support for actor-based programs, we proposed a taxonomy of concurrency bugs for actor-based programs. Although the actor model avoids data races and deadlocks by design, it is still possible to have lack of progress issues and message-level race conditions in actor-based programs.

Our literature review shows that actor-based programs exhibit a range of different issues depending on the specific actor model variant. In languages like Erlang and Scala programs can suffer from communication deadlocks because the actor implementation uses blocking operations. In languages that implement the event-loop concurrency model this issue cannot occur. However, they can suffer from other lack of progress issues such as behavioral deadlocks and livelocks. Behavioral deadlocks and livelocks are really hard to identify because actors are not blocked, but still do not make any progress. Both lack of progress issues can be seen in all variants of the actor model. Message order violations, bad message interleaving and memory inconsistencies are race conditions that can happen also in programs that implement any of the variants of the actor model.

Most work on identifying concurrency bugs is done in the fields of static analysis and testing. Current techniques are effective for some specific cases, but often they are not yet general and do not necessarily scale to the complexity of modern systems. Debugging support for actor languages currently provides features such as message-oriented breakpoints, inspecting the history of messages together with recording their casual relations, and support for asynchronous stack traces. However, better tools are needed to identify the cause of complex concurrency bugs.

Future work. For future work, there seems to be an opportunity for debuggers that combine strategies such as recording the causality of messages with message-oriented breakpoints and rich stepping. Today, few debuggers support a full set of breakpoints that for example, allows one to debug messages stepping on the sender and on the receiver side. From the debuggers investigated in Sect. 5.3 only Kómpos allows us to set breakpoints on promises to inspect the computed value before it is used to resolve the promise. We argue that the implementation of flexible breakpoints that adjust to the needs of actor-based programs is needed. For instance, a breakpoint set on the sender side of the message will suspend an actor's execution before the message is sent. This can be useful when debugging lack of progress issues such as livelocks and behavioral deadlocks because the developer will be able to see whether the message has the correct values. Ideally, a debugger does not only allow us to inspect the turn flow, but to also combine the message stepping with the possibility of seeing the sequential operations that the actor executes inside of a turn. This gives developers better ways to identify the root cause of a bug.

Currently, only few debuggers allow developers to track the causality of messages. However, we consider this an important debugging technique. Recording the causal relationships of messages can help diagnosing, e.g., message protocol violations. Back-in-time debugging techniques could be of great benefit for this. They are often used for postmortem debugging, because they allow developers to identify message order violations.

Moreover, visualization techniques could be explored to give developers a better understanding of the debugging information. To offer better visual support for actor systems, a combination of information about the actor's state and its objects, visualizing the order of execution of messages and including the happens-before relation between them, together with stack information should give the user better comprehension about the program that is debugged. Nevertheless, further research is needed that supports the tooling for identifying complex concurrency bugs. For example, a visualization is needed to distinguish between the stepping of messages that are exchanged by actors and stepping through the sequential code of each actor. Ideally, a visualization could also highlight, based on the source code, that certain messages are independent of each other, because there is no direct ordering relationship between them.

Acknowledgments. This research is funded by a collaboration grant of the Austrian Science Fund (FWF) with the project I2491-N31 and the Research Foundation Flanders (FWO Belgium) with the project number G004816N.

Appendix

Table 3. Catalog of bugs found in actor-based programs

Bug Type	Id	Bug Pattern	Observable Behavior	Source Reporting the Bug	Language
Message order violation	bug-1	incorrect execution order of two processes when registering a name for a pid in the Process Registry	runtime exception	Fig. 1 in [13]	Erlang
Memory inconsistency	bug-2	insert and write in tables of Erlang Term Storage with public access	inconsistency of values in the tables	Fig. 2 in [13]	Erlang
Memory inconsistency	bug-3	insert and write in tables (dirty operations in Mnesia database)	inconsistency of values in the tables	Fig. 2 in [13]	Erlang
Communication deadlock	bug-4	receive statement with no messages	process in waiting state due to an orphan message	Fig. 1 in [15]	Erlang
Memory inconsistency	bug-5	testing insert operations in parallel (Mnesia database)	exception or inconsistent return values	Sect. 5 of [33]	Erlang
Memory inconsistency	bug-6	testing open_file in parallel with other operations of dets API (Mnesia database)	inconsistency when visualizing the table's contents	Sect. 5 of [33]	Erlang
Memory inconsistency	bug-7	open, close and reopen the file, besides running three processes in parallel (Mnesia database)	integrity checking failed due to premature_eof error	Sect. 5 of [33]	Erlang

(continued)

Table 3. (*continued*)

Bug Type	Id	Bug Pattern	Observable Behavior	Source Reporting the Bug	Language
Memory inconsistency	bug-8	changes in the dets server state	integrity checking failed (Mnesia database)	Sect. 5 of [33]	Erlang
Communication deadlock	bug-9	receive statement with no messages	process in waiting state due to an orphan message (server waits for ping requests)	Program 2 and Test code 2 in [28]	Erlang
Communication deadlock	bug-10	message sent to a finished process, the finished process exit without replying	process blocks due to an orphan message	Test code 5 in [28]	Erlang
Message order violation	bug-11	spawned process that terminates before its Pid is register by the parent process	process will crash and exits abnormally due to an orphan message	Fig. 1 in [12]	Erlang
Bad message interleaving	bug-12	actor execute a third message between two consecutive messages	inconsistent values of variables	Fig. 2 in [35]	Actor-Foundry
Message order violation	bug-13	incorrect order of execution of two message receives	the program throws an exception because of a null value	Listing 1 in [55]	Scala
Message order violation	bug-14	the second message is executed with the value of the first message	actions are performed over the wrong variable	Fig. 4 in [60]	JavaScript
Bad message interleaving	bug-15	use of a variable not initialized by other methods before it was defined	out of bounds exception	Fig. 4 in [60]	JavaScript

(*continued*)

Table 3. (*continued*)

Bug Type	Id	Bug Pattern	Observable Behavior	Source Reporting the Bug	Language
Message order violation	bug-16	race between HTML parsing and user actions	application crash	Fig. 1 in [46]	JavaScript
Message order violation	bug-17	race between execution of a script and rendering of an input text box	inconsistency in the value of the variable (storing text the user entered)	Fig. 2 in [44]	JavaScript
Message order violation	bug-18	race between creation of HTML element and using the element	throw an exception that can lead the application to crash	Fig. 3 in [44]	JavaScript
Message order violation	bug-19	invocation of a function before parsing of the same function	application crash	Fig. 4 in [44]	JavaScript
Message order violation	bug-20	iframe's load event fires before the script executes	event handler will never run	Fig. 5 in [44]	JavaScript
Bad message interleaving	bug-21	execution of an operation (changing the workspace) between two other operations (starting the file transmission and the completion of the transmission)	exception of variable undefined	Fig. 6 in [31]	JavaScript
Bad message interleaving	bug-22	event handler updates DOM between two input events that manipulate the same DOM element	error because of a null value	Fig. 3 in [31]	JavaScript
Message order violation	bug-23	user input invokes a function before it has been defined/loaded	application crashes (due to unexpected turn termination)	Fig. 2 in [31]	JavaScript

References

1. Abbaspour Asadollah, S., Sundmark, D., Eldh, S., Hansson, H., Afzal, W.: 10 Years of research on debugging concurrent and multicore software: a systematic mapping study. Software Qual. J. **25**(1), 49–82 (2017). https://doi.org/10.1007/s11219-015-9301-7

2. Abbaspour Asadollah, S., Sundmark, D., Eldh, S., Hansson, H., Enoiu, E.P.: A study of concurrency bugs in an open source software. In: Crowston, K., Hammouda, I., Lundell, B., Robles, G., Gamalielsson, J., Lindman, J. (eds.) OSS 2016. IAICT, vol. 472, pp. 16–31. Springer, Cham (2016). https://doi.org/10.1007/978-3-319-39225-7_2

3. Agha, G.: ACTORS: a model of concurrent computation in distributed systems. Ph.D. thesis, MIT, Artificial Intelligence Laboratory, June 1985

4. Armstrong, J., Virding, R., Wikström, C., Williams, M.: Concurrent Programming in ERLANG. Prentice Hall, Englewood Cliffs (1993)

5. Aronis, S., Sagonas, K.: The shared-memory interferences of Erlang/OTP built-ins. In: Chechina, N., Fritchie, S.L. (eds.) Erlang Workshop, pp. 43–54. ACM (2017). http://dblp.uni-trier.de/db/conf/erlang/erlang2017.html#AronisS17

6. Artho, C., Havelund, K., Biere, A.: High-level data races. Softw. Test., Verif. Reliab. **13**(4), 207–227 (2003). http://dblp.uni-trier.de/db/journals/stvr/stvr13.html#ArthoHB03

7. Avizienis, A., Laprie, J.C., Randell, B., Landwehr, C.: Basic concepts and taxonomy of dependable and secure computing. IEEE Trans. Dependable Secur. Comput. **1**(1), 11–33 (2004)

8. Beschastnikh, I., Wang, P., Brun, Y., Ernst, M.D.: Debugging distributed systems. Commun. ACM **59**(8), 32–37 (2016)

9. Bracha, G., von der Ahé, P., Bykov, V., Kashai, Y., Maddox, W., Miranda, E.: Modules as objects in newspeak. In: D'Hondt, T. (ed.) ECOOP 2010. LNCS, vol. 6183, pp. 405–428. Springer, Heidelberg (2010). https://doi.org/10.1007/978-3-642-14107-2_20

10. Brito, M., Felizardo, K.R., Souza, P., Souza, S.: Concurrent software testing: a systematic review. On testing software and systems: Short Papers, p. 79 (2010)

11. Cassar, I., Francalanza, A.: On synchronous and asynchronous monitor instrumentation for actor-based systems. In: Proceedings 13th International Workshop on Foundations of Coordination Languages and Self-Adaptive Systems, pp. 54–68. FOCLASA 2014, September 2014

12. Christakis, M., Gotovos, A., Sagonas, K.: Systematic testing for detecting concurrency errors in Erlang programs. In: 2013 IEEE Sixth International Conference on Software Testing, Verification and Validation (ICST), pp. 154–163. IEEE (2013)

13. Christakis, M., Sagonas, K.: Static detection of race conditions in Erlang. In: Carro, M., Peña, R. (eds.) PADL 2010. LNCS, vol. 5937, pp. 119–133. Springer, Heidelberg (2010). https://doi.org/10.1007/978-3-642-11503-5_11

14. Christakis, M., Sagonas, K.: Detection of asynchronous message passing errors using static analysis. In: Rocha, R., Launchbury, J. (eds.) PADL 2011. LNCS, vol. 6539, pp. 5–18. Springer, Heidelberg (2011). https://doi.org/10.1007/978-3-642-18378-2_3

15. Christakis, M., Sagonas, K.: Static Detection of Deadlocks in Erlang. Technical report, June 2011

16. Claessen, K., et al.: Finding race conditions in Erlang with QuickCheck and PULSE. In: Proceedings of the 14th ACM SIGPLAN International Conference on Functional Programming, ICFP 2009, pp. 149–160. ACM (2009)

17. Colaço, J.L., Pantel, M., Sallé, P.: A Set-Constraint-based analysis of Actors. In: Bowman, H., Derrick, J., et al. (eds.) Formal Methods for Open Object-based Distributed Systems. IFIPAICT, pp. 107–122. Springer, Boston (1997). https://doi.org/10.1007/978-0-387-35261-9_8

18. Coscas, P., Fouquier, G., Lanusse, A.: Modelling actor programs using predicate/-transition nets. In: Proceedings Euromicro Workshop on Parallel and Distributed Processing, pp. 194–200, January 1995

19. Dagnat, F., Pantel, M.: Static analysis of communications in Erlang programs, November 2002. http://rsync.erlang.org/euc/02/dagnat.ps.gz

20. Dam, M., Fredlund, L.å.: On the verification of open distributed systems. In: Proceedings of the 1998 ACM Symposium on Applied Computing, SAC 1998, pp. 532–540. ACM (1998)

21. De Koster, J., Van Cutsem, T., De Meuter, W.: 43 years of actors: a taxonomy of actor models and their key properties. In: Proceedings of the 6th International Workshop on Programming Based on Actors, Agents, and Decentralized Control, AGERE 2016, pp. 31–40. ACM (2016)

22. Dedecker, J., Van Cutsem, T., Mostinckx, S., D'Hondt, T., De Meuter, W.: Ambient-oriented programming in ambienttalk. In: Thomas, D. (ed.) ECOOP 2006. LNCS, vol. 4067, pp. 230–254. Springer, Heidelberg (2006). https://doi.org/10.1007/11785477_16

23. Dijkstra, E.W.: Cooperating sequential processes. In: Genuys, F. (ed.) Programming Languages: NATO Advanced Study Institute, pp. 43–112. Academic Press (1968)

24. D'Osualdo, E., Kochems, J., Ong, C.-H.L.: Automatic verification of Erlang-style concurrency. In: Logozzo, F., Fähndrich, M. (eds.) SAS 2013. LNCS, vol. 7935, pp. 454–476. Springer, Heidelberg (2013). https://doi.org/10.1007/978-3-642-38856-9_24

25. Dragos, I.: Stack Retention in Debuggers For Concurrent Programs, July 2013. http://iulidragos.com/assets/papers/stack-retention.pdf

26. Garoche, P.-L., Pantel, M., Thirioux, X.: Static safety for an actor dedicated process calculus by abstract interpretation. In: Gorrieri, R., Wehrheim, H. (eds.) FMOODS 2006. LNCS, vol. 4037, pp. 78–92. Springer, Heidelberg (2006). https://doi.org/10.1007/11768869_8

27. Gonzalez Boix, E., Noguera, C., De Meuter, W.: Distributed debugging for mobile networks. J. Syst. Softw. **90**, 76–90 (2014)

28. Gotovos, A., Christakis, M., Sagonas, K.: Test-driven development of concurrent programs using concuerror. In: Proceedings of the 10th ACM SIGPLAN Workshop on Erlang, pp. 51–61. ACM (2011)

29. Haller, P., Odersky, M.: Scala Actors: unifying thread-based and event-based programming. Theoretical Computer Science **410**(2–3), 202–220 (2009)

30. Hewitt, C., Bishop, P., Steiger, R.: A universal modular actor formalism for artificial intelligence. In: Proceedings of the 3rd International Joint Conference on Artificial Intelligence, IJCAI 1973, pp. 235–245. Morgan Kaufmann Publishers Inc. (1973)

31. Hong, S., Park, Y., Kim, M.: Detecting concurrency errors in client-side JavaScript web applications. In: 2014 IEEE Seventh International Conference on Software Testing, Verification and Validation (ICST), pp. 61–70. IEEE, March 2014

32. Huch, F.: Verification of Erlang programs using abstract interpretation and model checking. In: Proceedings of the Fourth ACM SIGPLAN International Conference on Functional Programming, ICFP 1999, pp. 261–272. ACM, New York (1999). http://doi.acm.org/10.1145/317636.317908

33. Hughes, J.M., Bolinder, H.: Testing a database for race conditions with quickcheck. In: Proceedings of the 10th ACM SIGPLAN Workshop on Erlang, Erlang 2011, pp. 72–77. ACM (2011)

34. Lamport, L.: Time, clocks, and the ordering of events in a distributed system. Commun. ACM **21**(7), 558–565 (1978)

35. Lauterburg, S., Dotta, M., Marinov, D., Agha, G.A.: A framework for state-space exploration of Java-based actor programs. In: 2009 IEEE/ACM International Conference on Automated Software Engineering, pp. 468–479, November 2009

36. Lauterburg, S., Karmani, R.K., Marinov, D., Agha, G.: Basset: a tool for systematic testing of actor programs. In: Proceedings of the Eighteenth ACM SIGSOFT International Symposium on Foundations of Software Engineering, FSE 2010, pp. 363–364. ACM (2010)

37. Leesatapornwongsa, T., Lukman, J.F., Lu, S., Gunawi, H.S.: TaxDC: a taxonomy of non-deterministic concurrency bugs in datacenter distributed systems. In: Conte, T., Zhou, Y. (eds.) ASPLOS, pp. 517–530. ACM (2016). http://dblp.uni-trier.de/db/conf/asplos/asplos2016.html#Leesatapornwongsa16

38. Long, Y., Bagherzadeh, M., Lin, E., Upadhyaya, G., Rajan, H.: On ordering problems in message passing software. In: Proceedings of the 15th International Conference on Modularity, pp. 54–65. ACM (2016)

39. Lu, S., Park, S., Seo, E., Zhou, Y.: Learning from mistakes: a comprehensive study on real world concurrency bug characteristics. In: Proceedings of the 13th International Conference on Architectural Support for Programming Languages and Operating Systems, ASPLOS XIII, pp. 329–339. ACM, New York (2008)

40. Marr, S., Torres Lopez, C., Aumayr, D., Gonzalez Boix, E., Mössenböck, H.: A concurrency-agnostic protocol for multi-paradigm concurrent debugging tools. In: Proceedings of the 13th ACM SIGPLAN International Symposium on on Dynamic Languages, DLS 2017, pp. 3–14. ACM (2017)

41. Miller, M.S., Tribble, E.D., Shapiro, J.: Concurrency among strangers. In: De Nicola, R., Sangiorgi, D. (eds.) TGC 2005. LNCS, vol. 3705, pp. 195–229. Springer, Heidelberg (2005). https://doi.org/10.1007/11580850_12

42. Miriyala, S., Agha, G., Sami, Y.: Visualizing actor programs using predicate transition nets. J. Vis. Lang. Comput. **3**(2), 195–220 (1992)

43. Peierls, T., Goetz, B., Bloch, J., Bowbeer, J., Lea, D., Holmes, D.: Java Concurrency in Practice. Addison-Wesley Professional, Reading (2005)

44. Petrov, B., Vechev, M., Sridharan, M., Dolby, J.: Race detection for web applications. In: ACM SIGPLAN Notices, vol. 47, pp. 251–262. ACM (2012)

45. Prasad, S.K., Gupta, A., Rosenberg, A.L., Sussman, A., Weems, C.C.: Topics in Parallel and Distributed Computing: Introducing Concurrency in Undergraduate Courses, 1st edn. Morgan Kaufmann Publishers Inc., San Francisco (2015)

46. Raychev, V., Vechev, M., Sridharan, M.: Effective race detection for event-driven programs. In: Proceedings of the 2013 ACM SIGPLAN International Conference on Object Oriented Programming Systems Languages and Applications, OOPSLA 2013, pp. 151–166. ACM (2013)

47. Sagonas, K.: Experience from developing the dialyzer: a static analysis tool detecting defects in Erlang applications. In: Proceedings of the ACM SIGPLAN Workshop on the Evaluation of Software Defect Detection Tools (2005)

48. Sagonas, K.: Using static analysis to detect type errors and concurrency defects in Erlang programs. In: Blume, M., Kobayashi, N., Vidal, G. (eds.) FLOPS 2010. LNCS, vol. 6009, pp. 13–18. Springer, Heidelberg (2010). https://doi.org/10.1007/978-3-642-12251-4_2

49. Sen, K., Agha, G.: Automated systematic testing of open distributed programs. In: Baresi, L., Heckel, R. (eds.) FASE 2006. LNCS, vol. 3922, pp. 339–356. Springer, Heidelberg (2006). https://doi.org/10.1007/11693017_25

50. Shibanai, K., Watanabe, T.: Actoverse: a reversible debugger for actors (2017)

51. Stanley, T., Close, T., Miller, M.: Causeway: A message-oriented distributed debugger. Technical report, HP Labs, April 2009

52. Stiévenart, Q., Nicolay, J., De Meuter, W., De Roover, C.: Mailbox abstractions for static analysis of actor programs (artifact). DART 3(2), 11:1–11:2 (2017). http://dblp.uni-trier.de/db/journals/darts/darts3.html#StievenartNMR17

53. Tasharofi, S., Gligoric, M., Marinov, D., Johnson, R.: Setac: A Framework for Phased Deterministic Testing Scala Actor Programs (2011). https://days2011.scala-lang.org/sites/days2011/files/ws1-2-setac.pdf

54. Tasharofi, S., Karmani, R.K., Lauterburg, S., Legay, A., Marinov, D., Agha, G.: TransDPOR: a novel dynamic partial-order reduction technique for testing actor programs. In: Giese, H., Rosu, G. (eds.) FMOODS/FORTE - 2012. LNCS, vol. 7273, pp. 219–234. Springer, Heidelberg (2012). https://doi.org/10.1007/978-3-642-30793-5_14

55. Tasharofi, S., Pradel, M., Lin, Y., Johnson, R.E.: Bita: coverage-guided, automatic testing of actor programs. In: 2013 28th IEEE/ACM International Conference on Automated Software Engineering, ASE 2013, pp. 114–124, November 2013

56. Tchamgoue, G.M., Kim, K.H., Jun, Y.K.: Testing and debugging concurrency bugs in event-driven programs. Int. J. Adv. Sci. Technol. 40, 55–68 (2012)

57. Van Cutsem, T., Mostinckx, S., Gonzalez Boix, E., Dedecker, J., De Meuter, W.: AmbientTalk: object-oriented event-driven programming in mobile ad hoc networks. In: International Conference of the Chilean Computer Science Society (SCCC), pp. 3–12. IEEE Computer Society (2007)

58. Yonezawa, A., Briot, J.P., Shibayama, E.: Object-oriented concurrent programming in ABCL/1. In: Conference Proceedings on Object-oriented Programming Systems, Languages and Applications, OOPSLA 1986, pp. 258–268. ACM, New York (1986)

59. Zhang, M., Wu, Y., Chen, K., Zheng, W.: What is wrong with the transmission? A comprehensive study on message passing related bugs. In: ICPP, pp. 410–419. IEEE Computer Society (2015). http://dblp.uni-trier.de/db/conf/icpp/icpp2015.html#ZhangWCZ15

60. Zheng, Y., Bao, T., Zhang, X.: Statically locating web application bugs caused by asynchronous calls. In: Proceedings of the 20th International Conference on World Wide Web, WWW 2011, pp. 805–814. ACM (2011)

interActors: A Model for Separating Communication Concerns of Concurrent Systems

Hongxing Geng[1,2] and Nadeem Jamali[1(✉)]

[1] Agents Laboratory, Department of Computer Science,
University of Saskatchewan, Saskatoon, SK, Canada
`hongxing.geng@usask.ca, jamali@cs.usask.ca`
[2] Library and Scholarly Resources, Athabasca University,
Athabasca, AB, Canada
`billg@athabascau.ca`

Abstract. Concurrent computations increasingly require complex and diverse interactions. Although there is a growing body of work on separating communication concerns of such computations from their functional concerns, existing solutions offer static protocols, which cannot handle dynamically evolving numbers and sets of communicating processes, and complex initialization steps are left mixed with functional concerns.

This paper presents a model, *interActors*, and related mechanisms, to support programming of complex communications of applications separately from their functional concerns. These communications are self-driven and can dynamically evolve in response to changing communication needs as the computation progresses. New types of communications requiring aggregation and decision-making can be easily programmed, either directly or by composing existing communications. This leads to better modularity and reusability of software. The paper introduces formal semantics for interActors, followed by a prototype implemented in Scala. A number of examples and a case study are used to illustrate the ease with which this approach can be used for programming concurrent systems with complex communication requirements.

Keywords: interActors · Actors · Interaction · Separation of concerns

1 Introduction

Programming concurrent systems is difficult in part because they increasingly involve complex and diverse interactions. Consider a crowd-sensed restaurant recommendation service based on data collected from diners' smartphones. Or a finer-grained 21st century version of democracy, where instead of electing politicians for years, citizens can contribute to fine-grained decision-making directly by proposing policies and voting on them. Or message-passing implementations

© Springer Nature Switzerland AG 2018
A. Ricci and P. Haller (Eds.): Programming with Actors, LNCS 10789, pp. 186–215, 2018.
https://doi.org/10.1007/978-3-030-00302-9_7

of well-known parallel computations such as the gravitational n-body simulation. Computations of this type need to group together processes (including devices, people, etc.) based on notions of physical or logical locality, and then solicit input, and carry out required aggregations – sometimes over several stages – to achieve their goals. In addition to requiring mechanisms for transforming groups of messages into meaningful aggregates, and for deciding when enough information has been collected to come to useful conclusions, such computation often also require support for dynamically evolving sets of participants in the interaction.

Given the growing need for such multi-party interactions of various types and complexities, we argue for the need to identify these concerns as purely communication/interaction concerns, and to separate the mechanisms required to support them in separate layers or systems for better modularity and reusability.

Although the importance of interactions has long been established for open systems [24] – and process calculi [14,16,17] and Actors [1] abstract away some lower-level concerns – interaction protocols continue to be treated as a concept secondary to the computations requiring them [5]. Communication protocols are often mixed with functional code, so that, in order to interact, processes have to use the available communication primitives for message passing, remote procedure calls, etc., in increasingly complex ways.

There is a growing body of work separating interaction concerns from functional concerns (e.g., [4,21]); however, the setting up of an interaction and making changes to it continues to be cumbersome. Orchestration of the interaction is still left to the interacting processes, while the communication infrastructure sits passively. Participants in an interaction are also typically assumed to be known in advance.

Our approach is to: move the driving force for interactions between processes to the communication side of the divide, and have interactions drive themselves; enable the setting up of rendezvous between processes at run-time, and treat it as a communication concern; and enable creation of libraries of novel types of communications with required aggregation and decision-making requirements, which can be launched and used by applications at run-time.

The rest of the paper is organized as follows: Sect. 2 presents related work. Section 3 describes what we mean by communications. Section 4 presents our model, interActors, and its operational semantics. Section 5 introduces our prototype implementation using Scala [18] and the Akka Actors library [23]. Section 6 presents CSL, a specification language we have developed to aid programming of communications. Section 7 presents a case study, and finally Sect. 8 concludes the paper.

2 Related Work

The problem of separating communication concerns has traditionally been addressed in research on coordination and interaction protocols.

Linda [12] was the first language to separate coordination concerns of applications from their functional concerns. Processes interact with each other through shared objects called *tuples*, which reside in a shared place called *tuple space*. Synchronization is achieved through a blocking read primitive. Although Linda is said to offer *time-decoupling* (processes can communicate asynchronously) and *space-decoupling* (processes do not need to know each other), it still mixes communication protocols with functional behaviours because the communication primitives must be incorporated within the processes' code.

A number of works [8, 19, 25] extend Linda with the idea of programmable environments. For example, a *tuple center* [19] is a coordination medium, which extends the standard tuple space with a behavior, and associates a call to a communication primitive with a set of computational activities called a *reaction*. A reaction may manipulate tuples in the tuple center or trigger further reactions in a chain. Because reactions can be added or removed dynamically, the behaviors of a tuple center can be changed on the fly.

For multiagent systems, Reo [4] offers a channel-based dataflow-oriented interaction model. Agents can interact with each other through connectors, which are constructed by composing primitive channels of various types for synchronization, asynchronization, filtering, transformation, etc. Communications are orchestrated by using channels with special features to direct messages flowing through a connector; however, some coordinator/initiator agent has to construct the required connectors by performing operations such as create, connect, and join. Creating special purpose channels and putting them together in a connector is non-trivial for more complex interactions, and making changes is cumbersome. There is also an implicit requirement that the participating agents connected by a connector are known in advance and do not change at run-time. These requirements make it difficult to use Reo for supporting interactions as would be required for large-scale recommendation services, voting, etc.

BSPL [21] offers a way of building interaction protocols declaratively. Protocols are first-class entities and can be composed to form more complex protocols. BSPL is information-oriented, meaning that it makes information exchange explicit and it can impose the required flow of information. Although these are important features, it too implicitly constrains the number of participating agents in a communication, and the types of protocols to those involving fixed numbers of participants. Local State Transfer (LoST) [22] offers an approach to enact communication protocols written in BSPL.

A number of approaches have been developed to coordinate systems based on the Actors model [1], all of which use the idea of computational reflection [15]. Actors are primitive software agents which communicate using asynchronous messages. Coordination approaches for Actors include protocol stacks [7], Reflective Communication Framework (RCF) [13], and ARC (Actors, Roles and Coordinators) [20].

A protocol stack [7], for example, enables communications between agents to be customized through metaobjects. A metaobject implements a communication protocol and can only customize communications for one agent. A protocol enforced on a group of agents is implemented using the collection of metaobjects customizing each agent. A metaobject itself can be customized by a meta-metaobject so that an agent can be customized through a metaobject protocol stack. A stack can be changed on the fly by installing a new metaobject or removing an old metaobject, allowing two consecutive messages of an agent to use different protocols. In this sense, metaobjects can customize communications on a per-message base.

Despite its benefits, this approach is rigid in that protocols need to be explicitly added or removed from the stack in response to changing communication requirements. Furthermore, both incoming and outgoing messages for a protocol share the same protocol stack, which can lead to excessive overhead. Changes in communication requirements of a computation require explicit replacement of metaobjects with new ones. Finally, because the protocols are per-agent, and not per-message, the messages which do not require them still have to pass through the entire protocol stack.

Synchronizers [11] is a language framework for multi-object coordination, which enforces declarative synchronization constraints called *synchronizers* on a group of objects. Conceptually, a synchronizer is a special object which observes messages and restricts message dispatch for other objects in accordance with user-specified message patterns. In other words, messages matching a synchronizer's message pattern fall under the synchronizer's control. Synchronizers have a global effect and are imposed on receivers. Also, synchronizers may overlap, which means that different synchronizers can constrain the same object. Synchronizers support two types of constraints: (a) disabling constraints block the constrained objects from handling messages which match a given pattern, and (b) atomicity constraints ensure that bundled messages to multiple objects should succeed atomically. Scoped synchronizers [10] adapt synchronizers for Internet-scale systems where components cannot be trusted. Specifically, they limit the scope of application of synchronization constraints.

3   Communications

Our approach is to program complex communications for concurrent applications separately from their functional concerns, which are served by actor-like agents.

A communication is made up of a set of inlets and outlets through which agents can connect to the communication, and handlers, which carry out the communication's logic. Messages are sent out to agents by a communication from its outlets, and received by it at its inlets.

Outlets and inlets (referred to together as *oilets*) and handlers have behaviors which define how they handle messages received by them. These behaviors are intended to define *handling* of the messages which form the communication between agents, rather than *processing* them to achieve the computation's functional goals. The behaviors are therefore restricted with the intention of only allowing these handling actions. Figure 1 shows some examples of simple behaviors. Each behavior has a possibly dynamically evolving set of *target* agents to send the received messages to, individually or in aggregate form.

Behavior	Description
forwarder(msg, ts)	forwards a received message *msg* to targets *ts*.
counter(msg, ts)	counts the number of received messages so far and sends the result to targets *ts*.
timer(msg, ts, t)	temporally holds the received message *msg* for *t* milliseconds and then sends it to targets *ts*.
applier(msg, ts, f)	applies function *f* to a received message *msg* and then sends the result to targets *ts*.
filter(msg, ts, f)	filters a received message *msg* based on function *f*. If *msg* meets the requirements of *f*, it is sent to targets *ts*; otherwise, discarded.
selector(msg, ts, select)	sends the received message *msg* to a subset of targets *ts* selected by function *select*.
sequencer(msg, ts, parts)	a sequencer sends the received message *msg* to a list of participants *parts* one by one. Once all participants have responded, the received message is sent to the sequencer's targets.
aggregator(msg, ts, cond, aggr)	on the arrival of a message, the message *msg* is added into a message list; then function *cond* is applied to the message list to determine whether a certain condition is met or not. If it is, all received messages so far (stored in the message list) is aggregated using function *aggr* and the aggregated result is sent to targets *ts*.

Fig. 1. Examples of simple behaviors

3.1   Compositional Definition

We define communications compositionally.

A primitive communication (shown in Fig. 2) is called a *channel*, which simply connects an inlet to an outlet; the clear circle represents an inlet and the filled circle an outlet. A channel enables the sending of asynchronous messages from an agent connecting to the inlet to another connecting to the outlet.

More complex communications can be created by applying three composition rule on channels: inlet merge, outlet merge, and outlet-inlet merge. Recall that inlets and outlets together are referred to as oilets. An inlet merge composition combines a number of communications at their inlets; the purpose is to enable a single sender to send messages to a number of recipients. An outlet merge merges a number of communications at their outlets; the purpose is to enable

Fig. 2. Channel

a single outlet to receive the messages from a number of non-deterministically selected sources. An outlet-inlet merge connects some outlets of the composing communications to some inlets.

This way of constructing complex communications is primarily for definitional purpose: although communications can be composed for reusability, complex communications can always be programmed directly as will be shown later.

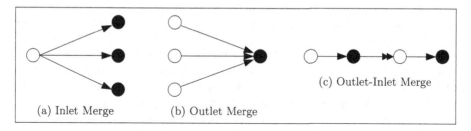

(a) Inlet Merge   (b) Outlet Merge   (c) Outlet-Inlet Merge

Fig. 3. Three composition rules

Inlet Merge. Figure 3a shows how an *inlet merge* composition merges a number of communications at their inlets. The number of communications being merged is not decided *a priori*, and is determined dynamically by the number of relevant recipients who fit some *pattern* [9]. The purpose is to enable a single sender to send messages to a number of recipients. A computation connecting to the composed communication's inlet can send messages, which are then delivered to the computations connected to its outlets. The inlet at the merging point has a behavior, which allows incoming messages to be processed before they are sent forward. This enables the communication to realize functions such as counting, aggregating, scattering (as in MPI scatter), etc. Furthermore, a message at the inlet may be sent selectively, which is similar to Akka routing [23].

Outlet Merge. Figure 3b shows an *outlet merge* composition, which merges a number of communications at their outlets. The purpose is to enable a single recipient to receive the messages sent by a number of non-deterministically selected senders in some order. The number of communications merging their outlets is not known *a priori*.

At the outlet of the composed communication, messages can be received by a computation. More interestingly, the outlet's behavior can also aggregate messages. In its degenerate form, the aggregation simply spits out each message received in its original form. In more interesting forms, it can process received messages in permitted ways, both to create aggregate messages to be forwarded, and to make decisions about whether and when to forward aggregates. For example, the aggregation could impose constraints on delivery of messages from different sources in a way similar to how the channels in Reo do [6], except that the number of computations participating in a communication do not have to be known *a priori*. Also, the protocols can be finer-grained and rely on decisions possible only at run-time. For example, a protocol could wait for a majority of voting computations to vote "yes" or "no," counting each vote equally, or weigh the votes of different voters differently.

Outlet-Inlet Merge. An *outlet-inlet merge* connects outlets of communications to inlets of other communications. These connections are specified as a set of bindings, each of which binds an outlet of one communication with an inlet of another communication. Figure 3c shows the simplest example of this, merging one outlet with one inlet. The double arrow in the figure depicts the *composition glue*, and shows the message flow from the outlet of one communication to the inlet of the other.

Figure 4 illustrates a more complex application of outlet-inlet merge on two communications, C_1 and C_2. Each communication has three inlets and three outlets. The two squares in the figure represent the two communications to be composed and the dashed rectangle between them represents the *composition glue* which composes them. The particular composition happens by connecting two of the outlets of C_1 to two inlets of C_2, and one outlet of C_2 to one inlet of C_1. The composed communication is represented by the biggest rectangle. To an external observer, the composition glue is invisible, as are the six oilets it connects. In other words, an external observer only sees three inlets and three outlets of the composed communication.

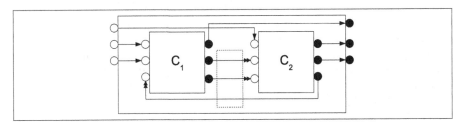

Fig. 4. Outlet-inlet merge of two communications

3.2   Example: A Simple Many-to-Many Communication

Consider a communication which somehow combines streams of messages from a number of senders, processes the combined stream and then somehow streams the outcome of this processing to several recipients. Let us say that there are three each of the senders and the recipients.

Such a communication can be constructed beginning with six primitive channel communications, C_1 through C_6, each simply able to transmit messages from one sender to one recipient. First, outlet merge can be applied to channels C_1 through C_3, with the senders at their inlets, and then inlet merge can be applied to channels C_4 through C_6, with the recipients at their outlets. At the time of application of these merges, the behavior for combining or sending forward the incoming streams would also be provided. Finally, these two communications can be composed by using outlet-inlet merge, which places some processing logic between the recipient of the first communication and the sender of the second. This is shown in Fig. 5.

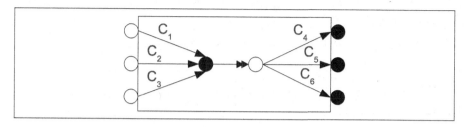

Fig. 5. Example: Simple many-to-many communication

4   The Model: interActors

interActors are defined in terms of – and extend – the Actors model of concurrency [1].

4.1   Actors

Actors [1] is a language-independent mathematical model for concurrent computing, which extends the concept of objects to inherently concurrent multiagent computations. An actor is a primitive software agent which encapsulates a thread of execution. Actors interact with each other using point-to-point asynchronous messages.

A snapshot of a system of actors [2] is represented as $\langle \alpha \mid \mu \rangle$, where α is a finite set of actors, and μ is a finite set of undelivered messages. An idle actor a with behavior b is represented by $(b)_a$; when active (i.e., processing message msg), it is represented by $[app(b, msg)]_a$, meaning that behavior b is being applied to msg. A message msg to actor a can be written as: $a \triangleleft msg$. Although message delivery is weakly fair, meaning that all messages are eventually delivered, the order of message delivery is not guaranteed.

Each actor has a unique name using which other actors can communicate with it. On receiving a message, an actor can evaluate lambda expressions, or carry out the following three types of primitive actions: it can send(a, v) an asynchronous message v to an actor named a; it can create(b, v) a new actor with behavior b and initialization parameter v, and returns the unique actor name for the newly created actor; or it can become(b) an actor executing behavior b.

4.2   interActors

interActors extend Actors with support for complex communications. The system can be seen as having two layers: the Actor Layer and the Communication Layer (see Fig. 6). Communications reside in the Communication Layer and the

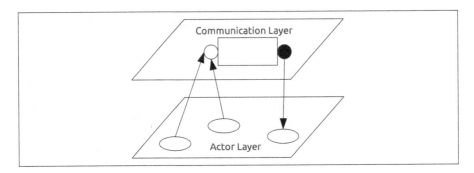

Fig. 6. Two-layer runtime system

actors – serving as computational processes – are in the Actor Layer. The black circle in the figure shows an outlet, and the white circle an inlet.

An actor in the Actor Layer interacts with a communication only by sending messages to inlets of the communication and receiving messages from the communication's outlets. Handlers of a communication are the driving force under the hood, and they can create more handlers, create more oilets, or change behaviors of oilets if necessary.

An instantaneous snapshot of a system of interActors is called a configuration, and is represented by a 5-tuple:

$$\langle C \mid M \mid \mathcal{B} \mid \alpha \mid \mu \rangle$$

The role of α and μ is essentially identical to that in an Actor configuration: α is the set of application actors in the Actor Layer, and μ is the set of undelivered messages to or from application actors. C is a finite set of communications, which are further elaborated as $(H : O : P)$, where H is a set of handlers, O is a set of oilets, and P is a set of mappings of the form (h, o) from handlers to oilets indicating which handler has names of which oilets. The oilets are what application actors connect to join the communication, and the handlers contain the communication's logic. M is a finite set of messages in the communication layer. $\mathcal{B}$ is a set of mapping of the form (a, o) from application actors to inlets indicating which application actors have names of which inlets.

Launching a Communication. An actor launches a communication by calling `launch(comm)`, where `comm` is a specification of the communication. As a result, `comm`'s oilets and handlers are created in the communication layer, and application actors are given the inlets' names. The following transition rule shows this:

$$\langle C \mid M \mid \mathcal{B} \mid \alpha, [R[\![\texttt{launch(comm)}]\!]]_a \mid \mu \rangle$$
$$\Longrightarrow \langle C, (H : O : P) \mid M \mid \mathcal{B} \mid \alpha, [R[\![nil]\!]]_a \mid \mu' \rangle$$

a is the actor launching the communication in some reduction context R. This creates the $(H : O : P)$ triple for the specification `comm`. $\mu' = \mu \cup m$, where m

is the initial set of messages to the application actors telling them which inlets they would be sending messages to.

Actor Sending Message to Inlet. When actor a sends a message to inlet o, the message is placed in μ.

$$\langle C \mid M \mid \mathcal{B} \mid \alpha, [R[\![\texttt{send(m)}]\!]]_a \mid \mu \rangle \Longrightarrow \langle C \mid M \mid \mathcal{B} \mid \alpha, [R[\![nil]\!]]_a \mid \mu' \rangle$$

where $\mu' = \mu \cup \{m\}$ and $m = o \triangleleft msg$, with content msg and oilet o as the message's recipient.

Actor Receiving Inlet Name. To participate in a communication, an actor has to send messages to the communication's inlets. Actor a receives the name of an inlet o in a message. app applies the behavior of an actor to the incoming message. a's knowledge of o is added to $\mathcal{B}$ to give $\mathcal{B}'$.

$$\langle C \mid M \mid \mathcal{B} \mid \alpha, (b)_a \mid \mu, a \triangleleft o \rangle \Longrightarrow \langle C \mid M \mid \mathcal{B}' \mid \alpha, [app(b,o)]_a \mid \mu \rangle$$

where o is an oilet, and $\mathcal{B}' = \mathcal{B} \cup \{(a,o)\}$; a's behavior b is applied to the incoming inlet name o to record it.

Oilet Sending Message. An inlet can send a message to a handler, and an outlet can send a message to an application actor. In the former case, a message is created in the communication layer; in the latter case, a message is generated in the actor layer. This scenario is depicted in the following equation:

$$\langle C, (H : O, [R[\![\texttt{send(m)}]\!]]_o : P) \mid M \mid \mathcal{B} \mid \alpha \mid \mu \rangle$$
$$\Longrightarrow \langle C, (H : O, [R[\![nil]\!]]_o : P) \mid M' \mid \mathcal{B} \mid \alpha \mid \mu' \rangle$$

where o is the oilet, $m = target \triangleleft msg$ and $target$ is the target of the message; $M' = M \cup \{m\}$ and $\mu' = \mu$ if the message recipient is a handler; $M' = M$ and $\mu' = \mu \cup \{m\}$ if the message recipient is an application actor.

Oilet Receiving Message. An inlet can receive a message from an application actor, and both inlets and outlets can receive a message from a handler. The oilet's behavior is then applied to the message. The receiving oilet applies the received message to its current behavior, which is depicted as follow:

$$\langle C, (H : O, (b)_o : P) \mid M \mid \mathcal{B} \mid \alpha \mid \mu \rangle$$
$$\Longrightarrow \langle C, (H : O, [app(b,msg)]_o : P) \mid M' \mid \mathcal{B} \mid \alpha \mid \mu' \rangle$$

where o is the oilet with behavior b. The message is removed from M or μ depending on whether it was from a handler or an application actor, respectively: $M' = M$ and $\mu' = \mu - \{o \triangleleft msg\}$ if the sender is an actor, $M' = M - \{o \triangleleft msg\}$ and $\mu' = \mu$ if the sender is a handler. app applies o's behavior b to the message.

  As a special case of this rule, if msg is of type $behv(b')$, applying b to it changes the oilet's behavior: $[app(b, msg)]_o = (b')_o$. These special messages can only be sent by handlers.

Handler Sending a Message. A handler h sends a message to another handler or to an oilet using **send**. As a result, a new message is created in the communication layer.

$$\langle C, (H, [R[\![\texttt{send(m)}]\!]]_h : O : P) \mid M \mid \mathcal{B} \mid \alpha \mid \mu \rangle$$
$$\Longrightarrow \langle C, (H, [R[\![nil]\!]]_h : O : P) \mid M' \mid \mathcal{B} \mid \alpha \mid \mu \rangle$$

where $M' = M \cup \{m\}$, $m = target \lhd msg$, and $target$ is a handler or an oilet in the same communication.

Handler Receiving Message. A handler h can receive a message from an oilet or another handler. As a consequence of receiving a message, the handler applies its current behavior to the message. Furthermore, if the message contains the name of an oilet not known to the handler, a new mapping from the handler h to the oilet msg is added to P.

$$\langle C, (H, (b)_h : O : P) \mid M, h \lhd msg \mid \mathcal{B} \mid \alpha \mid \mu \rangle$$
$$\Longrightarrow \langle C, (H, [app(b, msg)]_h : O : P') \mid M \mid \mathcal{B} \mid \alpha \mid \mu \rangle$$

where b is the handler's behavior. P' is $P \cup \{(h, oilet\text{-}names(msg))\}$ if msg contains oilet names, P otherwise.

Handler Creating Oilet. A handler h can create a new oilet using the **new_oilet** primitive. A new oilet with behavior b is created. At creation, only the handler h knows the oilet's name; it can send the name to other handlers and application actors subsequently.

$$\langle C, (H, [R[\![\texttt{new\_oilet(b)}]\!]]_h : O : P)_c \mid M \mid \mathcal{B} \mid \alpha \mid \mu \rangle$$
$$\Longrightarrow \langle C, (H, [R[\![o]\!]]_h : O, (b)_o : P')_c \mid M \mid \mathcal{B} \mid \alpha \mid \mu \rangle$$

where o is a fresh name for the new oilet and $P' = P \cup \{(h, o)\}$ to indicate h's knowledge of o.

Handler Creating Another Handler. A handler can create a new handler using the **new_handler** primitive. A new handler with behavior b is created. The newly created handler is only known to the creating handler, which may subsequently share the name with other oilets and handlers.

$$\langle C, (H, [R[\![\texttt{new\_handler(b)}]\!]]_h : O : P)_c \mid M \mid \mathcal{B} \mid \alpha \mid \mu \rangle$$
$$\Longrightarrow \langle C, (H, [R[\![h']\!]]_h, h' : O : P)_c \mid M \mid \mathcal{B} \mid \alpha \mid \mu \rangle$$

4.3   Composition

Finally, we look at the semantics of composing communications. Communications can be composed before being launched. A communication C is denoted by $(H : O : P)$, where H is a set of handlers, O is a set of oilets, and P is a set of mappings of the form (h, o) from handlers to oilets indicating which handler has names of which oilets. A handler with the name h, behavior b, and targets

t, is represented as $(b, t)_h$; an oilet with the name o, behavior b, and targets t is represented by $(b, t)_o$.

Recall that there are three ways of composing communications: inlet merge, outlet merge and outlet-inlet merge.

Inlet Merge. An inlet merge receives as parameters a set of inlets to be merged and a behavior. To be composed, the inlets are transformed into handlers which retain the inlets' behaviors and targets. A new handler is then created with the behavior provided as parameter. A new inlet is created with the forwarder behavior *fwd*, which becomes the new inlet of the composed communication. This new inlet forwards messages it receives to the newly created handler, which uses its behavior to decide how to forward messages to the handlers newly transformed from inlets. This can be formally represented as follows:

$$\underset{S,b}{\mid} {}_{i=1}^{n}(H_i : O_i : P_i) \Rightarrow \Big(\bigcup_{i=1}^{n} H_i \cup (b, T)_h \cup T : \big(\bigcup_{i=1}^{n} O_i - S \big) \cup \{(fwd, h)_{o'}\} :$$
$$\big(\bigcup_{i=1}^{n} P_i - P_M \big) \cup P_N \} \Big)$$

where S is the set of $n > 1$ inlets to be merged, $(fwd, h)_{o'}$ is the newly created inlet with forwarding behavior *fwd* and target h (the newly created handler). $(b, T)_h$ is the new handler h with provided behavior b, and targeting $T = \bigcup_{o \in S} \{tr((b_o, t_o)_o)\}$, the set of handlers transformed from inlets in S. The transformation function tr retains an inlet's behavior and its targets. The map tracking handlers' knowledge of oilets takes the mappings for the composing communications, removes mappings involving transformed inlets, P_M, and adds the newly created mappings, P_N.

Figure 7 shows an example of three communications, C_1, C_2, and C_3, being composed by applying inlet merge at inlets $\{in_1, in_2, in_3\}$.

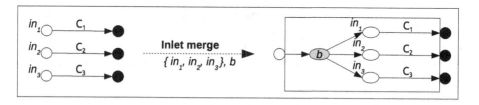

Fig. 7. Composition: Inlet merge

Outlet Merge. An outlet merge receives as parameters the set of outlets to be merged, a behavior, and targets. A new outlet is created with forwarding behavior *fwd* targeting the targets provided as parameter. A new handler is created with the behavior parameter, targeting the newly created outlet. Finally the outlets to be merged are transformed into handlers with the newly created handler as their target. This can be represented formally as follows:

$$|_{S,b,t}\,_{i=1}^{n}(H_i : O_i : P_i) \Rightarrow \Big(\bigcup_{i=1}^{n} H_i \cup (b,o')_h \cup T : (\bigcup_{i=1}^{n} O_i - S) \cup \{(fwd,t)_{o'}\} :$$

$$(\bigcup_{i=1}^{n} P_i - P_M) \cup P_N\Big)$$

where S is a set of $n > 1$ outlets to be merged, $(fwd,t)_{o'}$ is the newly created outlet with forwarding behavior fwd targeting t. $(b,o')_h$ is handler h with behavior b and target o'. $T = \bigcup_{o \in S}\{tr((b_o,h)_o)\}$ is the set of handlers transformed from S using transformation function tr. tr retains an outlet's behavior, but changes its target to h. The map tracking handlers' knowledge of oilets takes the mappings for the composing communications, removes those involving transformed outlets, P_M, and adds newly created mappings, P_N.

Figure 8 shows an example of communications C_1, C_2, and C_3 being composed by applying outlet merge at outlets $\{out_1, out_2, out_3\}$.

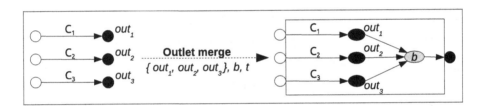

Fig. 8. Composition: Outlet merge

Outlet-Inlet Merge. An outlet-inlet merge binds some outlets of some communications to inlets of other communications. It takes as parameter the set of desired output-inlet bindings, B, each represented by the outlets and the inlets to be bound, plus the behavior for a new handler to be created to accept messages from the outlet and deliver them to the inlet. This can be represented formally as follows:

$$|_{B}\,_{i=1}^{n}(H_i : O_i : P_i) \Rightarrow \Big(\big(\bigcup_{i=1}^{n} H_i\big) \cup \bigcup_{j=1}^{m}\{(b_j,in_j)_{h_j}\} \cup \bigcup_{j=1}^{m}\{tr((b_{out_j},h_j)_{out_j})\}$$

$$\cup \bigcup_{j=1}^{m}\{tr((b_{in_j},t_{in_j})_{in_j})\} : (\bigcup_{i=1}^{n} O_i) - (\bigcup_{j=1}^{m}\{(b_{out_j},t_{out_j})_{out_j}\})$$

$$- (\bigcup_{j=1}^{m}\{(b_{in_j},t_{in_j})_{in_j}\}) : (\bigcup_{i=1}^{n} P_i - P_M)\Big)$$

where B is the provided set of bindings, where the jth binding (out_j, in_j, b_j), is a triple identifying the outlet and inlet to be merged, and the behavior b_j to be executed by the handler connecting the two. To compose the communications, for each of the binding triples in parameter B, both oilets are transformed into handlers, and a new handler h_j – with behavior b_j and target in_j – is created to connect them. h_j then becomes out_j's new target. The map tracking handlers' knowledge of oilets takes the mappings for the composing communications, and removes mappings involving transformed oilets, P_M; no new handler to oilet mappings are created as a result of an outlet-inlet merge composition.

Figure 9 illustrates this using the example of two communications, C_1 and C_2, being composed using the bindings set $\{(out_2, in_3, b_1), (out_4, in_2, b_2)\}$.

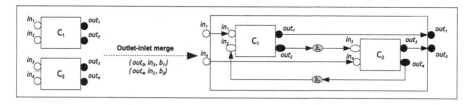

Fig. 9. Composition: Outlet-inlet merge

5   Implementation

We have implemented a proof-of-concept prototype of interActors, which can be used to program new types of communications. Our implementation is in Scala [18] using the Akka actor library [23].

5.1   Classes

A runtime interActors system is made up of a number of classes: CSL, Behavior, Handler, OutInlet, and Communication. The relationship between these classes is illustrated in Fig. 10. CSL implements methods which are used in defining behaviors or communications. Actor is Akka's Actor interface. Behavior has all the methods defined in CSL. Handler and OutInlet realize Actor. Communication inherits methods from CSL. Furthermore, handlers and oilets have behaviors, and communications have oilets and handlers.

5.2   Communication

Figure 11 shows the communication class. All programmer-specified communication types are subclassed from Communication. Each communication has attributes, inlets, outlets, and handlers. inlets, outlets and handlers are used to keep track of inlets, outlets, and handlers, respectively.

getInlets, getOutlets, and getHandlers return the inlets, the outlets, and the handlers, respectively, of a communication. addInlets, addOutlets, and `addHandlers` are used to add a list of inlets `ins`, a list of outlets `outs`, and a list of handlers `hdlers` to existing inlets, outlets, and handlers, respectively.

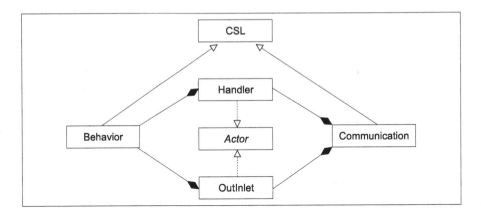

Fig. 10. interActors class diagram

```
 1  abstract class Communication (val context: ActorContext) extends CSL {
 2    var attributes = Map.empty[String, Any]
 3    var inlets = List[ActorRef]()
 4    var outlets = List[ActorRef]()
 5    var handlers = List[ActorRef]()
 6
 7    def getInlets = inlets
 8    def getOutlets = outlets
 9    def getHandlers = handlers
10    def addInlets(ins: List[ActorRef]) = {
11      inlets = inlets ::: ins
12    }
13    def addOutlets(outs: List[ActorRef]) = {
14      outlets = outlets ::: outs
15    }
16    def addHandlers(hdlers: List[ActorRef]) = {
17      handlers = handlers ::: hdlers
18    }
19
20    def setAttr(attrs: Map[String, Any]) = {
21      attributes = attrs
22      terminate()
23      init() // initialize oilets and handlers
24    }
25    def terminate() = {
26      inlets.foreach(context.stop(_)) // stop inlets
27      inlets = List[ActorRef]()
28      outlets.foreach(context.stop(_)) // stop outlets
29      outlets = List[ActorRef]()
30      handlers.foreach(context.stop(_)) // stop handlers
31      handlers = List[ActorRef]()
32    }
33
34    def launch()
35    def init()
36  }
```

Fig. 11. Abstract communication class

The method `terminate` terminates oilets and handlers if any. The run-time system can call this method in order to terminate a communication. The method is especially useful for resetting a communication's attributes which establishes the initial rendezvous between the communication and a set of actors participating in the communication.

After a communication is created, `setAttr` is called to customize the communication with attribute values and then initialize its oilets and handlers. Specifically, the `init` method creates the oilets and handlers.

`init` and `launch` are both abstract methods, which must be implemented by a concrete communication class. `init` initializes (or creates if they do not already exist) the oilets and handlers for a communication. The oilets and handlers which a communication type has are defined in a concrete subclass of the `Communication` class. A communication is launched by calling `launch`. Typically, `launch` sends a communication's participants the relevant names of its inlets. Once the participants know the inlets, they can send messages to them.

Life Cycle of a Communication. Figure 12 shows the life cycle of a communication object, which includes four states: *new, initialized, running,* and *terminated*.

A communication comes into existence once an application creates it. At this stage, although a communication exists as an object, its attributes are not yet set and its oilets and handlers do not exist yet. Its state becomes *initialized* through the initialization operation. Launching operation makes the communication *running*. For some long-lived communications, the *running* state is their final state. For others that should terminate, the final state is *terminated*, in which a communication may be garbage collected.

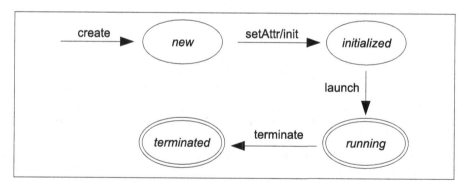

Fig. 12. Life cycle of a communication

6   Communication Specification Language

To ease the programming of communications, we have developed a specification language, CSL (Communication Specification Language), which is essentially a restricted version of the Scala programming language. In other words, although communications can also be coded directly in Scala, CSL makes it easier, both by dispensing with some of the boilerplate, as well as by restricting arbitrary computations from being included in a communication. Our goal is to allow specification of only the communications which can be constructed using the composition rules presented in Sect. 4.3. A simple source-to-source translator translates these CSL specifications into pure Scala code for actual execution.

CSL is styled after Scala for the ease of translation into Scala executable code. All valid Scala identifiers, types, variable declarations are allowed; however, not all Scala expressions are allowed. Programmers can additionally use CSL-specific statements to specify complex types of communications.

6.1 Syntax

The abstract syntax of CSL is presented in Fig. 13. The terms written in **bold italic** font should be self-explanatory; so they are not elaborated on further. Keywords are written in `monospace` font. Statements allowed in the initialization and behavior code are presented below in text.

A communication can be of two types: simple or composed. Either type of communication has a name, and is specified using a list of attributes, the logic of the communications – represented by lists of oilets and handlers for a simple communication, and represented by a list of existing communications for a composed communication – and finally an initialization method.

attributes declares a list of attributes, each of the form *attribute_name: Scala_type*. Scala types we have frequently used in specifying communications include *Int*, *Any*, *ActorRef*, and *List*. *Int* is obvious; *Any* is the supertype of any type, which is similar to Java's superclass *Object*; *ActorRef* is a reference to an agent; *List* is a list of objects.

oilet_list is a list of oilets of the communication. Each oilet has a type – `inlet` or `outlet` – and a *behavior*. Similarly, *handler_list* declares a list of handlers for the communication. Each handler has a *behavior*.

For composed communications, the list of composed communications *comm_list* and their composition *composition_decl* are specified. *comm_list* contains a list of communication type names (i.e., names of previously specified communications) with local variables to hold their instances. *composition_decl* contains details of how the communications are to be composed. For an outlet-inlet merge composition, a list of triples is specified. Each triple identifies the outlet and the inlet to be composed, as well as the behavior of the handler which goes between them (see Fig. 9). For the inlet and outlet merge compositions, the merging oilets are identified, along with the behavior of the new handler that these oilets connect to.

Initialization method *init* declares and initializes local variables, and sets up the initial *rendezvous* between the communication and the agents using it.

A variable declaration takes one of two forms: *val* defines a constant; *var* defines a variable. The only difference between *val* declaration and *var* declaration is that a constant cannot be modified and a variable can.

```
communication ::= communication name {
                       attributes:{attr_list}
                       comm
                       initialization
                   }

comm ::= simple | composed
simple ::= oilet_list
               handler_list^(0|1)
composed ::= comms:{comm_list}
                  composition:{composition_decl}

attr_list ::= attr_name: Scala_type; attr_list | attr_name: Scala_type;
oilet_list ::= oilet_decl; oilet_list | oilet_decl;
handler_list ::= handler_decl; handler_list | handler_decl;
oilet_decl ::= oilet_type oilet: oilet_name(behavior)
handler_decl ::= handler: handler_name(behavior)
oilet_type ::= inlet | outlet

initialization ::= init: {
                        var_list^(0|1)
                        statement;*
                   }

comm_list ::= comm_var: comm_type_name; comm_list |
                 comm_var: comm_type_name;
composition_decl ::= bindings: List(3_tuple_list) |
                         oilets: List(oilet_decl_list);
                         behavior: {behavior_var: behavior_type_name;}
3_tuple_list ::= (outlet, inlet, behavior), 3_tuple_list |
                    (outlet, inlet behavior)
oilet_decl_list ::= oilet, oilet_decl_list | oilet

var_list ::= var_decl; var_list | var_decl;

var_decl ::= val variable_name (: Scala_type | = Init_Value) |
                var variable_name (: Scala_type | = Init_Value)

behavior ::= behavior behavior_name( targets, para_list): {
                     var_list^(0|1)
                     receive(msg) = {
                        statement;*
                     }
                 }

para_list ::= var_decl, para_list | var_decl
```

Fig. 13. Abstract syntax for CSL

A behavior definition takes as parameters a list of targets and a list of additional parameters. Its body contains a **receive** method which defines the logic for handling the messages received by the oilet or handler executing the behavior.

CSL allows the following statements in the initialization and behavior code for a communication:

- **send**(*recipient*, *msg*) anonymously sends a message *msg* to a recipient named *recipient*
- **sendm**(*recipients*, *msg*) anonymously sends a message *msg* to multiple recipients named *recipients*

- tell(*sender, recipient, msg*) sends a message *msg* along with the sender's name *sender* to a recipient named *recipient* so that the recipient can reply to *sender*. Note that *sender* may be a third party other than the real sender.
- tellm(*sender, recipients, msg*) sends a message *msg* along with the sender's name *sender* to multiple *recipients* so that the recipients can reply to *sender*. Similar to tell, *sender* may be set to a party different from the real sender.
- multiSend(*recipients, data_list*) anonymously sends the first element of *data_list* to the first recipient in *recipients*, the second element to the second recipient, and so on. The number of recipients must match the length of *data_list*.
- multiTell(*sender, recipients, data_list*) sends the first element of *data_list* to the first recipient of *recipients* along with the sender's name, the second element to the second recipient, and so on. Recipient and data lists must be of the same size.
- createOilet(*oilet_type, behavior_name*) creates an inlet or outlet (depending on oilet_type) with behavior *behavior_name*.
- createHandler(*behavior_name*) creates a handler with behavior *behavior_name*.
- change(*oilet_name, behavior_name*) changes the behavior of oilet *oilet_name* with new behavior *behavior_name*.
- delay(*time*) delays the execution for defined *time* in milliseconds.
- subscribe(*trigger*) allows a communication to subscribe to an external trigger which sends a message to the subscribing communication. Possible types of triggers can be time, location, signal strength, magnetic field, amount of light, amount of noise, etc.
- *variable_name* = *expression* assigns the value of *expression* to a variable named *variable_name*.

Additionally, an inlet or outlet may not use createOilet, createHandler, or change, because although an oilet has a behavior, its role is primarily to serve as an interface between a communication and the agents using the communication.

CSL expressions include *variable_name*, list operations, and three types of Scala expressions: if, function calls, and mathematical expressions. List operations are functions for accessing or manipulating lists. Scala requires all elements of a list to be of the same type.

CSL explicitly does not support loops in an attempt to restrict oilet and handler behaviors from carrying out complex computations which could lead to mixing of computation concerns into communications. However, it does support possible periodic action through a triggering mechanism. Triggers can send messages to communications which subscribe to them. Subscribing to a trigger effectively makes a communication encapsulate the trigger within itself. Such a time trigger can send messages at required times to subscribing communications to trigger communication activity.

Finally, note that sendm, tell, tellm, multiSend, and multiTell are essentially syntactic sugar because they can all be implemented using send.

6.2   Examples

Here we show some examples of CSL specifications of behaviors (for oilets and handlers) and complete communications.

Behavior Examples

Forwarder. Figure 14 shows the `forwarder` behavior. A forwarder has `targets`. On receiving a message `msg`, a forwarder simply sends the message to its targets. Receiving of `msg` is handled by method `receive` method, inside which `sendm` sends the message to the `targets`.

```
1  behavior forwarder(targets): {
2    receive(msg) = {
3      sendm(targets, msg);
4    }
5  }
```

Fig. 14. Behavior: forwarder

Selector. Figure 15 shows the `selector` behavior, which uses a programmer-provided function `select`. Given message `msg` and a list of potential recipients `targets`, `select` picks out the recipients relevant to `msg`. The `selector` behavior forwards each message received to the relevant `targets` identified using `select`. The concept of *selector* is similar to the concept of *routing* in Akka.

```
1  behavior selector(targets,
2    val select: (Any, List[ActorRef]) => List[ActorRef]): {
3    receive(msg) = {
4      sendm(select(msg, targets), msg);
5    }
6  }
```

Fig. 15. Behavior: selector

Aggregator. Figure 16 shows the `aggregator` behavior. It accepts two functions: `cond`, used to determine whether the aggregator has received a sufficient number of messages to aggregate; and `aggr`, used to aggregate all messages received so far. On arrival, message `msg` gets placed in a list of messages `msgs`. The aggregator then uses `cond` to check if it is time to aggregate. If `cond` returns true, an aggregate of the messages in `msgs` – computed using `aggr` – is sent to `targets`, and `msgs` is reset for future use.

Communication Examples. Now we look at some examples of communication which use the defined behaviors.

```
 1  behavior aggregator(targets, val cond: List[Any] => Boolean,
 2                      val aggr: List[Any] => Any): {
 3    var msgs = List[Any]();
 4    receive(msg) = {
 5      msgs = append(msg, msgs);
 6      if (cond(msgs)) {
 7        sendm(targets, aggr(msgs));
 8        empty(msgs);
 9      }
10    }
11  }
```

Fig. 16. Behavior: aggregator

Broadcaster. Figure 17 shows the CSL code for a *broadcaster* communication, which enables one set of agents to send messages to another set of agents.

Broadcaster has two attributes: participants are the senders and recipients are the message targets. It has one outlet out executing forwarder behavior (Fig. 14) targeting recipients, and one inlet in, also executing forwarder behavior, but targeting out.

When a *broadcaster* is launched, it notifies participants of the name of the inlet, so that they can use it to send messages. Upon receiving a message at its inlet, Broadcaster forwards it to its outlet, which, in turn, forwards the message to recipients.

```
 1  communication Broadcaster {
 2    attributes: {
 3      recipients: List[ActorRef];
 4      participants: List[ActorRef];
 5    }
 6    outlet oilet: out(forwarder(recipients));
 7    inlet oilet: in(forwarder(out));
 8    init: {
 9      sendm(participants, in);
10    }
11  }
```

Fig. 17. Communication: Broadcaster

Router. Figure 18 shows the CSL specification of a *router* communication, which sends received messages to relevant recipients.

Router defines two sets of recipients recipients1 and recipients2. participants are message senders and select is a provided function for choosing the recipients relevant to a message. Router has two outlets out1 and out2, one handler chooser, and one inlet in. out1 and out2 execute the forwarder behavior (Fig. 14) with targets recipient1 and recipient2, respectively. The handler executes the selector behavior (Fig. 15) to pick a target from among out1 and out2 based on a received message. The selection criterion is defined in

```
 1 communication Router {
 2   attributes: {
 3     recipients1: List[ActorRef];
 4     recipients2: List[ActorRef];
 5     participants: List[ActorRef];
 6     select: (Any, List[ActorRef]) => List[ActorRef];
 7   }
 8   outlet oilet: out1(forwarder(recipients1));
 9   outlet oilet: out2(forwarder(recipients2));
10   handler: chooser(selector(List(out1, out2), select));
11   inlet oilet: in(forwarder(out1));
12   init: {
13     sendm(participants, in);
14   }
15 }
```

Fig. 18. Communication: Router

function **select**, which chooses a list of recipients, List[ActorRef], based on the received message of type Any.

When a *router* is launched, it informs **participants** of the existence of the inlet to which they can send messages.

Multi-Origin Many-to-Many (MOM2M) Communication. Figure 19 shows the CSL specification of an MOM2M communication, which has multiple participants and multiple recipients, where the goal is to receive messages from a group of senders, to aggregate them when appropriate, and to forward the aggregate to a set of recipients. This type of communication can have several uses, ranging from barrier synchronization to voting to recommendation services.

MOM2M has four attributes: **recipients**, which are the targets of the communication; **participants**, which are message senders; and **cond** and **aggr** functions, which are used for customizing the **aggregator** behavior (Fig. 16). The inlet **in** targets the handler **collector** executing the **aggregator** behavior, and targets the outlet **out**.

```
 1 communication MOM2M {
 2   attributes: {
 3     recipients: List[ActorRef];
 4     participants: List[ActorRef];
 5
 6     cond: List[Any] => Boolean;
 7     aggr: List[Any] => Any;
 8   }
 9   outlet oilet: out(forwarder(recipients));
10   handler: collector(aggregator(out, cond, aggr));
11   inlet oilet: in(forwarder(collector));
12   init: {
13     sendm(participants, in);
14   }
15 }
```

Fig. 19. Communication: MOM2M

On launching, an *MOM2M* communication invites the participants to send it messages, which it then passes on to the `collector` aggregator, which then forwards aggregates to `recipients` whenever `cond` is `true`.

7   Case Study: Gravitational N-Body Simulation

Here, to illustrate use of interActors, we develop a complete implementation of the message-passing solution to the classic gravitational n-body simulation problem. The problem involves several bodies in space, each with a mass and an initial position and velocity. The simulation then tracks the movement of these bodies as each exerts gravitational pull on others, finding the force exerted by each body on every other, and then moving the bodies for a small Δt, and then repeating these two steps for duration of time required.

Although a sequential implementation of this simulation is straightforward, a message-passing based concurrent implementation – typically using the manager-workers paradigm [3] – is fairly involved in its communication. It uses several worker agents, among whom the bodies are (roughly) equally divided, so that each worker is responsible for tracking its own *block* of bodies. Each worker is provided with the initial positions and velocities of *all* bodies. There is a manager agent whose job is to generate tasks for carrying out computations of all the required forces. These tasks are a list of pairs of blocks of bodies, from which the workers can repeatedly request one at a time from the manager, and compute the forces in the pair, until all tasks are completed. Once all forces have been calculated (indicated by all workers receiving (0,0) tasks from the manager), the forces have to be shared among all workers (because each body is subject to forces from every other body). Once all forces are available to all workers, each worker moves its own bodies as required. Next, the new positions and velocities of the bodies – which workers track only for their own block of bodies – have to be shared among all workers, so as to begin the next iteration in the simulation. Figure 20 shows the outline of code implementing the worker agents, where **STEPS** is the number of steps in the simulation, n is the number of workers, each of which receives its id in variable w.

An examination of this algorithm suggests two opportunities for separating communication concerns, corresponding to the two data collection/aggregation activities involved in sharing of forces and the new positions and velocities, respectively. In other words, workers can just work on computing the forces and new positions and velocities, and allow a separately programmed communication to handle the aggregation and sharing of forces and the new positions and velocities. Once a worker is finished with a task (i.e., calculating forces for a pair of blocks, or positions and velocities for its block of bodies), it simply sends the result to the communication, which is then responsible for aggregating and finally sending the aggregates to all workers. The communication is responsible for orchestrating the computation. Figure 21 graphically illustrates this solution

```
 1  task (int block1, int block2);
 2
 3  process Worker[w = 1 to n] {
 4     for (s = 1 to STEPS) {
 5        while (true) {
 6           t = get a task from the manager;
 7           if (t.block1 == 0) break;
 8           calculate forces;
 9        }
10        for (i = 1 to n st i != w) {
11           send local forces to ith worker;
12        }
13        for (i = 1 to n st i != w) {
14           receive forces from ith worker;
15           aggregate received forces to local forces;
16        }
17
18        calculate positions and velocities base on the aggregated forces;
19        for (i = 1 to n st i != w) {
20           send local bodies to ith worker;
21        }
22        for (i = 1 to n st i != w) {
23           receive bodies from ith worker;
24           move bodies;
25        }
26     }
27  }
```

Fig. 20. Code outline for workers in traditional manager-workers implementation

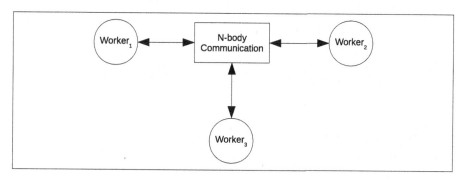

Fig. 21. Separating communication and functional concerns for N-body simulation

approach,[1] where $Worker_1$ through $Worker_3$ communicate only with the N-body Communication.

Communication Code. Although the communication required for this problem can be implemented as a single communication, we develop it here by composing three simpler communications, which were previously introduced in Sect. 6. This is to illustrate the usefulness of composition. Figure 22 shows this composition. *Router* (Fig. 18) is a communication with a handler executing the `selector` behavior (Fig. 15), which forwards received messages to one of two *MOM2M*

---

[1] Oilets have been abstracted out to simplify the figure.

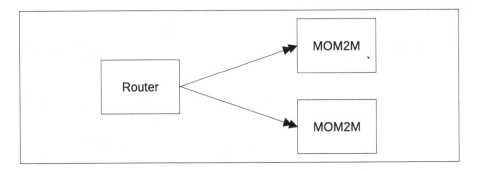

Fig. 22. Implementing N-body simulation using a composed communication

communications (Fig. 19): one handles aggregation and sharing of forces and
another handles collection and sharing of positions and velocities (PVs). We call
the one handling forces the force handler and the other the PV handler.

Once workers finish calculating forces or new PVs (Positions and Velocities),
they send their local copies to the router which – depending on whether messages
contain forces or PVs – sends received messages to either the force handler or the

```
 1  communication nbody {
 2    comms: { // communications to be composed
 3      rc: Router;
 4      fc: MOM2M;
 5      pvc: MOM2M;
 6    }
 7    composition: { // composition glue
 8      bindings:List((rc.out1, fc.in, forwarder(fc.in)),
 9                    (rc.out2, pvc.in, forwarder(pvc.in)));
10    }
11    attributes: {
12      workers: List[ActorRef];
13      condf: List[Any] => Boolean;
14      condpv: List[Any] => Boolean;
15      aggrf: List[Any] => Any;
16      aggrpv: List[Any] => Any;
17      select: (Any, List[ActorRef]) => List[ActorRef];
18    }
19    init: {
20      // set attributes
21      rc.attrs(Map("recipients"->workers,  "participants"->workers,
22                   "select"-> select));
23      fc.attrs(Map("recipients"-> workers, "participants"->workers,
24                   "cond"-> condf, "aggr"-> aggrf));
25      pvc.attrs(Map("recipients"-> workers, "participants"->workers,
26                    "cond"-> condpv, "aggr"-> aggrpv));
27      // compose
28      OutIn(List(rc, fc, pvc), bindings);
29      // notify participants
30      sendm(workers, rc.in);
31    }
32  }
```

Fig. 23. N-body composed communication

PV handler. The force handler aggregates forces (by adding them) and the PV handler aggregates positions and velocities of the bodies (by collecting them). After the aggregation is done, the handlers send the result to their corresponding outlets, which, in turn, forward them to all workers.

Figure 23 shows the CSL definition of the composed communication. In the code, we can see that nbody is composed from three communications rc, fc and pvc by connecting rc's out1 to fc's in and rc's out2 to pvc's in.

To use this communication, we create an instance of it, set up its attributes, and launch it. Figure 24 shows the code for doing this, which assumes that the variables assigned to attributes have already been defined by the application programmer.

Workers Code. Finally, Fig. 25 shows an outline for the code for the workers, which assumes that the workers have already been told of the communication's inlet, to which they are to send their results.

```
1 nb = new nbody();
2 nb.setAttr(Map("workers"->workers, "condf"->condf, "condpv"->condpv,
3               "aggrf"->aggrf, "aggrpv"->aggrpv, "select"->select));
4 nb.launch();
```

Fig. 24. Using the N-body communication

```
1  task (int block1, int block2);
2  Communication c;
3  process Worker[w = 1 to n] {
4      for (s = 1 to STEPS) {
5          while (true) {
6              t = get a task from the manager;
7              if (t.block1 == 0) break;
8              calculate forces;
9          }
10         send local forces to c's inlet;
11         receive aggregated forces from c;      // in one message
12         calculate PVs of own bodies based on received forces;
13         send local bodies to c's inlet;
14         receive PVs for bodies from c;          // in one message
15         move bodies;
16     }
17 }
```

Fig. 25. Code outline for workers using N-body communication

7.1   Discussion

Separation of Concerns. In the interActors-based solution, the communication concerns are successfully separated from the functional concerns, because the workers only need to compute the forces and the PVs, without worrying about the aggregation, which we argue is essentially a communication concern. Plus, the communication is constructed by composing existing general purpose communications: `Router` and `MOM2M`. The resulting solution better separates the functional and communication concerns of the application, delivering better reusability and modularity.

System Overhead

Processing. Both the traditional and the interActors solutions carry out identical force and PV calculations at the workers. What is different, however, is the aggregation. In the traditional solution, each worker would aggregate all the forces relevant to its block of bodies. This would mean that the results of each task calculation would be added twice, once for each of blocks in the pair. In the interActors solution, all forces collected at the communication would be added only once. Updating the bodies would have identical costs in both solutions.

That said, in the traditional solution, the local aggregations at the workers of only the relevant forces would happen in parallel; in comparison, in the interActors-based solution, the complete aggregation in the communication happens sequentially.

Number of Messages. Both solutions have identical interactions with the manager agent. We focus on the remaining messages.

If there are n workers, in the traditional implementation, the number of messages required for sharing forces is $n(n-1)$. This reduces to only $2n$ for the interActors solution. The same analysis applies to the process of exchange positions and velocities. The *interActors*-based solution therefore leads to fewer messages in the system.

Data Communicated. Here again, both solutions have identical interactions with the manager agent, so we ignore that in the comparison.

Let us say we have b bodies, and n workers. Dividing the bodies evenly among the workers, we would have n blocks, each of size b/n (let's call this s). This would lead to $(n \times (n+1))/2$ tasks in all.

In the traditional solution, all communication would be between the workers.

– Forces: Each task would compute s^2 forces, which the worker would send to every other worker. In all $(n \times (n+1))/2 \times s^2$ forces would be so communicated $n-1$ times each. This leads to:

$$\frac{n \times (n+1)}{2} \times s^2 \times (n-1) = \frac{n \times (n^2-1)}{2} \times \left(\frac{b}{n}\right)^2 = \frac{(n^2-1) \times b^2}{2n} \quad (1)$$

– PV: Each worker would send its bodies to every other worker, 2 values for each body. This would add up to $2 \times b$. Adding this to (1), we get:

$$\frac{(n^2-1) \times b^2}{2n} + 2b = O(b^2 \times n) \quad (2)$$

In comparison, in the *interActors* solutions, for both the forces and the PVs, the network traffic has two parts: messages from workers to the communication and from the communication to the workers.

- Forces: For the first part, the network traffic is essentially the same as in discussion above, except that only one message is sent per task, to the communication. This leads to:

$$\frac{n \times (n+1)}{2} \times s^2 = \frac{n \times (n+1)}{2} \times \left(\frac{b}{n}\right)^2 = \frac{(n+1) \times b^2}{2n} \qquad (3)$$

  For the second part, the network traffic involves the aggregated forces from the communication to each of the workers. This is simply $b \times n$. Adding this to (3) above, we get:

$$\frac{(n+1) \times b^2}{2n} + (b \times n) \qquad (4)$$

- PV: For the first part, the network traffic would be a single message sent by each worker to the communication, containing $2 \times s$ values (one each per body in block for position and velocity), where s is the size of a block. This ultimately leads to a total of $2 \times b$ values communicated. For the second part, there are $2 \times b$ values sent to each worker by the communication, amounting to a total of $2 \times n \times b$ values.

Adding the force and PV values gives:

$$\frac{(n+1) \times b^2}{2n} + (b \times n) + (2 \times b \times n) = O(b^2 + 3(b \times n)) \qquad (5)$$

In other words, for a fixed number of workers, both have $O(b^2)$ amount of network traffic.

Programming Complexity. The traditional solution does not have the additional abstraction complexity of a communication, whereas the interActors solution obviously does. We argue that the resultant better separation of concerns, modularity and reusability of the interActors solution more than pay for this added complexity.

8   Conclusion

In a variety of emerging applications, the interactions in concurrent computations are becoming more complex and varied, often requiring aggregation and decision-making at run-time. Leaving such complex interactions to be managed by the processes complicates their code, and hampers reusability. Significant advances have been made in separating communication concerns of computations from their functional concerns; however existing approaches create static protocols which cannot evolve over the course of an interaction. In this paper, we presented the idea of communications which are self-driven, and which can respond to the changing state of an interaction. We presented operational semantics for interActors, a model which separates complex communication concerns of concurrent computations from their functional concerns. A prototype implementation was developed using Scala and the Akka Actors library. A specification language called CSL allows programmers to program such communications. Finally, we illustrated the modularity and reusability advantages of an interActors based approach using a set of examples, culminating in a case study involving the classic gravitational n-body simulation. We also discussed performance implications of using interActors in the context of the case study.

References

1. Agha, G.: Actors: A Model of Concurrent Computation in Distributed Systems. MIT Press, Cambridge (1986)
2. Agha, G.A., Mason, I.A., Smith, S.F., Talcott, C.L.: A foundation for actor computation. J. Funct. Program. **7**(1), 1–72 (1997)
3. Andrews, G.: Foundations of Multithreaded, Parallel, and Distributed Programming. Addison-Wesley, Reading (2000)
4. Arbab, F.: Reo: a channel-based coordination model for component composition. Math. Struct. Comput. Sci. **14**(3), 329–366 (2004)
5. Arbab, F.: Puff, the magic protocol. In: Agha, G., Danvy, O., Meseguer, J. (eds.) Formal Modeling: Actors, Open Systems, Biological Systems. LNCS, vol. 7000, pp. 169–206. Springer, Heidelberg (2011). https://doi.org/10.1007/978-3-642-24933-4_9
6. Arbab, F., Aştefănoaei, L., de Boer, F.S., Dastani, M., Meyer, J.-J., Tinnermeier, N.: Reo connectors as coordination artifacts in 2APL systems. In: Bui, T.D., Ho, T.V., Ha, Q.T. (eds.) PRIMA 2008. LNCS (LNAI), vol. 5357, pp. 42–53. Springer, Heidelberg (2008). https://doi.org/10.1007/978-3-540-89674-6_8
7. Astley, M., Sturman, D.C., Agha, G.: Customizable middleware for modular distributed software. Commun. ACM **44**(5), 99–107 (2001)
8. Cabri, G., Leonardi, L., Zambonelli, F.: Reactive tuple spaces for mobile agent coordination. In: Rothermel, K., Hohl, F. (eds.) MA 1998. LNCS, vol. 1477, pp. 237–248. Springer, Heidelberg (1998). https://doi.org/10.1007/BFb0057663
9. Callsen, C.J., Agha, G.: Open heterogeneous computing in actorspace. J. Parallel Distrib. Comput. **21**(3), 289–300 (1994)
10. Dinges, P., Agha, G.: Scoped synchronization constraints for large scale actor systems. In: Sirjani, M. (ed.) COORDINATION 2012. LNCS, vol. 7274, pp. 89–103. Springer, Heidelberg (2012). https://doi.org/10.1007/978-3-642-30829-1_7
11. Frølund, S.: Coordinating Distributed Objects: An Actor-Based Approach to Synchronization. MIT Press, Cambridge (1996)
12. Gelernter, D., Carriero, N.: Coordination languages and their significance. Commun. ACM **35**(2), 96–107 (1992)
13. Gutierrez-Nolasco, S., Venkatasubramanian, N.: A reflective middleware framework for communication in dynamic environments. In: Meersman, R., Tari, Z. (eds.) OTM 2002. LNCS, vol. 2519, pp. 791–808. Springer, Heidelberg (2002). https://doi.org/10.1007/3-540-36124-3_53
14. Hoare, C.A.R.: Communicating sequential processes. Commun. ACM **21**(8), 666–677 (1978)

15. Maes, P.: Computational reflection. In: Morik, K. (ed.) GWAI-87 11th German Workshop on Artifical Intelligence. Informatik-Fachberichte, vol. 152, pp. 251–265. Springer, Heidelberg (1987). https://doi.org/10.1007/978-3-642-73005-4_27
16. Milner, R.: A Calculus of Communicating Systems. Springer, Heidelberg (1980). https://doi.org/10.1007/3-540-10235-3
17. Milner, R.: Communicating and Mobile Systems: The π-Calculus. Cambridge University Press, New York (1999)
18. Odersky, M., et al.: An overview of the Scala programming language. Technical report (2004)
19. Omicini, A., Denti, E.: From tuple spaces to tuple centres. Sci. Comput. Program. **41**(3), 277–294 (2001)
20. Ren, S., Yu, Y., Chen, N., Marth, K., Poirot, P.-E., Shen, L.: Actors, roles and coordinators — a coordination model for open distributed and embedded systems. In: Ciancarini, P., Wiklicky, H. (eds.) COORDINATION 2006. LNCS, vol. 4038, pp. 247–265. Springer, Heidelberg (2006). https://doi.org/10.1007/11767954_16
21. Singh, M.P.: Information-driven interaction-oriented programming: BSPL, the Blindingly Simple Protocol Language. In: AAMAS 2011, Richland, SC, pp. 491–498 (2011)
22. Singh, M.P.: Lost: local state transfer - an architectural style for the distributed enactment of business protocols. In: 2011 IEEE International Conference on Web Services, pp. 57–64, July 2011
23. Typesafe: Akka Framework. http://www.akka.io
24. Wegner, P.: Why interaction is more powerful than algorithms. Commun. ACM **40**(5), 80–91 (1997)
25. Weyns, D., Omicini, A., Odell, J.: Environment as a first class abstraction in multiagent systems. Auton. Agents Multi-Agent Syst. **14**(1), 5–30 (2007)

A Homogeneous Actor-Based Monitor Language for Adaptive Behaviour

Tony Clark[1], Vinay Kulkarni[2], Souvik Barat[2(✉)], and Balbir Barn[3]

[1] Sheffield Hallam University, Sheffield, UK
[2] Tata Research Development and Design Centre, Pune, India
souvik.barat@tcs.com
[3] Middlesex University, London, UK

Abstract. This paper describes a structured approach to encoding monitors in an actor language. Within a configuration of actors, each of which publishes a history, a monitor is an independent actor that triggers an action based on patterns occurring in the histories. We define a monitor language based on linear temporal logic and show how it can be homogeneously embedded within an actor language. The approach is demonstrated through a number of examples and evaluated in terms of a real-world actor-based simulation.

Keywords: Monitors · Actors · Linear temporal logic
Homogeneous language embedding · Simulation

1 Introduction

1.1 Background

Software system monitors are instruments that are added to applications in order to collect data, diagnose problems and influence behaviour, for example to collect training data [21], recognise health issues [19], control of energy networks [7], dynamically verify system requirements [14] and to adapt to environmental changes [12]. Monitors are typically orthogonal to the system that is monitored and, as such, manage their own thread of control. Our particular interest in monitors arises within the field of simulation to support decision-making [4,20] where levers that control a simulation need to be adapted by monitoring the behaviour of system components as shown in Fig. 1.

The actor model of computation [2] would seem to be a good candidate for representing both systems to be monitored and their associated monitors because an actor has autonomous behaviour and new actors can be added or deleted without significant architectural disruption. Figure 2a shows a simple model of a monitor actor that is attached to a monitored actor. Adaptation occurs by regularly checking the history exported by the monitored actor and taking action when monitor conditions are satisfied by the data in the history.

© Springer Nature Switzerland AG 2018
A. Ricci and P. Haller (Eds.): Programming with Actors, LNCS 10789, pp. 216–244, 2018.
https://doi.org/10.1007/978-3-030-00302-9_8

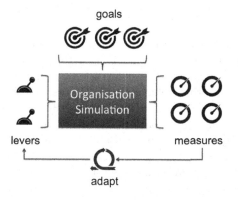

Fig. 1. System adaptation

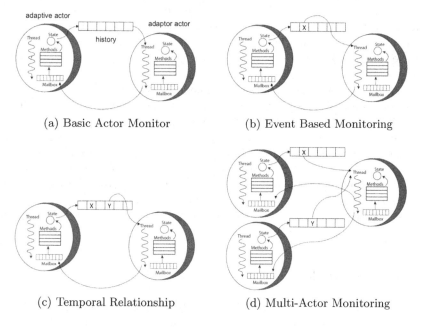

(a) Basic Actor Monitor

(b) Event Based Monitoring

(c) Temporal Relationship

(d) Multi-Actor Monitoring

Fig. 2. Actor monitors

Several patterns emerge from the actor arrangement shown in Fig. 2a. An individual monitored actor that publishes events on its history can be monitored so that when the monitoring actor detects the event-data it can take action as shown in Fig. 2b. If the monitoring actor also takes into account the timing of events, it may compare the relative times of two or more events as shown in Fig. 2c. A single monitor may be attached to two or more actors as shown in Fig. 2d in which case we can define *intra-* and *inter*-actor relationships between events that occur over multiple actors.

1.2 Requirements and Contribution

The patterns described in Fig. 2 lead to technical requirements for actor-based monitors: (1) It must be possible to define an actor interface so that monitored actors provide a history in the correct format for monitor actors and are otherwise unaware of monitoring behaviour. (2) Events that are published via histories should have temporal information that monitor actors can use for intra- and inter-actor reasoning. (3) Monitors should be actors to allow them to be added and removed dynamically during system execution (and to support meta-monitoring where that is appropriate). (4) There should be a monitor language, whose denotation is defined in terms of actors, that is open to static analysis.

Our contribution is to show how monitors can be encoded within an actor language in a way that achieves the requirements listed above. In particular, we achieve a homogeneous representation by defining a sub-language of a broader actor language that supports monitors and define a general purpose interface for monitored actors. We perform static analysis, in terms of actor interfaces, and outline in the conclusion how we intend to check that monitors are consistent with the histories published by monitored actors. As described in [9], monitors can themselves be actors and we demonstrate this by defining the semantics of monitors as an homogeneous language embedding [23].

Section 2 describes existing work on actors, agent languages and software monitoring in general. Languages employing temporal operators are often used to specify the behaviour of actor systems, but we employ such operators to define a language of dynamic monitors in Sect. 3. Our work on simulation has led to the implementation of a new actor-based language called ESL that is used to present our contribution; Sect. 4 introduces that part of ESL necessary to understand how monitors are encoded. Section 5 describes how monitors are defined in ESL and Sect. 6 shows how ESL and monitors are used to implement a simulation for a real-world case study.

2 Related Work

The concept of a *monitor* that observes the behaviour of a system and detects the violations of safety properties is well studied area [16]. The early work on monitors focused on off-line monitoring where the historical data or program trace is statically analysed post-execution [13] to detect anomalies. In contrast, the recent research trend primarily addresses on online monitoring that dynamically validates the observed system execution against a specification to achieve preventive and corrective measures.

Monitoring-related research challenges include: (1) the use of an appropriate foundational model for system specification (this can be mapped to Monitoring-Oriented Programming[1]); (2) an efficient implementation of monitors; (3) monitor control patterns. Existing monitor technologies are largely based on temporal logic which has led us to use the same underlying formalism. For example, the

---

[1] http://fsl.cs.illinois.edu/index.php/Monitoring-Oriented_Programming.

past-time linear temporal logic (PTLTL) is recommended as specification language [18,22] where monitor properties are expressed using the notion of time, as introduced by LTL, with both past and future modalities including *next, previous, eventually* in the future or past, *always* in the future or past, *etc.* The PTLTL is further extended with call and returns in [24], the Eagle Logic (where the temporal logic is extended with *chop* operator) is proposed in [5], and the Meta Event Definition Language (a propositional temporal logic of events and conditions) is used in the Monitoring and Checking (MaC) toolset [26]. In contrast, an extended regular expression and context free grammar based language is proposed and implemented in [9].

From an implementation dimension, online monitoring technologies are implemented either by adopting an inline approach [25] or a centralised approach [15]. A centralised approach is applied to the system under observation using either a synchronous [10] mode or an asynchronous mode [11]. In general, the inline monitors are computationally efficient as they have access to all system variables, whereas the centralised monitors are better in other dimensions as they enable clear separation of concerns (and thus less error-prone), facilitate distributed computation, and exhibit compositional characteristics.

As part of our work on system simulation, we propose a variant of monitor technology that can be used to evaluate agent goals (similar to monitoring safety properties) and make decisions about appropriate system adaptation. A restricted form of centralised asynchronous monitor is implemented in Akka [3] to realise the monitoring behaviour of supervisor actors of a hierarchical actor system. Recently, a prototype of asynchronous centralised monitor implementation is presented in [9]. In the context of multi-agent systems, the concept of monitor is used for one of the two purposes - (a) to support heterogeneous agent implementations, and (b) to introduce a clear separation of concerns between core agent behaviour and other aspects such as adaptation. With respect to (b) the core agent behaviour (or behavioural specification) is considered to be a black-box, and adaptation is defined as monitor that observes the execution of core behaviour and reacts to specific observations [9].

ESL, simulation and adaptive behaviour are active areas of our research. Work in this area by [28] is likely to prove useful in efforts to specify the structure of histories, perhaps using pattern based rules, and then to verify that monitors are consistent with the monitored actors to which they are applied.

Our proposed language also provides centralised asynchronous monitors. The Akka implementation monitors the occurrence of events within its sub-actors and uses a fixed set of operations such as *stop actor, suspend actor* as an adaptation strategy. In contrast our proposed implementation evaluates the historical data to produce adaptation without using a restricted set of operations, effectively achieving a combination of [9] with the adaptation strategy presented in [8] augmented with temporal features and the extensions presented in [22] (*i.e.,* past and future modalities).

3   An Actor-Based Monitor Language

We have motivated a requirement for an actor-based monitor language that can be used in a variety of applications including diagnosis and adaptive behaviour. Since monitors need to reason about behaviour over time, it is reasonable to follow existing approaches to both actor behavioural specification and system monitoring that are based on linear temporal logic (LTL). We show how the proposed LTL-based monitor language can be encoded using actors. This section describes the monitor language and provides a simple example. The rest of the paper provides the semantics of the language by embedding it in an actor language called ESL, and then evaluates the language using a real-world case study.

3.1   Language Definition

Figure 3 defines a monitor construction language. A monitor p is applied to a monitored actor that exposes a history as a sequence of data elements. The monitor p can *hold* for the supplied history *at a given time*, where time is an integer that indexes the data in the history. Typically time will start with the first element of the history and the modal operator **N** is used to advance time so that p; **N**(q) holds for a history starting at time 0 when p holds at time 0 and q holds at time 1. The formula □(p) is equivalent to p;**N**(p;**N**(p;...)).

The language allows arbitrary conditions ?(c) to be applied to data in a history at a given time. In order to support actions and system instrumentation, a monitor may be an action !(a) where a is a function of 0-arguments. The intention is that we use guard monitors of the form: p ⇒ !(a).

In order to support multi-actor monitoring as shown in Fig. 2d we allow monitored actors to be aggregated using a binary operator. Monitors can manipulate such actors using the disaggregation operator _ ↑ _ (split) and its inverse _ ↓ _ (join). For example two monitored actors a and b can be aggregated to create Fork(Leaf(a),Leaf(b)). When such an actor is monitored by (p ↑ q);r, p monitors a, q monitors b and r monitors both a and b. Note that the _ ↓ _ operator

```
p,q ::=                     monitors.
         n                  a named monitor.
      |  ε                  holds for any history.
      |  □(p)               holds when p holds at all times.
      |  μ(λ(n)p)           provides recursive definitions: [μ(λ(n)p)/n]p
      |  p;q                holds when p and q both hold now.
      |  p|q                holds when p or q (or both) holds now.
      |  p ⊕ q              holds when p or q (but not both) holds now.
      |  p ⇒ q              if p holds then q must hold now.
      |  N(p)               holds when p holds for time now + 1.
      |  P(p)               holds when p holds for time now - 1.
      |  ?(c)               holds when the condition c is true now.
      |  !(a)               always holds and performs action a.
      |  p ↑ q              splits two merged histories between p and q.
      |  p ↓ q              (re)merges two split histories.
```

Fig. 3. Actor monitor language

is implicitly inserted between (p ↑ q) and r thereby ensuring that the monitor types are consistent.

3.2   A Simple Application of Monitors

The monitor language is influenced by LTL since it uses modal operators to range over time within histories. LTL is used by Bulling *et al.* to specify agent behaviour [6] with respect to an example involving traffic queues. We will use this example to show that an LTL-based monitor language can be used to help adapt traffic-light behaviour.

Traffic flow at an east-west bottle-neck along a single-carriage road is controlled by traffic lights. The bottle-neck can only accommodate one car and therefore the job of the traffic-lights is to ensure that the queues on either side do not become too large. Furthermore, traffic approaches from the east more frequently than that from the west.

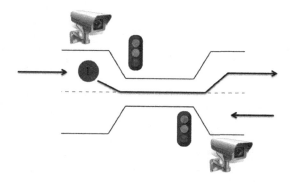

Fig. 4. Traffic flow at a bottle-neck (Color figure online)

Figure 4 shows the situation. The approaches from east and west are represented as actors whose autonomous behaviour supplies cars to their respective queues. The traffic lights are assumed to be in-sync and are passive actors. A single monitor combines data from the cameras that detect the current queue levels at the two approaches.

We will consider the simulation under three levels of monitor control: (1) To test the simulation we leave one of the traffic lights stuck on red and the other on green; (2) The monitor is even-handed and allows traffic to pass where there is a queue; (3) The monitor gives preference to the traffic from the east unless a queue has formed on the western approach and has not moved for a given time period.

The simulation has been encoded in ESL which includes a facility to produce a *filmstrip* consisting of a sequence of diagrams generated from simulation data. Figure 5 shows filmstrips generated using the three different monitor strategies. Figure 5a shows three snapshots at times 0, 6 and 40: the lights are stuck on green

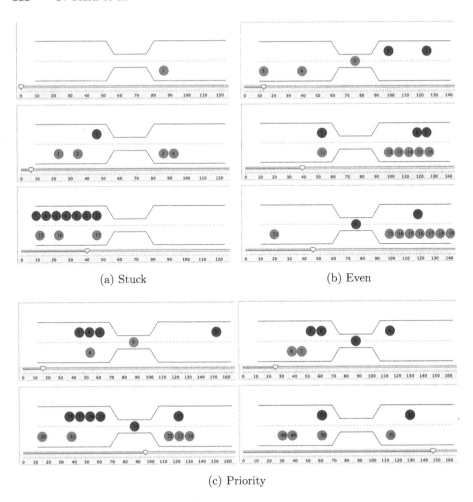

(a) Stuck   (b) Even

(c) Priority

Fig. 5. Actor monitors (Color figure online)

for east-west and red for west-east and therefore a queue soon builds up on the western approach. Figure 5b shows the situation with an even-handed monitor where, since the east-west traffic is more frequent, a queue quickly builds up. Figure 5c shows the situation at four different times where the monitor prefers east-west traffic, but attempts to prevent queues lingering for too long at the west-east approach. At time 17 a queue has developed and the monitor adapts the traffic light behaviour to clear it by time 25. At time 96 queues have built up on both approaches, but the strategy has cleared them by time 148. Based on the assumptions made by the simulation, the third monitor strategy would seem to be a good one and can be encoded in the monitor language as follows:

```
P0(p) = p                                                                    1
Pn(p) = p;P(Pn-1(p))                                                         2
□(PmaxQueueDuration(?(gre(maxQueueSize)))) ↑ ε ⇒ !(westEast) ⊕             3
                        ε ↑ ?(gre(0)) ⇒ !(westEast) ⊕                        4
                    ?(gre(0)) ↑ ε ⇒ !(eastWest) ⊕                           5
                    ε)                                                       6
```

The definition **Pn** is used to define a monitor that must hold over **n** previous time units. The monitor consists of three rules that hold at all times and is applied to a pair of monitored actors (the west and east traffic cameras) whose histories can be indexed using the split operator _ ↑ _. The first rule on line 3, states that if the west approach has a queue length `maxQueueSize` that has been waiting for `maxQueueDuration` time units then the lights should be changed `westEast`. The rule on line 4 gives queuing traffic on the eastern approach precedence over that queuing on the western approach. A monitor must be satisfied, so ε on line 6 ensures that we can move on to the next time unit.

4   ESL

The previous section has introduced a language for actor based monitors. The language has been implemented as a library using ESL[2] which is an actor language designed to support simulations. ESL combines functional and actor-based programming and provides a number of novel features that we believe are important when representing systems with emergent behaviour. The rest of this paper introduces ESL and uses it to define the monitor library. We will conclude with a real-world simulation written in ESL that uses monitors. Section 4.1 provides a brief overview of ESL syntax, Sect. 4.2 describes the operational semantics of ESL in terms of a system executive, and Sect. 4.3 implements a standard actor-based example and shows how it executes concurrently in ESL.

4.1   Syntax

The syntax of ESL is shown in Fig. 6. It is statically typed and includes parametric polymorphism, algebraic types and recursive types. Types start with an upper-case letter. An ESL program is a collection of mutually recursive bindings. Behaviour types **Act** { ... } are the equivalent of component interfaces and behaviours **act** { ... } are equivalent to component definitions. A behaviour **b** is *instantiated* to produce an actor using **new** **b** in the same way that class definitions are instantiated in Java. Once created, an actor starts executing a new thread of control that handles messages that are sent asynchronously between actors. Pattern matching is used in arms that occur in **case**-expressions and message handling rules. Uncertainty is supported by **probably(p)** x y that evaluates x in p% of cases, otherwise it evaluates q. Functions differ from actors because they are invoked synchronously.

---

[2] http://tonyclark.github.io/ESL/.

```
exp  ::= name                              variable   type ::= Name                              type var
     |   num | bool | str                  constant        |   Act { export dec* Mes* }          behaviour
     |   self                              receiver        |   (type*) → type                    λ-type
     |   null                              undefined       |   Term                              term type
     |   new name[type*] (exp*)            creation        |   Int | Bool | Str                  constant
     |   become name[type*] (exp*)         change          |   Void                              undefined
     |   exp op exp                        binexp          |   [ type ]                          lists
     |   not exp                           negation        |   Fun(Name*) type                   type op
     |   λ(dec*)::type exp                 operation       |   ∀(Name*) type                     poly
     |   let bind* in exp                  locals          |   rec Name . type                   recursion
     |   letrec bind* in exp               recursion
     |   case exp* arm*                    matching   bind ::= dec = exp                         bind
     |   for pat in exp { exp }            looping         |   name(pat*)::type=exp when exp     λ-bind
     |   { exp* }                          block           |   type Name[Name*] = type           type dec
     |   if exp then exp else exp          tests           |   data Name[Name*] = Term*          algebraic
     |   [ exp* ]                          list            |   act name(dec*)::type {            behaviour
     |   []                                empty                   export name*                  interface
     |   exp(exp*)                         apply                   bind*                         locals
     |   Name(exp*)                        term                    → exp                         initial
     |   exp ← exp                         message                 arm*                          behaviour
     |   name := exp                       update              }
     |   exp . name                        reference
     |   probably(exp)::type exp exp       uncertain  Term ::= Name(type*)                       term type
     |   exp[type*]                        app type
                                                      dec  ::= name[Name*] :: type               declare
pat  ::= dec                               variable
     |   dec = pattern                     naming     arm  ::= pat* → exp when exp               guarded
     |   num | bool | str                  const
     |   pat : pat                         cons pair
     |   [ pat* ]                          list
     |   [][type]                          empty
     |   Name[type*](pat*)                 term
```

Fig. 6. ESL syntax

A minimal ESL application defines a single behaviour called `main`, for example:

```
1 type Main = Act{ Time(Int) };
2 act main::Main {
3    Time(100) → stopAll();
4    Time(n::Int) → {}
5 }
```

An ESL application is driven by time messages. The listing defines a behaviour type (line 1) for any actor that can process a message of the form `Time(n)` where `n` is an integer. In this case, the `main` behaviour defines two message handling rules. When an actor processes a message it tries each of the rules in turn and fires the first rule that matches. The rule on line 3 matches at time `100` and calls the system function `stopAll()` which will halt the application. Otherwise, nothing happens (line 4).

4.2   Operational Semantics

ESL compiles to a virtual machine code that runs in Java. Each actor is its own machine and thereby runs its own thread of control. Figure 7 shows the ESL executive that controls the pool of actors. When the executive is called, the global pool `ACTORS` contains at least one actor that starts the simulation. Global time and the current instruction count are initialised (lines 3 and 4)

```
 1 stop := false;
 2 exec() {
 3   time := 0;
 4   instrs := 0;
 5   while(!stop) {
 6     actors := copy(ACTORS);
 7     clear(ACTORS);
 8     for actor ∈ actors do {
 9       if terminated(actor) then schedule(actor);
10       run(actor,MAX_INSTRS);
11     }
12     instrs := instrs + MAX_INSTRS;
13     ACTORS := ACTORS + actors;
14     if instrs > INSTRS_PER_TIME_UNIT
15     then {
16       time := time + 1;
17       instrs := 0;
18       for actor ∈ ACTORS do sendTime(actor,time)
19     }
20   }
21 }
```

Fig. 7. The ESL executive

before entering the main loop at line 4; the loop continues until one of the actors executes a system call to change the variable stop.

Lines 6–7 copy the global pool ACTORS so that freshly created actors do not start until the next iteration. If an actor's thread of control has terminated (line 9) then a new thread is created on the actor's VM by scheduling the next message if it is available. The operation run continues with the actor's thread of control on a machine that runs a call-by-value functional language [1] extended with actor-based features such as asynchronous message passing.

The executive schedules each actor for MAX_INSTRS VM instructions. This ensures that all actors are treated fairly. Once each actor has been scheduled, the existing actors are merged with any freshly created actors (line 13).

The executive measures time in terms of VM instructions. Each clock-time in the simulation consists of INSTRS_PER_ TIME_UNIT instructions performed on each actor. When actors need to be informed of a clock-tick (line 14), global time is incremented (line 16), the instruction counter is reset (line 17) and all actors are sent a clock-tick message.

4.3   Factorial

ESL Messages are sent asynchronously between actors. An actor that is at rest selects a new message and processes it in a thread that is independent of other actor threads. When the thread terminates, the actor is ready to process the next message. Consider the concurrent processing of factorials:

```
type Customer = Act { Value(Int) };
type Fact = Act{ Get(Int,Customer) };

act fact::Fact {
  Get(0,c::Customer) → c ← Value(1);
  Get(n::Int,c::Customer) →
```

```
    let cc::Customer = new cust(n,c)
    in self ← Get(n-1,cc)
}

act cust(n::Int,c::Customer)::Customer {
  Value(m::Int) c ← Value(n*m)
}

act main::Customer {
  f::Fact = new fact;
  computeFact(n::Int)::Void = f ← Get(n,self);
  → { computeFact(6); computeFact(6); computeFact(6) }
  Value(n::Int) → print[Int](n)
}
```

An actor of type `Customer` receives an integer value `Value(n)`. An actor of type `Fact` receives a request `Get(n,c)` for the value `!n` to be sent to the customer c. The behaviour `main` implements `Customer` and is the end-point for factorial-calculations: when it receives `Value(n)` it prints out the result.

The behaviour `fact` implements `Fact` using two message-handling rules. The first handles 0 and just passes the value 1 to the supplied customer. The second rule receives a request for a factorial of a non-0 number n. An actor with behaviour `fact` is able to handle multiple factorial requests at the same time. To do this it creates an auxiliary customer `cc` that is used to handle the return value from `!(n-1)`: this is equivalent to distributing the linked stack-frames of conventional singly-threaded computation to an equivalent number of concurrent customer actors. The behaviour `cust` implements `Customer` and forwards `n*m` to the pending customer c.

An actor with behaviour `main` calls `computeFact(6)` three times. Figure 8 shows the resulting message traces as a sequence diagram. Each of the actors is shown as a box with a life-line. Messages sent between actors are shown as arrows between life-lines and are labelled using the following convention `TIME:[THREAD]MESSAGE` where `TIME` is the time at which the message is sent and `THREAD` is a label used to identify each separate calculation of `computeFact(6)`. Messages are encoded to show the different steps: `Start` is the initial message, `Get(n,c,cc)` is a message to calculate `!n` with `cc` as the intermediate customer and c as the requesting customer, `One` is the recursion termination step, and `Return(n)` shows the return values between customers.

The sequence diagram shows that the three factorial calculations occur concurrently. The customer actors correspond to conventional stack frames in a singly-threaded language where the calls to factorials occur in sequence and are appropriately nested. Mapping actors to conventional languages has been the subject of several research projects [17,27] where monitors such as those described in this article may be an interesting implementation consideration.

5   Monitor Implementation in ESL

Section 3 introduced an actor-based monitor language and Sect. 4 describes the actor language ESL. This section shows how monitors can be implemented as actors by defining a pair of actor types: `Mtd[T]` for a class of behaviours that

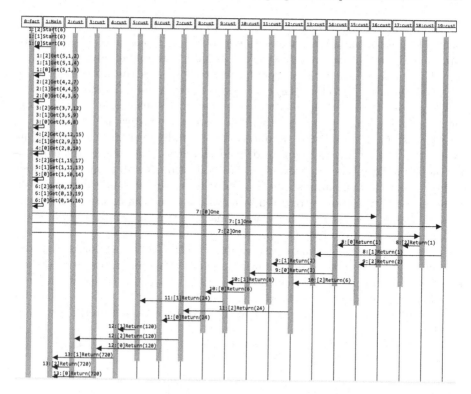

Fig. 8. Concurrent factorial

export histories over type T, and Mtr[T] for a class of behaviours that monitor histories of type T.

Given that actors are autonomous, we require a mechanism to synchronise monitors and actor histories. The basic mechanism is described in Sect. 5.1 and then encoded in ESL as described in Sect. 5.2.

5.1 Processing Histories

A history is a list of public state information and as such each monitor processes a list of data. For example, suppose that we want to express a monitor fff that causes action a to be performed every time a sequence of 3 fails, 000, is detected:

```
anF(0)::Bool = true                                          1
anF(1)::Bool = false                                         2
aT(n::Int)::Bool = not(anF(n))                               3
any(n::Int)::Bool = anF(n) or aT(n)                          4
                                                             5
pxn[T](n::Int,p::(T) → Bool)::Mtr[T] =                       6
  case n {                                                   7
    0 → idle                                                 8
    else ?(p) ; N(pxn(n-1,p)))                               9
  }                                                          10
                                                             11
fff::Mtr[Int] = □((pxn(3,anF) ⇒ !(a)) ⊕ ?(any))             12
```

The predicates `anF` and `any` are defined to detect the appropriate state elements. The history formula `fff` uses the operator `_;_` to compose three `F` detectors one after another in the history. The operator **N** is used to advance through the history. Finally, the history predicate `fff` combines the three `F` detector with an alternative detector `?(any)` that skips a state value. The monitor `p ⇒ q` checks `p` first, if `p` fails then `q` is checked, so line 12 will use three `F`'s as a guard on the action `a`, if the guard fails then the head of the history is skipped.

The history of an actor is produced incrementally over time. Therefore an expression written in the language defined in Fig. 3 must continually monitor the actor's history. The expression can be thought of as a state machine whose nodes correspond to monitor states and whose transitions consume parts of actor histories. Each transition is triggered by a clock-tick and can proceed when there is some history to consume, otherwise the machine must stay in its current state and try again when the next tick occurs.

Figure 9 shows the machine corresponding to `fff`. Each transition is triggered by a clock-tick, the labels on the transitions are: ϵ when no history is available; `F` occurs when the next state element in the history is an `F`; $\bigcirc$ occurs when there is at least one element at the head of the history and causes the element to be consumed; * denotes the situation when the next state element in the history is anything but `F`.

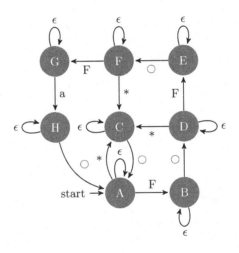

Fig. 9. A monitor state machine

5.2 Monitor Implementation

The implementation of monitors in ESL has four parts: (1) An actor type for a class of monitored behaviours, (2) A compositional data type that allows monitored actors to be combined, (3) An actor type for a class of monitors,

(4) The definition of the operators in Fig. 3. This section addresses each of these parts in turn.

Monitored Behaviours: An actor that can be monitored must export a list of data values called `history`. The order of the values in the history is important since it corresponds to the temporal operators in the monitor language. The actual type of the data elements in the list is not important so the definition of the type `Mtd` is parametric with respect to the type `T`:

```
type Mtd[T] = Act {
  export history::[T];
  Time(Int)
}
```

Composition: As shown in Fig. 2, monitors may be attached to single or multiple actors. Therefore, we require a mechanism that will combine the histories of two actors into a single history. Such a binary operator, can then be used successively to compose an arbitrarily large history that can be processed by a single monitor.

The type `MTree[T]` is the type of potentially aggregated monitored actors. Given a single monitored actor `m::Mtd[T]`, we create an aggregate singleton `Leaf(m)`. Given two aggregate monitored actors: `m1::MTree[T]` and `m2::MTree[T]` the composition `Fork(m1,m2)::MTree[T]` is also an aggregate monitored actor. The data type is defined below:

```
data MTree[T] = Leaf(Mtd[T])  |  Fork(MTree[T],MTree[T])
```

Monitor Behaviours: A monitor `m::Mtr[T]` can be sent a message `Check(a,c,s,f)` that causes it to check whether it holds for the monitored actor `a`. The integer `c` is an index into the history that is exported by `a` and represents the *current time*. Checking whether the monitor is satisfied or not by `a` at time `c` may be delayed while `m` waits for `a` to produce the required amount of history. Therefore, `m` must keep polling `a` for its history until it can determine whether it is satisfied. At this point `m` is either satisfied with the history or not. These two outcomes are handled by the arguments `s` and `f` in terms of *success* and *fail* continuations. The argument `s` is a monitor to which `m` will send `a` when it is satisfied. The argument `f` is an operation that is invoked in the case that `m` is not satisfied with `a` at time `c`. The data type is as follows:

```
type Fail = () → Void
type Mtr[T] = rec M. Act {
  Check(Mtd[T],Int,M,Fail);
  Time(Int)
}
```

Operator Definition: The monitor behaviours are defined in Fig. 10, note that where the clock-tick handler is `Time(n::Int) → {}` it is omitted. A monitor of type `T` is created by instantiating a behaviour with type `Mtr[T]`; for example, `new ε[T]()`. A monitor is activated by sending it a `Check(a,c,s,f)` message where `a` is a tree of monitored actors, `c` is the current history-index (initially 0), s is a success-monitor, and f is a failure-monitor. The behaviour of each type of monitor, as defined in Fig. 10, is outlined below:

```
act ε[T]::Mtr[T] {
    Check(a::MTree[T],c::Int,s::Mtr[T],f::Fail) →
        s ← Check(a,c,self,f)
}

idle[T]::Mtr[T] = new ε[T]()

act ![T](command::() → Void)::Mtr[T] {
    Check(a::MTree[T],c::Int,s::Mtr[T],f::Fail) → {
        command();
        s ← Check(a,c,idle[T],f)
    }
}

act (_;_)[T](p::Mtr[T],q::Mtr[T])::Mtr[T] {
    Check(a::MTree[T],c::Int,s::Mtr[T],f::Fail) →
        p ← Check(a,c,new (q;s)[T],f)
}

act (_|_)[T](p::Mtr[T],q::Mtr[T])::Mtr[T] {
    Check(a::MTree[T],c::Int,s::Mtr[T],f::Fail) →
        p ← Check(a,c,s,λ()::Void q ← Check(a,c,s,
        f))
}

act (_⊕_)[T](p::Mtr[T],q::Mtr[T])::Mtr[T] {
    Check(a::MTree[T],c::Int,s::Mtr[T],f::Fail) → {
        p ← Check(a,c,s,f);
        q ← Check(a,c,s,f)
    }
}

□[T](p::Mtr[T])::Mtr[T] =
    new μ[T](λ(q::Mtr[T])::Mtr[T]
        new seq[T](p,new next[T](q)))

act N[T](p::Mtr[T])::Mtr[T] {
    Check(a::MTree[T],c::Int,s::Mtr[T],f::Fail) →
        p ← Check(a,c+1,s,f)
}

act (_ ⇒ _)[T](p::Mtr[T],q::Mtr[T])::Mtr[T] =
    Check(a::MTree[T],c::Int,s::Mtr[T],f::Fail) →
        p ← Check(a,c,new (q;s),λ()::Void s ←
            Check(a,c,idle[T],f)
}

act P[T](p::Mtr[T])::Mtr[T] {
    Check(a::MTree[T],c::Int,s::Mtr[T],f::Fail) →
        p ← Check(a,c-1,s,f)
}

act ?[T](pred::(T) → Bool)::Mtr[T] {
    Check(t::MTree[T],c::Int,s::Mtr[T],f::Fail) →
        case t {
            Leaf(a::Mtd[T]) →
                if length[T](a.history) > c
                then {
                    if pred(nth[T](a.history,c))
                    then s ← Check(t,c,idle[T],f)
                    else f()
                } else self ← Check(t,c,s,f)
        }
}

act μ[T](g::(Mtr[T]) → Mtr[T])::Mtr[T] {
    Check(a::MTree[T],c::Int,s::Mtr[T],f::Fail) →
        g(new rec[T](g)) ← Check(a,c,s,f)
}

act (_↑_)[T](p::Mtr[T],q::Mtr[T])::Mtr[T] {
    Check(t::MTree[T],c::Int,s::Mtr[T],f::Fail) →
        case t {
            Fork[T](t1::MTree[T],t2::MTree[T]) →
                let j::Mtr[T] = new (t1 ↓ t2)
                in {
                    p ← Check(t1,c,j,f);
                    q ← Check(t2,c,j,f)
                }
        }
}

act (_↓_)[T](t1::MTree[T],t2::MTree[T])::Mtr[T]{
    done::Bool = false
    Check(a::MTree[T],c::Int,s::Mtr[T],f::Fail) →
        if not(done)
        then done := true
        else s ← Check(Fork(t1,t2),c,s,f)
}
```

Fig. 10. ESL monitor behaviours

- ε() immediately activates the success-monitor by sending it a message. The global actor idle can be used as the identity monitor.
- !(c) receives a Check message, performs the command c, and then activates the success-monitor.
- p;q forwards the Check message to p and creates a new success-monitor q;s.
- p|q forwards the Check message to p using q as the fail-monitor. Therefore, q will be tried in the case that p fails. Both p and q will use f as their fail-monitor.
- p ⊕ q tries both p and q in parallel and assumes that only one will succeed.

- $\square$(p) checks the monitored actor using p with respect to history-indices c, c+1, c+2 *etc.* Note that checking occurs in parallel with all other monitors and any check with respect to a particular history-index will wait, due to the definition of ?(_), until the indexed history element has been generated by the monitored actor.
- N(p) checks the monitored actor using p with respect to history-index c+1.
- p $\Rightarrow$ q if p holds then q should also hold, otherwise the fail-monitor is used.
- P(p) checks the monitored actor using p with respect to history-index c-1.
- ?(g) when this monitor is activated by a Check message, the history element at index c is checked using guard g. If the result is true then the success-monitor is activated, otherwise the fail-monitor is activated. Note that if an element at index c is not yet available, the monitor sends itself a Check message that will be processed at some time in the future, thereby delaying the guard. Note also that the monitored actor is actually a tree: it is the responsibility of the monitor to use _↑_ and _↓_ to access a leaf of the tree when applying a guard.
- μ(g) recursive monitors are created by supplying a function g whose argument is a cyclic monitor. For example:

μ[Int](λ(fStar::Mtr[Int])::Mtr[Int]   isF; N(fStar))

is a monitor that will expect a history to contain an infinite sequence of 0s.

5.3   Traffic Monitoring

Section 3.2 describes a simple use of monitors to achieve adaptive behaviour at a traffic light. This section provides the ESL implementation of the simulation and shows how the adaptor language works by providing a fragment of the resulting sequence diagram.

The ESL program in Fig. 11 is a slightly simplified version of that which generates the outputs shown in Fig. 5 where the details of generating sequence diagram output have been omitted. The behaviour type Approach is a sub-type of Mtd[Int] and exports a history of integers being the time-sequenced number of cars queuing at an approach. An approach actor is created by supplying the behaviour approach with an identifier, a traffic light and the probability of new car arrival. Two approaches called left and right are created and the operations westEast and eastWest are used to control the traffic lights.

Each approach is autonomous and receives a Time(n) message at regular intervals. When this occurs, either a new car will arrive or the next available car will move from the approach if the lights are green.

The monitor defined in Sect. 3.2 is attached to the monitored actors left and right by creating an aggregate Fork(Leaf(left),Leaf(right))::MTree[Int]. Figure 12 shows the initial steps performed by the simulation and its associated monitor. The actors are labelled with their unique identifier and behaviour where E stands for the behaviour nothing, L is the left approach and R is the right approach. Messages of the form Check(a,c,s,f) are represented on the sequence diagram as C(a,c,s) since the failure continuation is not particularly informative. Message passing starts at actor 14:rec which is created by the monitor definition

```
type TrafficLight = Act { export colour::Str; change::() → Void }
type Approach = Act < Mtd[Int] { export history::[Int]; Time(Int) }

act light(colour::Str)::TrafficLight {
  export colour, change;
  change()::Void =
    case colour {
      'RED' → colour := 'GREEN';
      'GREEN' → colour := 'RED'
    }
}

act approach(id::Str,light::TrafficLight,probOfNewCar::Int)::Approach {
  export history;
  history::[Int] = [0];
  Move            → if light.colour = 'GREEN' and head[Int](history) > 0 then self ← DeQueue;
  DeQueue         → queue := (head[Int](history) - 1) : history;
  Queue           → queue := (head[Int](history) + 1) : history
  Time(n::Int) → probably(probOfNewCar) self ← Queue else self ← Move
};

l1::TrafficLight = new light('RED');
l2::TrafficLight = new light('GREEN');
left::Approach = new approach('left',l1,10);
right::Approach = new approach('right',l2,20);

westEast()::Void =  if l2.colour = 'RED' then { l2.change(); l1.change() }
eastWest()::Void =  if l1.colour = 'RED' then { l1.change(); l2.change() }
```

Fig. 11. The traffic simulation

for □. The **rec** behaviour creates a loop that is used to increment the history counter c that starts at 0 and is incremented twice by successive messages from 18:next to 14:rec. Notice that the left and right approach actors concurrently queue and de-queue cars at the same time that the monitor is processing their histories.

6   Evaluation

Our claim is that actor-based systems can benefit from monitors that meet the requirements outlined in Sect. 1.2 and in particular actor-based simulations can use monitors to encode adaptive behaviour. We have proposed a monitor-language and shown how it can be encoded in an actor language called ESL. This section evaluates the claims by describing a real-world case study that we have implemented in ESL and that uses monitor-based adaptation to influence actor behaviour.

6.1   Case Study Overview

The cash in circulation in the Indian economy has steadily been increasing over the years. In 2001, the total cash in circulation was 2.1 trillion rupees and by early November it had reached 15.4 trillion. On November 8, 2016, the dominance of cash-based transactions and the relentless growth of a shadow economy triggered a sudden fiscal intervention by the Indian government with the withdrawal from circulation of 500 Rupees and 1000 Rupees notes. This action resulted in 87% of the total cash in the system being pulled out. The primary objective of this

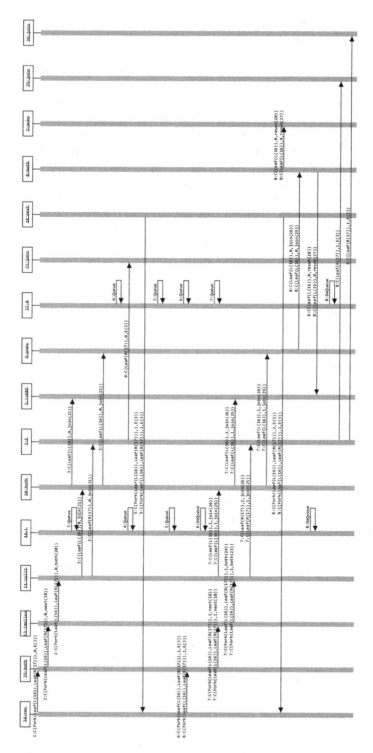

Fig. 12. Initial messages sent by traffic monitor

demonetisation was seen as a way of purging black money from the system with the key assumption that such a large amount of money would not come back to the system as holders of illicit wealth would be wary of prosecution by tax authorities. Further, cash would be slowly replenished with newly minted currency notes.

The initiative involved several financial restrictions. For example, a limitations were imposed on the exchange of old notes wherein the citizens were allowed to exchange up to 4000 rupees with the remaining deposited to their bank account; ATM withdrawal limits were reduced to 2000 rupees in a day for Indian citizens, and there was a cap of 10,000 rupees on bank withdrawal in a day along with a weekly withdrawal restriction of 20000 rupees per citizen. In addition to these restrictions, cash-less payment modes, such as mobile wallet and card payments, were incentivised. For example, on Dec 8, e-transactions for fuel included a 0.75% discount. Despite all preventative measures, the demonetisation initiative resulted into prolonged cash shortages. Citizens were inconvenienced due to non-availability of new currency notes in the banks and ATM machines. Even as recently as Feb 16, estimates indicate that at least 30% of ATMs still run dry. Overall, the initiative has faced a lot of criticism as being poorly thought through, inadequately planned, inefficiently executed and unfair to a significant segment of cash dependent citizen[3].

6.2   Adaptation

When creating a simulation of the demonetisation case study, adaptation occurs in a number of ways. The banks, commercial suppliers, and citizens were continuously monitoring and adopting their behaviour to cope with the emerging situation. For example, banking transaction limits were changed multiple times to control cash flow, commercial suppliers adopted alternative payment options to stay viable, and citizens changed their behaviour to avoid undesired consequences.

The behaviour of citizens changed along multiple dimensions: (1) individuals started using alternate payment modes such as mobile wallet and credit/debit cards; (2) individuals changed their needs and suppliers catering to those needs so as to support cash-less transactions; (3) some individuals felt a greater sense of security in having cash-in-hand in excess of their requirements, *i.e.* hoarding behaviour emerged.

These adaptations to individual behaviour collectively impacted the overall system in a non-linear manner. In particular, the frequent changes to banking transaction limits, uncertainty in availability of cash with banks and ATM machines, circular dependencies between availability of cash and behaviour of individuals, and non-linearity in cash-in-hand of an individual and cash hoarding tendency led to an emergent system behaviour.

---

[3] http://bit.ly/2mpgGRb.

The use of actors and actor-monitors within a simulation can help to understand the effect of demonetisation. Actors are used to encode the individual behaviours and monitors are used for post-demonetisation adaptations.

6.3   Case Study Model

We formulate a society comprised of three key identities: Citizens, Banks, Shops, and a basic element termed Item as shown using a class diagram in Fig. 13. The term Item represents the needs of citizens that include merchandise and services; shops are the locations where items can be purchased and services can be acquired. The activities that we consider: citizens consume items to cater to daily needs; citizens purchase items from shops when the item quantity dips below a threshold value; citizens withdraw cash when cash-in-hand dips below a threshold value. A citizen may hold Cards, and a citizen who holds a card may choose to pay by cash or by card for a purchase, and may withdraw cash from ATM machine or bank counter. In contrast, a citizen without a card always pays by cash and withdraws cash from bank counters. The purchase behaviour and cash withdrawal behaviour are illustrated using state-machines in Fig. 14 (the firm lines describe the pre-demonetisation behaviour).

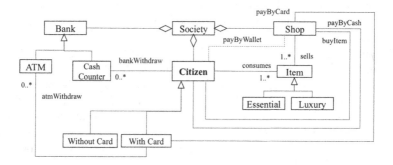

Fig. 13. Structural representation of society

We assume citizens are able to satisfy their daily needs *i.e.*, poverty and other societal aspects are not considered in the case study. We further consider: there is sufficient cash with the banks to service citizens through ATMs and Bank counters *i.e.*, no denial of service from bank; there is sufficient stock in shops; and citizens are able to withdraw cash when in need during pre-demonetisation phase. We replicate demonetisation by eliminating cash abruptly from banks and citizens, and replenishing cash at slow rate (around 0.7% of cash in circulation at pre-demonetisation) up to a certain percentage (*e.g.*, 70% of cash in circulation at pre-demonetisation). The key identities of society start behaving differently during post-demonetisation phase. They adopt different strategies which are very

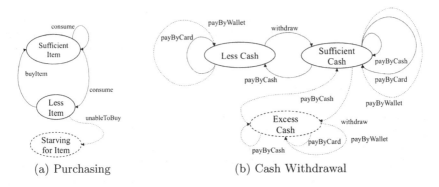

(a) Purchasing   (b) Cash Withdrawal

Fig. 14. Citizen behaviour

specific to individuals. The adaptation strategies considered in this case study are:

(1) Bank: banks impose restrictions on cash withdrawals *e.g.*, ATM withdrawal limit is 2000 rupees in a day for a citizen, bank withdrawal limit is 10,000 rupees in a day for a citizen, and the weekly withdrawal limit is 20000 rupees per citizen. These changes are deterministic and associated with the demonetisation event.

(2) Shop: shops may (a stochastic behaviour) adapt themselves to accept alternate payment options such as mobile wallet and card payment whenever they observed a drop in sales record.

(3) Citizen: a citizen, as an individual, may adopt (as a stochastic behaviour) an appropriate strategy (with multiple options selected based on personal intuition and experience) to avoid entering an undesired state. The strategies can be visualised along two independent dimensions: **Payment Pattern:** Citizens start using mobile wallet and/or card as a payment option to save cash for the future. However, not everyone will start using alternate option, an individual's decision will be based on several factors such as availability and familiarity with payment technology, and whether the citizen is an early or late adopter. **Cash Withdrawal Pattern:** A group of citizens may start making attempt to withdraw cash (from ATM machine and/or Bank counter) even when the cash is not required (temporary hoarding behaviour) to safe guard from future consequences.

6.4   Case Study Monitors and Adaptation

The case study exhibits a variety of adaptive behaviour each of which is realised using monitors of the types shown in Fig. 2. For example, a shop tries to understand the situation in terms of its sales target, and adapts if the sales target is not met. A citizen observes the financial status (of itself and others) and adapts depending on circumstances; for example, one citizen may choose an alternate payment option as a mobile wallet, whereas another citizen may adapt to cash hoarding behaviour to avoid a cash shortage.

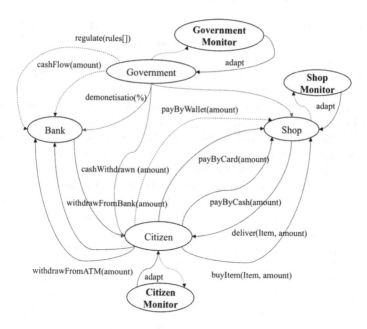

Fig. 15. Case study adaptors

In this case study, the shops and citizens exhibit significant individualistic behaviours and often adapt new strategies to deal with changing situations. A set of shops may change their behaviour proactively immediately after the demonetisation event, whereas another set of shops may wait until they observe a significant decline in sales before changing their behaviour. We attach a single event based monitor to represent the former scenario, and a simple history based monitor to represent latter.

A citizen may adapt their behaviour (a) right after the demonetisation event, (b) on demonetisation followed by several consecutive failures to authorise transactions, (c) when they observe low cash-in-hand for a given number of days and are unable to withdraw cash, or (d) when they observe a given number of citizens with multiple authorisation failures. Thus we see the need for all types of monitors to represent citizen adaptation. In contrast to citizen and shop actors, the bank actor primarily follows standard regulations that are defined by a government actor. Hence we associate a monitor actor with the government actor and allow government to control banks through their event interactions.

6.5   Simulation Organisation

We set up a simulation by forming a society with actors representing the government, citizens, shops, and banks. Monitors are attached to shop and citizen actors for specifying the individualistic adaptation. The simulation progresses with a time event that represents a 'day'. Each day, citizen actors consume items, buy items from shops if any item is below a certain threshold, pay for the purchases, and make an attempt to withdraw cash if needed. Similarly, bank actors try to stock up cash to fulfil ATM and Bank withdrawal requests, and shop actors stock up the items for their customers. The government actor triggers 'demonetisation' at specific day of a simulation run.

We divide a simulation run into three phases: setup, pre-demonetisation, and post-demonetisation. Figure 16 shows part of the simulation: the levers are displayed in the top left hand corner and the measures are displayed in real-time as the simulation progresses. Pre-demonetisation is an observation phase to validate conditions that include (a) cash at banks are adequate to serve all citizens *i.e.*, no denial of service at ATM machines and Bank counters; (b) the stock are sufficient at each shops to serve their citizens; and (c) citizens can buy items and withdraw cash as needed. This phase also monitors the cash-flows to the banks, and cash in circulation.

In this simulation setting, we firstly observe the impact of demonetisation by removing cash and reducing cash-flows. We then explore various what-if scenarios by changing the parameters and/or by attaching different actor monitors to understand the impact of courses of action. For example: the impact of demonetisation if the government replenishes cash at a faster rate, or the impact if the government decides to replenish 60% cash instead of 70%. Similarly, one can explore the impact if none of the citizen exhibits cash hoarding behaviour by detaching the monitors that are responsible for cash hoarding behaviours. In this paper, we limit our analyses to two scenarios (a) understand the effect of demonetisation for standard setting that closely represents the real Indian demonetisation event, and (b) understand the positive/negative effect on overall society when there is no hoarders. We have chosen these two relatively intuitive scenarios to illustrate the efficacy of using actors and monitors.

6.6 Simulation Results

We simulated the demonetisation case study with one government, one bank, 15 shop and 1710 citizen actors for 150 days, where the first 15 days are considered for setup phase, next 30 days are the pre-demonetisation phase, and 105 days are the post-demonetisation phase. A snapshot of ESL simulation dashboard at the day of 115 (*i.e.*, after 70 days of demonetisation) is depicted in Fig. 16. The dashboard shows useful states of the society and its identities: the 'Citizen Type' table describes the citizens and their card/wallet usage capabilities, (b) the 'Payment Distribution' pie chart shows distribution of Card (green), Wallet (blue) and Cash (red) payments, (c) the 'Payment Transaction Volume' chart describes the history of overall payment transactions where card transactions are green, wallet transactions are blue, and cash transactions are red, (d) the 'Cash Availability in Bank and ATM' graph shows the history of cash availability at Banks and ATMs using red and blue respectively, (e) the 'Transaction Declined Rate' graph describes the denial of service at Banks and ATMs using red and blue respectively. In addition, the 'Citizen with no Cash' and 'Citizen with excess Cash' charts describe the financial condition of the citizens: the former chart

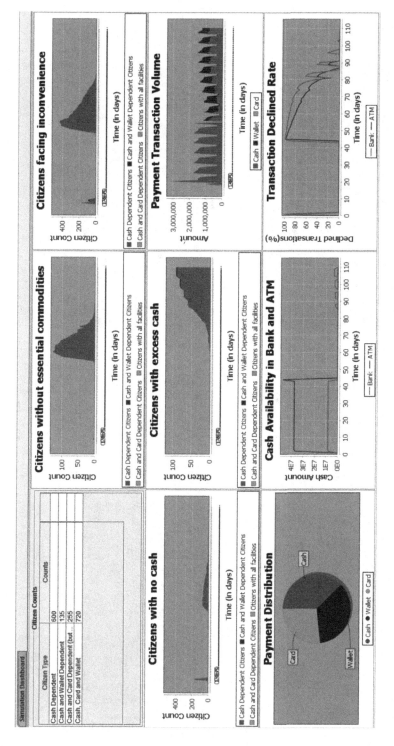

Fig. 16. Case study dashboard

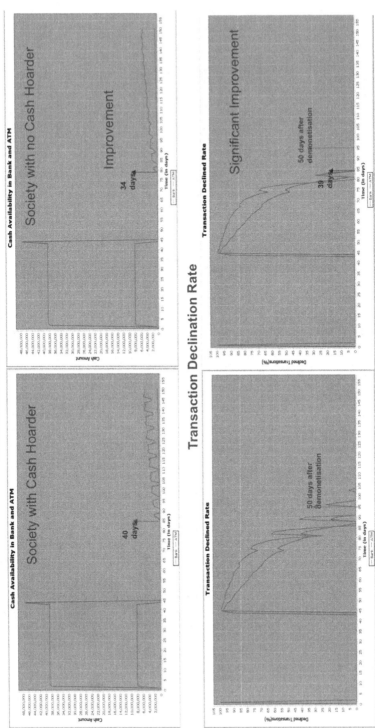

Fig. 17. Case study results

describes the number of citizens having considerably less cash, and the latter represents the number of cash hoarders (the red, blue, green and yellow colours signify the cash dependent citizens, cash and wallet dependent citizens, cash and card dependent citizens, and citizen with all facilities respectively as classified in table). The 'Citizens without essential commodities' and 'Citizen facing inconvenience' charts represent the number of citizens starving for essential items and luxury items respectively.

We observe that the graphs are unstable for first 15 days of the simulation runs as the simulator is trying to set the values based on actor behaviours and their interactions. The simulation outcomes for pre-demonetisation phase is stable: no bank withdrawal request is denied, no citizen is facing any financial crisis, and citizens are not having any deficiency for essential or luxury items. The demonetisation event is triggered at day 45, causing a sudden reduction of cash from the bank and ATM machines. Subsequently, the withdrawals from bank and ATM decline whilst wallet payment and card payment increase significantly: the citizens have started facing a financial crisis and the citizens who are solely dependent on cash have started starving for essential and/or luxury items. The adverse effects continue for almost 50 days and then the situation returns to normal.

As we can observe in graph with title 'Citizen with excess cash' in Fig. 16, 115 citizens started hoarding cash when the situation is on the verge of returning back to normal. One may hypothesise that cash hoarding behaviour is significantly slowing down the stabilisation process. We validate the hypothesis on hoarding behaviour by removing the monitors that are responsible for turning a citizen into a cash hoarder. We simulated the same society with no hoarders, and relevant simulation results are depicted in Fig. 17. We observe improvements in 'cash in bank and ATM' and 'transaction declination rate' for the society with no hoarders. The cash condition is returning back to normal in 40 days instead of 50 days. Thus the result is supporting the hypothesis regarding hoarding behaviour and also providing an indication of possible improvement.

7   Conclusion

This paper has proposed a homogeneous actor-based language for monitors that achieve adaptive behaviour. It is interesting because we have used the prevailing LTL-based approach to expressing behaviours in actor and multi-agent systems in order to define monitors that are also actors and therefore can be freely mixed with other actors at run-time. The language has been given a semantics by defining it using ESL which is a function-oriented actor language and we have demonstrated the utility of the approach using a real-world case study based on the recent demonetisation event in India. The case study demonstrates how monitors are used in the context of a simulation that exhibits emergent behaviour.

A number of limitations are identified in this work. The example described in Sect. 6 involves several thousand actors, and completes a simulation in roughly 30 s. We recognise the need to scale up to more realistic actor configurations which may then require further investigation in how to make actor behaviour, including adaptation, more efficient. A larger simulation model of our case study would also allow us to calibrate more precisely the simulation results with real world events as documented in the Indian national newspapers. As with all actor based simulations, the results need to be carefully interpreted given the underlying assumptions which we make given the complexity of the example. Regardless, the ability of the language to define actors with their own behaviours and adaptations and the flexibility for testing different conditions provide a means evaluating different policies and options. The ability to visualise and quantify the simulations results is also promising but again, we recognise that much more work on visualisation is required. Time in this simulation remains challenging however, we are similar in our approach to other efforts to map simulation time with real world time. Our monitor language semantics is currently defined using ESL which is currently in use in our research groups. It may be appropriate to document other options for defining the semantics of the monitor language to demonstrate other external validity routes.

ESL, simulation and adaptive behaviour are active areas of our research. An interesting extension of this work would be to specify the structure of histories, perhaps using pattern based rules, and then to verify that monitors are consistent with the monitored actors to which they are applied. Other case studies are also being explored to validate the technology and to produce a simulation development method based on ESL.

References

1. Ager, M.S., Biernacki, D., Danvy, O., Midtgaard, J.: A functional correspondence between evaluators and abstract machines. In: Proceedings of the 5th ACM SIGPLAN international conference on Principles and practice of declaritive programming, pp. 8–19. ACM (2003)
2. Agha, G.: Actors: A Model of Concurrent Computation in Distributed Systems. MIT Press, Cambridge, MA, USA (1986)
3. Allen, J.: Effective Akka. O'Reilly Media Inc. (2013)
4. Bharat, S., Kulkarni, V., Clark, T., Barn, B.: A simulation-based aid for organisational decision-making. In: Maciaszek, L.A., Cardoso, J.S., Ludwig, A., van Sinderen, M., Cabello, E. (eds.) Proceedings of the 11th International Joint Conference on Software Technologies (ICSOFT 2016), ICSOFT-PT, Lisbon, Portugal, 24–26 July 2016, vol. 2, pp. 109–116. SciTePress (2016)
5. Barringer, H., Goldberg, A., Havelund, K., Sen, K.: Rule-based runtime verification. In: Steffen, B., Levi, G. (eds.) VMCAI 2004. LNCS, vol. 2937, pp. 44–57. Springer, Heidelberg (2004). https://doi.org/10.1007/978-3-540-24622-0_5
6. Bulling, N., Dastani, M., Knobbout, M.: Monitoring norm violations in multi-agent systems. In Proceedings of the 2013 International Conference on Autonomous Agents and Multi-agent Systems, pp. 491–498. International Foundation for Autonomous Agents and Multiagent Systems (2013)

7. Cahn, A., Hoyos, J., Hulse, M., Keller, E.: Software-defined energy communication networks: from substation automation to future smart grids. In: 2013 IEEE International Conference on Smart Grid Communications (SmartGridComm), pp. 558–563. IEEE (2013)

8. Cassar, I., Francalanza, A.: Runtime adaptation for actor systems. In: Bartocci, E., Majumdar, R. (eds.) RV 2015. LNCS, vol. 9333, pp. 38–54. Springer, Cham (2015). https://doi.org/10.1007/978-3-319-23820-3_3

9. Cassar, I., Francalanza, A.: On implementing a monitor-oriented programming framework for actor systems. In: Ábrahám, E., Huisman, M. (eds.) IFM 2016. LNCS, vol. 9681, pp. 176–192. Springer, Cham (2016). https://doi.org/10.1007/978-3-319-33693-0_12

10. Chen, F., Roşu, G.: MOP: an efficient and generic runtime verification framework. In: ACM SIGPLAN Notices, vol. 42, pp. 569–588. ACM (2007)

11. Colombo, C., Francalanza, A., Gatt, R.: Elarva: a monitoring tool for Erlang. In: Khurshid, S., Sen, K. (eds.) RV 2011. LNCS, vol. 7186, pp. 370–374. Springer, Heidelberg (2012). https://doi.org/10.1007/978-3-642-29860-8_29

12. D'Ippolito, N., Braberman, V., Kramer, J., Magee, J., Sykes, D., Uchitel, S.: Hope for the best, prepare for the worst: multi-tier control for adaptive systems. In: Proceedings of the 36th International Conference on Software Engineering, pp. 688–699. ACM (2014)

13. Dodd, P.S., Ravishankar, C.H.: Monitoring and debugging distributed real-time programs. Softw., Pract. Exper. **22**(10), 863–877 (1992)

14. Fotrousi, F., Fricker, S.A.: QoE probe: a requirement-monitoring tool. In: REFSQ Workshops (2016)

15. Francalanza, A.: A theory of monitors. In: Jacobs, B., Löding, C. (eds.) FoSSaCS 2016. LNCS, vol. 9634, pp. 145–161. Springer, Heidelberg (2016). https://doi.org/10.1007/978-3-662-49630-5_9

16. Goodloe, A.E., Pike, L.: Monitoring distributed real-time systems: a survey and future directions (2010)

17. Haller, P., Odersky, M.: Scala Actors: unifying thread-based and event-based programming. Theoret. Comput. Sci. **410**(2), 202–220 (2009)

18. Havelund, K., Roşu, G.: Synthesizing monitors for safety properties. In: Katoen, J.-P., Stevens, P. (eds.) TACAS 2002. LNCS, vol. 2280, pp. 342–356. Springer, Heidelberg (2002). https://doi.org/10.1007/3-540-46002-0_24

19. Juen, J., Cheng, Q., Prieto-Centurion, V., Krishnan, J.A., Schatz, B.: Health monitors for chronic disease by gait analysis with mobile phones. Telemed. e-Health **20**(11), 1035–1041 (2014)

20. Kulkarni, V., Barat, S., Clark, T., Barn, B.: Toward overcoming accidental complexity in organisational decision-making. In: 18th ACM/IEEE International Conference on Model Driven Engineering Languages and Systems, MoDELS 2015, Ottawa, ON, Canada, 30 September–2 October 2015, pp. 368–377 (2015)

21. Müller, H., Bosse, S., Wirth, M., Turowski, K.: Collaborative software performance engineering for enterprise applications. In: Proceedings of the 50th Hawaii International Conference on System Sciences (2017)

22. Pradella, M., San Pietro, P., Spoletini, P., Morzenti, A.: Practical model checking of LTL with past. In: ATVA03: 1st Workshop on Automated Technology for Verification and Analysis (2003)

23. Renggli, L., Gîrba, T., Nierstrasz, O.: Embedding languages without breaking tools. In: D'Hondt, T. (ed.) ECOOP 2010. LNCS, vol. 6183, pp. 380–404. Springer, Heidelberg (2010). https://doi.org/10.1007/978-3-642-14107-2_19

24. Roşu, G., Chen, F., Ball, T.: Synthesizing monitors for safety properties: this time with calls and returns. In: Leucker, M. (ed.) RV 2008. LNCS, vol. 5289, pp. 51–68. Springer, Heidelberg (2008). https://doi.org/10.1007/978-3-540-89247-2_4

25. Sen, K., Vardhan, A., Agha, G., Rosu, G.: Efficient decentralized monitoring of safety in distributed systems. In: Proceedings of the 26th International Conference on Software Engineering, pp. 418–427. IEEE Computer Society (2004)

26. Sokolsky, O., Sammapun, U., Lee, I., Kim, J.: Run-time checking of dynamic properties. Electron. Notes Theoret. Comput. Sci. **144**(4), 91–108 (2006)

27. Srinivasan, S., Mycroft, A.: Kilim: isolation-typed actors for Java. In: Vitek, J. (ed.) ECOOP 2008. LNCS, vol. 5142, pp. 104–128. Springer, Heidelberg (2008). https://doi.org/10.1007/978-3-540-70592-5_6

28. Yasutake, S., Watanabe, T.: Actario: a framework for reasoning about actor systems. In: Workshop on Programming based on Actors, Agents, and Decentralized Control (AGERE) (2015)

Author Index

Printed in the United States
By Bookmasters